PATIENTS ARE PEOPLE LIKE US

PATIENTS ARE PEOPLE LIKE US

THE EXPERIENCES OF HALF A CENTURY IN NEUROPSYCHIATRY

by

HENRI BARUK

MEMBER OF THE FRENCH MEDICAL ACADEMY

with the assistance of
JEAN LABORDE

TRANSLATED FROM THE FRENCH BY EILEEN FINLETTER AND JEAN AYER

WILLIAM MORROW AND COMPANY, INC.

NEW YORK   1978

French edition published by Éditions Robert Laffont under the title Des Hommes Comme Nous: mémoires d'un neuropsychiàtre. © Opera Mundi, 1976

Printed in the United States of America.

1   2   3   4   5   6   7   8   9   10

Library of Congress Cataloging in Publication Data

Baruk, Henri (date)
    Patients are people like us.

    Translation of Des hommes comme nous.
    Includes index.
    1. Baruk, Henri, 1897– 2. Psychiatrists—
France—Biography. I. Laborde, Jean, 1918– joint
author. II. Title.
RC339.52.B37A3312   616.8'9'00924 [B]   77–13692
ISBN 0-688-03271-0

BOOK DESIGN   CARL WEISS

DEDICATED TO:

MY PARENTS,

MY FATHER,

WHO INTRODUCED ME

TO PSYCHIATRY,

MY DEAR WIFE,

SUZANNE

CONTENTS

PATIENTS
ARE PEOPLE
LIKE US

MY EARLY DEVELOPMENT

I was born on August 15, 1897, at Saint-Avé in the Morbihan, but my childhood was spent at Sainte-Gemmes-sur-Loire in the psychiatric hospital of which my father, Jacques Baruk, was the director for forty years.

The hospital was an eighteenth-century château, a sort of Versailles in miniature, with French gardens, an English park, an artificial river, an orange grove, and a majestic staircase which led to the Loire through luxuriant green lawns. The Department of the Maine-et-Loire had bought the château and its outbuildings in 1842 and had turned it into a nursing home and psychiatric hospital. The doctors and other hospital personnel were lodged in the château proper.

Day after day I saw my father organize and administer his colony of the mentally ill after a model which at the time constituted the prototype of a modern psychiatric center. There was little restraint at Sainte-Gemmes. The patients were left as free as possible—a revolutionary concept at the end of the last century and the beginning of this one. Assisted by the understanding attitude of the doctors and nurses, the mentally ill felt safe and content in such a calm and beautiful environment.

Thus, my childhood was passed amid men who disturb, frighten, or cause shame. To be sure, society no longer classed them among the diseased, the lepers. But often they appeared to reflect a taint infecting the blood of an entire family. Nothing could have been more contrary to reality. I believe that a deranged mind, for one of the many reasons that I shall describe, should be neither more terrifying nor more humiliating in a family than a broken leg, and that it can often be as well cured as the body.

PATIENTS ARE PEOPLE LIKE US

A great alienist of the nineteenth century, Jean Esquirol, stated what I believe to be a fundamental truth when he described the mentally ill as men like others, but men who simply lack the ability to control and dissimulate their thoughts more effectively. At a very early age, because of long conversations with such people, conversations which did not much differ from those children have with so-called healthy people, I had the good fortune to discover that they belong to the same world as we.

Because of his origins, my father had enjoyed a rather adventurous life. Born in Alexandria, Egypt, into a large, poor, Jewish family of French nationality, he had left for Paris after graduating from preparatory school, sailing fourth class on a ship with only ten francs in his pocket.

He made a wretched living in the French capital by giving Hebrew and Arabic lessons. Studying very hard on his own, he succeeded in winning a scholarship in a competitive examination. He studied with the great psychiatrists of the time, but did not neglect the other branches of medicine—a lesson which was to be extremely useful to me when I followed in his footsteps and attempted to become the completely well-rounded doctor that he wanted me to be.

My father married very young. My mother's father was a Tunisian Jew who had married a French Catholic. He was a profoundly religious man who attended the synagogue every Saturday to read the Torah. My grandmother loved him deeply and later transferred that affection to me. She was an admirable woman, endowed with extraordinary intuition and an ardently warm heart. Also, she was free of any pettiness or small-mindedness, representing the best and noblest of what France has produced at the highest moments of our history. However, there were many difficulties, not the least of which was the revulsion—and the word is not too strong—in some circles against mixed marriages.

I lived with her and my sister on the rue Cacheux near the Parc Montsouris when I first arrived in Paris and during my internship at Sainte-Anne. When the war began in 1939, I was mobilized, so I took her to my parents, then living in Angers. Alas, they were going to be arrested by the Germans and fled to Paris, while my grandmother was obliged to take refuge in a home for the aged run by nuns in Angers. I was heartbroken when my grandmother died of the flu in 1945, and, because of my yellow star, I could not go to her without endangering my parents.

My mother, entirely devoted to Judaism, had inherited its great virtues. She was a constant support for my father with her ardent and combative character, her devotion to him and to their children, and her lofty conception of duty. She had a magnificent voice and was artistically talented as well. Shortly before her death, when she was very old and weakened by two leg fractures which confined her to her bed, she still would ask me to play the Pleyel grand piano in the salon of the rue Mirabeau in Angers when I came to visit her. I can still see her, exhausted and in pain, but transfigured by the variations of Suite Number 7 by Handel and in particular the Passacaglia.

I owe so much to my parents, who made me what I am and from whom I inherited the love of humanity without which it would have been impossible for me to fulfill my task.

But later it was my wife on whom I depended for the love and support so necessary to my well-being. She belonged to an illustrious French-Jewish family named Sorano, whose ancestors had come from Spain and settled first in Bayonne, then in Bordeaux and later in Toulouse. We were very close and, alas, our only child, a little girl, died at birth. My wife, a physics professor at the Lycée Camille Sée in Paris, was a brilliant woman as well as one deeply involved in humanity, and I could not have done my work without her.

My father was a man completely dedicated to medicine. He was not only responsible for the administration of the Sainte-Gemmes establishment but also for the medical treatments carried out there. I profited enormously from our long discussions during my childhood and, without being aware of it, thus became initiated into the profession which has dominated my entire life.

My father had already become concerned with the problems of social readaptation. He had peopled a small islet in the Loire, called the Île-aux-Chevaux, with convalescent patients, the majority of whom were peasants, who came there to prepare for their return to normal life. It was a familial colony where the farmers worked in the fields and began to taste the pleasures of freedom.

He did not limit himself to the psychiatric battle, but also performed emergency surgical operations. Also, at that time the region was ravaged by typhoid fever and bacillary dysentery during the summer months. A rigorous hygienist, he took steps to purify the water and to provide for defense against the mosquitoes. Finally, making use of his law studies, he set about trying to reform the 1838 law regarding the insane, whereby the indigent mentally ill were automatically placed in asylums by the police—voluntary confinement being reserved only for the mentally ill who were able to pay. He succeeded in abolishing this practice in the Maine-et-Loire region. I myself succeeded in extending that reform over all of France in 1937. Yes, I had received a fine example and profitable lessons on the banks of the Loire at the beginning of the century!

I had always been struck by my father's attitude toward his patients. He listened attentively and patiently, was kind but firm, and, above all, was available to them at all times. The mentally ill knew that whatever happened, they could call on him as director of the establishment at any hour of the day or night. I have always tried to follow in his steps in this regard.

He was also concerned with amusing his patients. On the Fourteenth of July, Bastille Day, all the park gates giving on to the Loire were opened and a crowd of people from the neighboring villages would invade the illuminated gardens.

The patients roamed freely in the park, mingling with the visitors. Of course a close but discreet eye was kept on them. The patients talked for years of those fêtes, which were not resumed after the First World War.

At first I had no idea of becoming a doctor or a psychiatrist at all. I was attracted by literature, philosophy, Greek, and Latin. Along with my comrade, Paul Meignant, I intended to prepare for the École Normale. We were so intent on studying Greek philosophy that a special class was created for us in the lycée at Angers, so that we might perfect ourselves in Plato's language.

But the War changed everything. In 1914, Paul and I were just about to pass our baccalaureate examination. Paul had left for Germany to perfect his German, and he was placed in an internment camp for many months. I decided that I should choose a more practical profession which would give me a chance to render service. So I began to study medicine, to my father's great delight. When Paul returned to France, he too took up the study of medicine and later became an eminent psychiatrist at Nancy. He died several years ago.

I entered the medical school in Angers, and my father insisted that I study general medicine before concentrating on psychiatry. That is why when I was mobilized in 1917 at the age of twenty, I was an intern in the medical and surgical services of the Angers hospital.

My first war experience was extremely disagreeable—an encounter with anti-Semitism. Of course, I had heard vague remarks from time to time at the university, but they were of no importance and quickly forgotten; this was different. At the station, when we were leaving for the front lines, I was surrounded by a group of medical students who were members of a right-wing royalist party, *Action française*. Their remarks were intolerable, and I was on the point of replying in a forceful manner when a young seminarian appeared beside me, expressed his indignation, and left with me.

I was appointed auxiliary doctor to the twelfth infantry regiment and took part in the operations in Lorraine and the defensive action against the German march toward Paris, as well as the battles which led to the Armistice. My regiment was decimated during the attack on the Hindenburg line before Saint-Quentin. There were so few officers left that I quit my role as doctor and became a company commander. I received the Military Cross and three citations.

When the War ended, I returned to my medical studies, but in Paris rather than Angers. After studying general medicine, pediatrics, dermatology, and neurology, I began to take courses in psychiatry. My father's dream had come to pass.

Trousseau, Tenon, Bicêtre—it was in the latter hospital that my future calling became clear to me. The neuropsychiatric service for children at Bicêtre, which had been created fifty years earlier by Bourneville, and was headed at the time of which I write by Dr. Roubinovitch, had seven hundred and fifty beds for boys and two hundred and fifty for girls, a children's museum and, what was most important of all, a first-rate staff of nurses and orderlies who brought to the care of their young patients a quasi-maternal devotion.

It was at Bicêtre that the great eighteenth-century alienist, Philippe Pinel, had brought about an early revolution in the treatment of the mentally ill. Until then, the accepted custom the world over had been to chain them in place by the leg, like dogs. Pinel was not praised for abolishing practices such as this, but instead was almost universally vilified.

The lives we led at the hospital followed a rigorous schedule, with only rare excursions outside its walls. Our days were spent in the picturesque doctors' and interns' lounge, not far from the court in which Dr. Guillotin first tried out his famous invention.

Bicêtre's chief physician, Dr. Roubinovitch, a comrade of mine, Bariéty, and I worked together in 1922 to take stock of the existing state of neuropsychiatry for children, an extraordinarily fascinating field. I have yet to explore fully those aspects of it dealing with the psychomotor development of infants, catalepsy in the newborn, and epilepsy in young people.

The last year of my internship was spent in what was then considered the temple of neuropsychiatry, Salpêtrière. Scholars from all over the world met there. Americans were especially attracted to it by the spirit of liberal discussion which reigned in the former general hospital, constructed by Le Vau under Louis XIV.

At Salpêtrière, I wrote my thesis on mental illnesses caused by cerebral tumors, and thereby uncorked a controversy that still lies at the heart of the science of psychiatry: Are the causes of mental disease psychological or physiological? When I appeared on the scene, the accepted doctrine was that of Charcot, which called for a clear and distinct separation between neurology and psychiatry. Charcot believed that all nervous or mental illness was caused by disturbances in the brain—either lesions, which gave rise to paralysis or motor dysfunction, or functional ailments, which led to psychic disorders. This concept is known as the organodynamic theory of Charcot.

However, a student of Charcot's, Joseph Babinski, who practiced at the same time as Freud, had an idea fundamentally different from his mentor's. Babinski contended that maladies of the brain centers, of whatever origin or kind, whether stemming from physical injury or other causes, engendered only motor disorders. He put aside the study of malfunctions of the personality as another branch of the science entirely—pure psychiatry. An illustration will point up this distinction. An automobile functions poorly for one of two reasons: Either the carburetor or some other part of the motor does not work, or the driver is at fault. Neurology is that part of science which takes into account breakdowns of the engine; psychiatry deals with the weaknesses of the driver. But then everyone, following the example set by Charcot, concentrated on the engine and ignored the driver.

My thesis, which bore the title "Mental Illnesses and Cerebral Tumors," laid the groundwork for a bridge to be constructed between neurology and psychiatry. At that time, when cerebral tumors were not yet so well understood as they are today, I followed closely not only every case of brain tumor at Salpêtrière in the practice of Achille Souques, the great neurologist who was my teacher, but also in that of Professor Guillain, and I also examined examples of this disease that were brought to my attention in the Paris hospitals. At the same time I began work in neurosurgery, under De Martel, the prestigious father of neurosurgery in France, who had himself interned with Souques.

De Martel was not then practicing in the hospitals, but cared for his patients in his own clinic in the rue Vercingétorix and paid out of his own pocket the expenses of those who lacked means. Besides an extraordinary competence not only in his field but in all branches of medicine and surgery, he possessed singular moral conviction and was a true Renaissance man. At the unbearable news that the Germans had entered Paris, this admirable and unusual figure, who lived by the code of honor of the old French aristocracy, put an end to his life!

Later on I worked in the field of neurosurgery with Clovis Vincent, Babinski's gifted student and De Martel's close friend. Vincent created the first neurological service at the Pitié and held the first chair in neurosurgery ever to be set up at the Faculty of Medicine in Paris. I also worked with my friend Professor Petit Dutaillis, who later occupied the chair in neurosurgery.

The study of brain tumors, specifically the anatomical and anatomicopathological examinations that we and our friend Ivan Bertrand, the great anatomist, made on these growths at Salpêtrière, led us to the discovery of a hitherto unknown syndrome, the phenomenon of cerebral edema, or excessive cerebro-spinal fluid in the brain, which causes the mental confusion observed in cases of brain tumor. Such disorientation manifests itself in a slowing down of the mental processes, in dreams, and in a sort of blockage of the will, which itself, contrary to what takes place in psychosis, is not altered. Neither, as I have demonstrated in tests, is the personality changed, but merely disturbed, obstructed by a barrier external to itself.

I should like here to interrupt the chronological continuity of my story in order to show the reader clearly, via a series of specific cases, the nature of an astonishingly precise and complex cerebral geography. Everyone is acquainted with the phenomenon of hemiplegia, which is brought about by the destruction of certain convolutions in one side of the brain that are linked to movements in the opposite side of the body. Similar phenomena also exist whose origin is psychic, or functional, and which are given the name of hysterical hemiplegia. In the latter instances, the mechanism of execution, the "engine," remains intact, and it is the personality, the "driver," whose will to accomplish the movement is impaired.

However, not only movement may be affected. Named according to the area or geography of the brain that is involved, we have *alexia*, or the inability to understand ideas represented by the written word; *aphasia*, or powerlessness to translate thoughts into words; *amusia*, which is a disorder of the musical sense, whether in reading or in execution; *agraphia*, or the incapacity to write; *acalculia*, impairment of the ability to use figures in even the simplest mathematical operations; *apraxia*, or inability to execute ordinary acts or movements.

Let us take a look at alexia. A woman getting off a streetcar feels dazed and suddenly dizzy. She can see street signs but is unable to read them. She buys a newspaper, finds that the words signify nothing to her. All memory of the letters which make them up has been lost to her.

Where does alexia come from? This question has given rise to interminable arguments. Thanks, however, to a patient who suffered from this disorder as the result of a craniocerebral bullet wound, I was able to make some extremely accurate observations. The ophthalmologist Hartmann, my friend Ivan Bertrand, and I first reconstructed the exact trajectory of the projectile, then used precise radiographic clues to enable us to make a valuable contribution toward pinpointing the origin of the alexia.

The patient was a thirty-three-year-old woman who had been shot by a revolver in the left occipital, lower and posterior region of the skull. After several days in a coma, she recovered consciousness, but she could not read a single word and was scarcely able to recognize letters, though she could distinguish a few numbers. When a newspaper was placed before her, she could give its name, not because she was able to read but because she recognized the typographical layout of its masthead. An interesting detail was that she could write but not read what she had written, and so we understood that only the area of the brain governing reading power was affected. The patient spoke, understood and executed even complicated acts, and, with some hesitation, designated certain objects as requested. When shown a pen, she at first said, "That's a pencil," but on her own initiative rectified her mistake. She could tell time, recognize places, and knew the season of the year.

We tried every trick we knew to cure her. Our hopes of teaching her to read through the act of writing, as Charcot had succeeded in doing in cases of pure word-blindness, failed utterly. When we asked her to trace printed characters with her finger, she was unable to do so. A procedure which we had employed successfully in another case, consisting of making the patient trace printed letters in the air, then translate them into cursive writing, proved no more efficacious. It became apparent that her alexia was directly connected to the destruction of the lower part of the brain at the level of the temporo-occipital region.

Was it possible to reeducate her? Alas, the answer was no. In that case the "engine" had been put out of commission forever.

I have also come across many cases of aphasia, a disorder which I was able to approach with confidence since I had been practicing both neurology and psychiatry. An aphasiac is not a lunatic, as today's psychiatrist who has not studied neurology may be led to conclude; such a conclusion illustrates, in fact, the extreme danger of the specialization so dear to our time.

In aphasia a very limited region of the brain is involved—called Wernicke's zone—from which spring all the words we need to express ourselves. An alteration in this part of the brain causes the meanings of words to be lost; they signify nothing when the patient hears them spoken by another person, but seem to be part of a foreign language. Wernicke's zone is situated in the first and second temporal regions of the left hemisphere.

Aphasia takes several forms and is called "motor" when, to the difficulty of finding words, is added that of pronouncing them. Wernicke's aphasia is the term used when the patient can neither bring words to mind nor comprehend them. Aphemia means that the patient is able to use words but cannot express ideas with them.

Reeducation is almost impossible in cases of Wernicke's aphasia. In instances of pure motor aphasia, that is to say aphemia or anarthria, in which the comprehension of language remains intact, reeducation can be achieved. With the help of her son, who devoted infinite pains to teaching her how to speak again, I successfully treated a patient suffering from this latter malady. My victory was obvious when she read aloud to me Voltaire's letters to Signor Theodoti de Tavazzi on the respective merits of the French and Italian languages!

Amusia, or the disorder of the musical sense, has been little observed by science. It is possible that, in order to cure stricken musicians, doctors are needed who are as devoted to the art as are their patients. This happens to be my case, and the strangest patient along this line that I have had occasion to treat I came across while working with Professor Souques. It was a woman who—disturbing paradox—was a piano teacher. Hers was a case of Wernicke's aphasia, total, complete, covering every aspect of language. At the same time, she retained, to a degree, her musical gift.

Her disease came upon her in the course of one of her lessons. Suddenly, in the presence of her students, she began to utter gibberish. You can imagine the children's dismay and their reports to their parents afterward: "Our piano teacher has gone crazy."

They probably added that she was "deaf" too, for she talked without stop, replacing words she failed to find with meaningless chatter, which made it impossible for her to hear what her pupils might be saying. On her arrival at Salpêtrière, the consensus of the interns was no different from that of our students: "Completely mad," they said.

It seemed that they must be right. The patient's speech was utterly incoherent and illogical; there was no connection between any of the sentences she uttered, and she substituted one word for another, employing clichés that had nothing to do with the thoughts she wished to express. We call such a condition "paraphasia," or, even more colorfully, "jargonophasia." The center of language was definitely affected. Her fate was to become one of those patients we nickname "chatterbox aphasiacs," who overwhelm their hearers with incoherent jabbering and so are mistakenly considered to be genuinely insane.

Now, appearances to the contrary, it happens that the personality of such a patient remains unchanged. I proved this to be the case on the day that I led my piano teacher into the only place in Salpêtrière where a piano existed: the lounge. I sat her down before the instrument and asked her to perform. She began with a dance tune which she rendered with a well-marked rhythm, a certain agility of execution, but also with a few false notes and an occasional jerky passage. I knew nothing about the professional standing of my patient, but I was aware that her entire professional life had been spent in preparing students for the conservatory.

When I made her repeat the test, she insisted on playing the same dance tune, as though she remembered nothing else. Since she was suffering from total auditory aphasia, that is, she could hear words but not identify them, I could not convey to her how poor her performance was. I was, however, able to make her understand that I wished her to play a few scales, and she obeyed, though without enthusiasm.

I then took her place at the piano and played two well-known, simple tunes: the "Marseillaise" and "Au Clair de la Lune." Her face remained impassive, as if those melodies reminded her of nothing. Since "Au Clair de la Lune" was the easier of the two tunes, I played it for her a second time, then I made a sign to indicate that it was her turn. She produced something that had nothing at all to do with the famous refrain. I began again at the beginning and, by dint of patience, was able to get her to play an air which reproduced the rhythm but not the exact notes, after which she literally massacred the "Marseillaise" and some other works.

Next I played scales, into which I introduced false notes. To my astonishment, she rapped my knuckles, as though I were one of her students, and reproached me very seriously. Then she played the scale herself.

I took over the keyboard once more and played the C major scale instead of the C minor with which I had begun. She seemed annoyed. When I went back to the C minor she showed her approval, making it clear that she could distinguish the major from the minor key. But I observed that she could not notice mistakes nearly so readily when she could not see the keyboard, and so I realized that her musical hearing was on the whole rather badly affected.

On the other hand, although she could not tell a vowel from a consonant, she read a sonata of Clementi's perfectly and played it reasonably well. She labored over a Bach prelude, playing it slowly and hesitantly, as a beginner might. I found that she retained a good memory of the rudiments of music and of musical writing.

When I stopped the experiment, the patient rose from the bench and looked around as if seeing for the first time the designs, for the most part pretty scabrous, which ornamented the walls of the lounge.

"How disgusting," she remarked clearly.

I have recorded this comment in order to demonstrate that her personality did remain unchanged.

In spite of all we tried to do, we were unable to help her. She died in 1927, and the autopsy performed on her body revealed a large area of degeneration in the left hemisphere of the brain, occupying the temporal lobe almost exclusively. Such cases of amusia caused by an arterial obliteration or a circulatory disorder in a narrowly localized zone are common.

I also took care of a great musician, one of the most famous of our century, whose symptoms were those of the typical amusiac, without any trace of aphasia or any disorder of the personality. The onset appeared as he was in the midst of writing a concerto. Suddenly his hand stopped writing notes. The latter ceased to have any meaning for him. When he went to the piano, he found that he could not play, although he was an extraordinary virtuoso.

He first went to consult Professor Alajouanine, who called me in on the case because he knew that I was a musician. I received the celebrated composer with great emotion. Not only did I admire him deeply, but he was a man of exceptional sensitivity, tact, and instinctive judgment, qualities which his disease had in no way altered.

When we sat down together at the piano, it was he who asked me to play one of his works. I was reluctant to do so, as the piece was not easy and I did not feel capable of rendering its spirit, let alone its form. However, at his insistence, I plunged in. At each of my innumerable false notes or errors of style or nuance he stopped me. I was provided, of course, with a score, but he was guided by his ear alone.

I confess that I was unable to restore to that great man, whose fame has grown since his death, the gift, nay the genius, that had once been his. Alas, Professor Alajouanine and I lost sight of him. Perhaps he had lost patience; it is also possible that we, in any case, would never have succeeded in really helping him. However that may be, he later on consulted a celebrated neurosurgeon who performed an exploratory operation on his brain, in the hope of determining which area was affected. The composer of so many masterpieces died of complications following the operation.

Where does amusia come from? Does it originate in the same center as language itself? Like aphasia, it constitutes a disorder of automatism localized in the brain, but does the musical sense occupy an independent seat? Certain clinical facts would seem to indicate that it does, and Charcot made comments on this subject which I find fascinating.

He had as a patient a forty-five-year-old former member of the *Garde républicaine* of Paris who had given up his military career in order to play the trombone in an orchestra. At the same time, he was employed as a copyist, work which required not only an extensive knowledge of music but also quick and sure reflexes in setting down notes for scores and correcting errors. Great composers such as Massenet used his services.

One summer, after playing at the casino at Trouville, he returned to Paris feeling rather fatigued. He discovered that he could no longer copy music. He could read it, decipher it, sing it, but he found it impossible to set it down on paper. However, he was still able to write words, which means that he was suffering from musical agraphia. When he took up his trombone, the sound he made resembled nothing at all, and certainly not music.

"In my mind," this man was to remark, "I could hear the notes perfectly. I could see the melody form itself in my head, but I could not reproduce it."

He went to see Charcot, who examined him, made a note of his symptoms and diagnosed the disorder. Unfortunately, the great physician did not resort to any anatomical verification of his findings. However, as a result of his description of the case, I found it possible to make an interesting hypothesis: Given the connection between common aphasia and disturbances of musical language, though it cannot be proven, amusia points to the existence of lesions in the area of Wernicke's zone.

It is in relation to cases of apraxia, that is, to disorders of movement, that the controversy about these afflictions, whether they are or are not of organic origin, can be understood most clearly. Apraxia involves the loss of automatism in life's most ordinary gestures— waving a hand in greeting, blowing a kiss, striking a match, lighting a cigarette—all motions which we accomplish without conscious thought. Apraxia takes two forms: Either the patient, though his intelligence remains unaffected, is not able to execute movements, or he no longer knows how to accomplish them. Thus, in lighting a candle, he may be incapable of governing the movement of his hand, or he may try to do so but no longer remembers what he should do: Instead of striking the match on the box, he may strike it on the candle.

"Praxes," or everyday gestures, which have been so well studied by my friend Morlaas, who worked under Charles Foix, must not be confused with reflexes. The former are situated in the upper lobes of the brain and their loss is linked for the most part to localized cerebral lesions. The affliction is thus organic, caused either by a lesion or by a process of degeneration—a clogged artery, for example. But certain authors attempted to apply the principles learned from the sensational discoveries made in relation to praxes to the entire psyche, making man a creature composed merely of automatisms and totally ignoring the idea of personality. I took issue with this narrow —but generally accepted—concept.

It must be pointed out that at the time the disagreements among scholars reached a degree of intensity which is difficult to imagine today. I remember an argument I had with Dr. Meyerson, a highly distinguished psychologist who wished to extend this concept of automatism to cover all human activity. One day, we met in a small café near the Opéra Comique. Soon, to the astonishment of the other patrons, we found ourselves on our feet looking for all the world as though we were about to engage in a boxing bout. We were promptly asked to leave the premises.

Such was the atmosphere in the world of psychiatry when, my thesis written, I left Salpêtrière to join Professor Henri Claude as Clinic Head at Sainte-Anne Hospital. My life there was to prove enthralling and dramatic for the young doctor enamored of his calling I then was.

Professor Henri Claude was the neurologist par excellence, a devout disciple of Charcot and totally convinced of the validity of his teacher's organodynamic theory. I can set this concept forth in a word: In Charcot's opinion, a lesion in the center of the brain gave rise to a series of organic symptoms, while a functional affliction caused mental illness. This was a clever and simple idea to which I did not subscribe even at that early date. Claude believed that a lesion in Wernicke's zone produced aphasia, while a functional disorder brought about only the loss of speech—a psychic or hysterical muteness. Now, the works of Babinski had already shown that these two classes of disorders—hysterical syndromes and organic symptoms —had nothing in common, that indeed an abyss yawned between the two sorts of ailments.

Torn as he was between neurology and psychiatry (to which he had come quite late), Claude did not feel at ease with his theory and never succeeded in synthesizing the two sciences with anatomicoclinical and biological methods. Babinski, on the contrary, had pushed his clinical research extremely far regarding organic symptoms in illness, inventing numerous tests in order to bring them to light. The examinations he carried out were very long indeed and called for infinite patience on his part as he made tests designed to uncover organic disturbances, for example, reflexes involving the labyrinth of the ears, the soles of the feet, and the base of the neck. Their goal was to bring to light every symptom which, not being able to be brought about by the will, indicated an organic or functional affliction of the brain centers; to follow, through the body and the mind of a patient, the path of the impulse so as to discover whether his "breakdowns" were or were not the result of a lesion.

One day a young girl, evidencing all the manifestations of a hysterical crisis, turned up in Professor Claude's service at Sainte-Anne. Her body was bent in such an extreme arc that the back of her head nearly touched her heels, and in this position she bounded straight up to the ceiling, then fell back on her bed—an impressive example of the "major hysteria" described by Charcot.

All the doctors were intrigued by her and she became the center of professional attention. Each of us had his own idea, and we sometimes contradicted each other fiercely. Claude himself was fascinated.

PATIENTS ARE PEOPLE LIKE US

The poor girl became a real obsession for all of us, as we hoped to discover, through her, the origin of and the cure for epilepsy. A passionate curiosity is the true motivating force of medical research.

Professor Claude finally delivered his opinion of the case. He had noticed that the girl kept her arms rigidly at her sides, like two splints, with the palms of her hands turned outward. He believed that the cause of the trouble was a functional disorder in the midbrain, the mesencephalon, and from this he argued that Charcot had been right in attributing all pathology to organic or functional causes. He even urged the celebrated Tinel, my friend Lamache, and me to make a presentation of the case before the French Medical Society. That unforgettable session marked me for life. Envision if you will a hall filled to overflowing with the most eminent doctors of the time—an audience which by its very definition would certainly not be lenient in its judgment—and, on the rostrum, with Tinel at our head, three young men, their hearts pounding with apprehension.

I arrived at the same moment as Babinski, whom I knew and who had always been friendly toward me. He was a giant of a man, well over six feet tall, with an extraordinarily deep and resounding voice. He was furious before the meeting was even called to order, for he was in total disagreement with the thesis Claude was about to present. Upon seeing me, he leaned forward and declared in a voice that struck terror in my heart:

"You're going to get your ears pinned back, young man!"

The arguments began and immediately turned acrimonious. Babinski refused to accept Claude's interpretation, as given by Tinel, and the two men exchanged bitter remarks. The audience of specialists plunged into the fray, but the real contest was between Babinski and Tinel. I must admit that I was shaken by Babinski's assurance.

At eight o'clock, at the end of a session that had begun early in the afternoon, Babinski rose to his feet and proposed that we adjourn, saying that it would take another session to settle the matter.

On the agreed date, we found ourselves once again in the same room, which was even more jammed than it had been the first time.

Babinski, who arrived with several of his assistants, was backed by an impressive array of his friends, and I had the distinct impression that we were confronting an army bent on our destruction. I was terrified above all by Babinski. We fought him and his friends for five hours, at the end of which neither camp had given an inch.

"There's no point in continuing," Babinski declared at last. "Perhaps when we are rested Professor Claude will permit us to meet on his premises and examine the patient."

Professor Claude, though none too enthusiastic, could scarcely refuse. On the given day, Babinski presented himself, and we—Claude, Percival Bailey, a Chicago doctor who was working with us, some other students, and I—received him. That was the first occasion on which I had an opportunity to observe an examination by Babinski. It was one of the most impressive sights it has been my privilege to witness.

He was an extremely meticulous diagnostician. I can see him still, surrounded by students in the presence of a difficult case. First he would invite one or another of us to look for reflexes. While the person called on gave his opinion, Babinski would don a special monocle, an accessory permitting him to see in greater detail, which terrified his assistants. When the student had finished, Babinski would announce:

"Our turn to examine the patient."

We would wait in terror for his verdict. If our fellow student had been wrong, Babinski would heap opprobrium on the miscreant in his most cutting voice.

It took me a long time—you will soon see under what conditions —to understand Babinski's method. He was capable of spending hours examining a single patient without uttering a word. The principle he adhered to was obvious. He had, as I have said, invented numerous tests designed to distinguish between symptoms independent of the will, which are therefore manifestations of pathological cerebral localization, and the aggregate of symptoms which would show that the will was involved. Thus, I cannot voluntarily move an isolated muscle, but I can open or shut my hand. If an individual muscle contracts, this has occurred independently of the will. If, however, volition enters into the action, we may consider that to be a mental symptom, the sign of a hysterical disorder. Babinski did not say, as did the authors of his time, that this was a matter of shamming, but rather a disorder which took the guise of a voluntary movement.

Let us return to our young girl patient. Babinski spent the entire afternoon examining her. He turned her in every direction, placed her in extraordinary positions, tested her reflexes, set her upside down, then right side up. He finally declared that he could find nothing wrong with the mesencephalon.

Claude, of course, received this diagnosis with embarrassment. What then, he asked, did Babinski think the girl was suffering from? Babinski was only able to answer that a localized disorder existed in the central nervous system, and that it did not matter whether the disturbance was organic or functional.

It has happened in, let us say, a patient suffering from cerebral uremia that one of Babinski's symptoms would crop up, only to disappear when the poisoning had ceased. The only difference between organic (bodily) and functional (mental) disorders lies in their severity and their duration. However, in both cases "localization" is involved.

Now, a fundamental difference that was not understood at that time is that in cases of hysteria, both neurotic and psychotic, it is impossible to find any localization. Everything points to the personality and the will, and not to a lesion, as being at the origin of the trouble, and therein lay the mystery. If one dismissed the notion of the patient faking, how could one explain the transformation of a purely psychic disorder into a motor reaction? How could the patient behave as he did without consciously deciding to do so? This translation of a mental illness into a physical affliction remained an enigma. How, for example, could that young girl, Professor

Claude's patient, perform her astonishing somersaults if she was not suffering from a lesion? We were at an impasse.

That incursion of Babinski's into Professor Claude's domain, however, was to shake my life to its foundations. The direction my career was to take was changed by that encounter with a man who was undoubtedly one of the great geniuses of modern psychiatry.

After he had examined the girl, Babinski took my arm and said, "Drop by some evening and we'll go into all this again."

I, of course, accepted with alacrity. At his home on Boulevard Haussmann I met Jarkowski, the great neurologist of equal eminence, who espoused Babinski's ideas and was also of Polish origin. My interest in Babinski's ideas was so evident that he invited me to visit him at the Pitié. After spending two or three mornings there, I found it impossible not to return again and again. It soon became clear that Claude was displeased by my intimacy with the man who had contradicted him so violently.

I had just passed my examinations for appointment to a teaching post, and Claude had intended that I should be his successor in the professorship at Sainte-Anne. But after his clash with Babinski and my friendship with the latter, Claude soon conceived a horror of my very presence. I remarked that the mere sight of me seemed to inspire in him such aversion that whenever I entered the room he actually grimaced, and one day I suggested that my presence appeared to distress him.

"That's an understatement," he replied.

I immediately left Sainte-Anne and never saw him again. When he was very old and ill, I attempted to call on him, but he sent word that it was useless for me to take the trouble. His hostility never faded, so that I continued to work with Babinski, a decision which I have never regretted.

Babinski taught me to conduct examinations such as are no longer made today, a regrettable loss to both science and to patients. He carried the art of clinical inquiry to the highest degree of rigor and perfection and was unsparing in effort and in time. He did not rule out the use of technical aids, of course, such as X ray, physiological testing, and so on, but the picture he built up was ceaselessly corrected and completed by clinical study.

After the War, laboratory work advanced so prodigiously that some doctors looked condescendingly on clinical observations as "subjective." A conflict grew up between fierce partisans of clinical examination and adepts of the new techniques. As is often the case, everyone took extreme positions, though the truth lay somewhere in between, and once again Babinski was at the heart of the controversy. The question to be solved was the exact localization of tumors of the spinal cord.

Common sense would tell us that in order to operate on them one must know their exact position. Babinski had perfected a method involving the modification of reflexes in order to determine whether such reflexes are present or have been destroyed. Let us suppose, for example, that we have a person afflicted with a growth on the spinal cord. A series of pinches applied to the skin from the foot to the groin induces a contraction of the lower limb. The foot as well as the leg bends uncontrollably. Let us say that the phenomenon stops at one spot. In the entire region below the site of the tumor the patient will feel nothing—neither touch nor friction nor heat nor cold nor pain—as it is completely anesthetized. One then calculates the difference between the level of the destruction of the reflexes and that of the area of sensitivity. The location of the tumor will be found within a millimeter.

But Professor Sicard and his student Forestier had perfected another procedure in which a needle was introduced into the cephalo-spinal fluid and a substance called Lipiodol injected, after which the patient was placed in different positions—head down, head up, legs in the air and so on—and the path of the substance traced by X ray. When an obstacle was encountered, the location of the tumor was discovered.

Violent arguments raged in the Neurological Society between Babinski and the technocrats of the period. The former brought in a patient suffering from a growth on the spinal cord which caused him to be incontinent. Without causing the man any pain, Babinski examined him, calculated the position of the tumor and had it removed by surgery. A month later he brought the patient back to show that he was walking normally and was completely recovered, never once having been subjected to painful or traumatizing examinations.

The technocrats, on the other hand, gave their patients a disagreeable injection, forced them to make difficult and painful movements and to adopt awkward positions, only to come up with no better results than Babinski. In my opinion, Babinski personally applying his own method was infinitely superior to all the machines or gadgets in the world.

Alas, Babinski isn't with us anymore, and I regret his loss every day. Technology has triumphed and clinical observation is rarely practiced nowadays. There is no end to the testing, which is agonizing, sometimes traumatic, for the patient.

Today, imagine a man who complains of severe headaches and is suspected of having a brain tumor. A doctor like Babinski would have reassured the sufferer very quickly, but now he is subjected to a succession of X rays and injections (first of air and then of liquid) into the ventricles of his brain, then to interminable manipulations, often extending over periods of several weeks. All this is done in order to tell the patient that he has no tumor.

"But I still have the headaches," he protests.

"Go and consult a psychiatrist," he is told.

I once treated a woman of nearly eighty who had been attacked by a dog in a street in Charenton. The dog had not injured her, but it had torn her dress, and her emotional reaction had been intense. Soon afterward she began to suffer great pain in her lower limbs. I was called in to examine her, and, to my astonishment, while evaluating her neurological state, I discovered radicular areas of anesthesia which led me to suspect an organic injury. My observation was ignored, and the patient was sent to a mental hospital to be treated by psychoanalysis. At the end of three months she was completely paralyzed and incontinent.

When I examined the woman a second time, using Babinski's method, I observed signs of medullary compression. I sent her to Professor Alajouanine at Salpêtrière, who confirmed my diagnosis and saw to it that she was operated on by Dr. Thurel. Thurel found a benign tumor pressing on the medulla in the region of the lower backbone. He removed it and the patient recovered completely.

This story shows how important it is for psychiatrists to have neurological training.

Thus, the true solution is to apply first the clinical method and, if that is found to be insufficient, to resort then to technological testing. Babinski's method must be preserved, for its loss would have grave consequences. Even in America, there are many admirers of his clinical method who believe as I do that to jettison it completely would be abominable. But I hardly see signs of a revival in this direction.

I still feel the deepest admiration for Babinski, who brought me to such an important stage in my intellectual development and in my career. However, at that time, and in spite of Babinski's magnificent contribution, we still had a mystery to solve: How did a psychological disorder become converted into a physical illness?

CHAPTER

CATATONIA:
AWAKENING FROM THE DREAM

Before me lies an inert body. I lift an arm; the arm obediently takes and holds the position in which I place it. I pull it to the right, push it back to the left; it does just as I wish. I can make that sleeping being accomplish any movement, as though he were a doll. I can even place him in strange, uncomfortable positions and he will hold them with admirable docility. This state is what we call catalepsy.

Another patient, or the same one a while later, refuses to do anything I wish. If I push him, he resists fiercely; if I pull him, he clings desperately to his place. This is called negativism.

Or he may start brusquely from his sleep and become agitated, even violent, flailing his arms and throwing his legs about. On a sudden impulse, and for no apparent reason, he may assault his neighbor; or else he may faint, assuming some ecstatic attitude, generally that of the Crucifixion. This is called hyperkinesia, that is to say, an abnormal amount of uncontrolled muscular action.

It is not only the minds of the patients I have described which are affected; they also suffer from disorders involving the sympathetic nervous system. For example, they salivate so copiously that puddles form around them. Their faces are extraordinarily pale, since their blood vessels have contracted, and their legs may become scarlet or white as linen. Their stomach and intestines contract; even the rate of their heartbeat changes. In short, the ailment from which they suffer is accompanied by important changes in their bodily functions as well as in their mental state.

I became interested very early on in the study of catatonia, the condition just described, for I sensed obscurely that it could furnish me with clues as to what links existed between the functional and the organic in certain illnesses.

Since at that time neurology and psychiatry were considered to be separate sciences, catatonia was treated either as a neurological illness, which implied an injury to the central nervous system, or as a psychological malady, which meant that the patient was either shamming or that he was suffering from a delusion.

Thanks to a technique which had only lately come into use at the time—the recording of the electrical currents that accompany muscular and nervous activity—I discovered rather quickly that neither of those approaches was valid. Working under Professor Claude and with the help of two close friends, Thévenard (a neurologist and student of Charles Foix) and Mademoiselle Mouel de Kérangué (a student of Laugier at the Sorbonne), I experimented with the new method. We paid the utmost attention to details, insisting on absolute meticulousness, and every result that we obtained showed us that catatonia could in no sense be considered a neurological affliction. We found in the muscles of catatonics currents comparable to those of voluntary contractions, which, however, disappeared once the patient awoke from his psychic sleep. The immobility of catatonics is also entirely different from that of patients suffering from organic problems. The catatonic's dysfunction is linked to what can only be described as a psychic torpor.

But this does not mean that the malady is a purely psychic phenomenon, since the will is incapable, for example, of reproducing the changes recorded on the electrocardiogram, just as it cannot produce spasms of vessels and capillaries or respiratory disorders. As soon as the patient is awakened, all those anomalies vanish. We had made the important discovery of a new kind of psychosomatic affliction, a special sleep governing the inhibition of both volition and initiative and causing cardiovascular and respiratory irregularities, a cataleptic sleep found in both schizophrenia and hysteria, which varies only in degree. In cases of hysteria, the cataleptic sleep is lighter, which explains the "miraculous" cures, the patient finding himself cured after the administration of electroshock—a treatment which I replaced by the administration of a drug called scopochloralose.

But I still had to learn the reasons for the torpor itself. I observed that it was accompanied by vivid dreams which often had as their subjects the patient's former cares and preoccupations. These very active hallucinations would be transformed into delirium, the patient's psychological symptoms being determined by the nature of his visions.

At that point, with the help of De Jong, a Dutch neurologist whom I had met by chance at a Neurological Society lecture on the use of bulbocapnine in the treatment of tremors, I succeeded in reproducing catatonia clinically. The substance in question was a plant extract not found in man, an alkaloid derived from a bulb, *Corydalis cava,* which was discovered by Gadamer in Germany in 1902.

Until then, De Jong, who was familiar with the work done in Germany by Peters, Shaltenbrand, and others on bulbocapnine and the cataleptic immobility which it seemed to induce (Peters had noticed that animals injected with this substance suddenly became motionless), had failed to relate this state of immobility, which is accompanied by currents of muscular action, to human catatonia because he did not know whether catatonia was a muscular or a mental phenomenon; and he had trusted in the erroneous conclusions of Froehlich and Mayer in Vienna, who believed that currents of action were absent in this condition.

Now Thévenard and I, in our extensive studies on a series of catatonic patients, had not only discovered the existence of such currents of muscular action in human catatonia but had used bulbocapnine to create the first experimental state of catatonia. I referred De Jong to the reports that Claude, Thévenard, and I had written and at the same time showed him our charts of identical curves of currents of action produced by administration of the drug. I also informed him of the other symptoms we had found in catatonia: negativism, hyperkinesis, fits of Kahlbaum's gesticulations, disorders involving the autonomic nervous system, especially salivating. Thereafter, he and I worked together, discovering all these symptoms in animals as well, and in September 1928 the first report on the creation of experimental catatonia through the agency of bulbocapnine was presented by De Jong and me before the Neurological Society.

This step forward was the outcome of the discovery by Thévenard and me (described above) of currents of action in the electromyograms of catatonics. Our auxiliary troops were an army of animals of every species, ranging from the lower vertebrates (amphibians, reptiles, and so on) up to birds, cats, monkeys, and the like.

De Jong, who had treated pathological tremors with bulbocapnine, had felt just as I had that the substance would be capable of reproducing catatonia clinically. But his lack of thorough knowledge of catatonia itself had prevented him from carrying his research to a successful conclusion, until our meeting provided the "shock" that sent us far along on our path.

When De Jong came to Paris, I staged a real gathering of catatonics for him, bringing them all together at Sainte-Anne, so that he could see for himself all the symptoms of the disorder. For his part, he revealed to me all he knew about the drug bulbocapnine. We agreed then and there to experiment on a cat.

The results were most impressive, for the cat reacted to bulbocapnine in the same way that our catatonics reacted to their malady. Like my patients, the animal kept the positions in which we placed him. If we set him between two chairs, he stayed there. If we pushed him, he would jump with alacrity but then become petrified as before, his eyes dulled, with no more sign of life in him than if he had been stuffed. His eyes were open, he was not asleep; he seemed instead to have been almost literally turned to stone. We could pinch him, make threatening gestures, even hold a flame to his whiskers; still he would sit unmoving as a statue. When we pushed him, he gripped the floor. If we did manage to be so insistent as to force him to move, he would resume his Buddha-like immobility immediately afterward. An hour and a half after we had given him his injection, we forced him to descend a staircase, but that involved pushing him down each step. He showed exactly the same negative attitude as had my human catatonics. Babinski was extremely interested in the work that De Jong and I were doing, and for the first time he admitted that one could pass from a purely neurological concept to a biological doctrine. It was our research, moreover, which provided the impetus for the Rockefeller Foundation's work in biopsychiatry.

De Jong invited me to continue our studies in Amsterdam, where there was an institute for the study of the brain and where we would receive the help of such organizations as Professor Brouwer's physiology laboratory, the Institute of Tropical Medicine, and the zoo. I was able to accept his offer thanks to a grant from the Rockefeller Foundation, which was directed at that time by Messrs. Gregg and O'Brien. These two men later backed me in setting up at Charenton my laboratory for the study of experimental catatonia and experimental neurosurgery, attached to the School of Higher Applied Studies.

Those fascinating days at the Wilhelmina Hospital in Amsterdam were not without their tense moments. One day we were experimenting with boa constrictors, and as I left for lunch I forgot to close the laboratory door. Our subjects, immobile as rocks until left to their own devices, came to and undertook a tour of the hospital. You can well imagine the panic up and down the corridors and in the waiting rooms.

The observations we made there led to valuable discoveries, such as the fact that in the lower vertebrates life oscillated continuously between a total absence of motion and violent movement. We found that among the more evolved vertebrates, birds for example, akinesia was not total. A bird is always in movement, be it only a matter of quivering, and of its own accord takes flight. Such movement arising from within the animal, and not merely in response to an external stimulus, is what we call initiative.

Now bulbocapnine produced no catatonia in the lower vertebrates, which possess no initiative, but only in birds and mammals, which do have initiative and lost it under the effects of this drug.

Later on at Charenton, I often made the following experiment at conferences. I would inject a pigeon with bulbocapnine, place it on my head and then take a long walk out in the streets. The bird never once flew away. I once put the pigeon on the head of one of my students who was a very good dancer and told her to dance as she pleased without regard for the bird. It never budged. When I pushed it, it did not fall but simply flew normally. This retention of automatic movement, and at the same time suspension of initiative, in animals under the influence of bulbocapnine proved to be identical to that found in catatonics.

Another significant finding I made while in Holland was that the phenomena obtained with bulbocapnine varied according to the dosage. When the drug was injected in small amounts it brought about only sleep, from which the animal could be awakened by a mere touch. Stronger doses made the animal cataleptic, and thus able to remain in the most difficult possible positions. In my laboratory, I used to put cats on the top of a column near the ceiling, where they would remain with their bodies arched—a truly astonishing sight. Still larger doses of bulbocapnine produced epilepsy with its entire range of convulsions, and a maximum injection brought on the well-known decerebrate rigidity. We had succeeded perfectly in producing experimental catatonia.

I kept Babinski informed of the minutest details of our work, the worth of which he readily recognized, even when it proved him to have been wrong. Indeed, experimental catatonia became accepted the world over and opened the way not only to the development of the science of neuropsychiatry but also to a pharmacology useful in the treatment of mental illnesses.

In order to apply to human illness the knowledge we had gained from our experiments, it now became necessary to discover the nature of the substances secreted by the organism that produced catatonia. What poisons flowing in our blood gave rise to such a curious affliction, which affected not only the mind but the body as well? At this juncture, Dr. Antoine Laporte, a doctor working in the Paris hospitals, and I had occasion to treat a patient who was to point me in the direction of an answer.

Her body totally flexed, arched rigidly on her bed, her eyes vacant as a corpse's, the patient appeared to be utterly at the mercy of some mysterious force. She was the wife of a great Parisian industrialist, and many doctors had unsuccessfully attempted to cure her. At last my friend Dr. Laporte, who knew of my work, called me in on the case.

I walked around the bed where the patient lay, noting all the symptoms of catatonia. When Laporte and I approached her, she seemed to be unaware of our presence. I took her arm and tried to move it, but she countered my attempt with savage resistance. I questioned her, but she neither replied nor even seemed to hear me.

Then, without warning, she looked straight at us and screamed, "Russian doctors!"

The ray of light in her eyes died as quickly as it had come and she lapsed back into unconsciousness almost instantly. At that moment, the door opened and her husband, who had been waiting in the next room and had become alarmed at her cry, appeared. His wife awoke a second time from her comatose state, saw her husband and screamed, "It's a ghost!"

Laporte told me that his patient had suffered for many years from an intestinal disorder and that recently she had contracted pyelonephritis, an infection of the urinary tract caused by intestinal coliforms (colon bacilli), with pus in the urine. The coliforms had then entered her bloodstream and she had developed septicemia, quite a serious condition in those days. Soon she had fallen into a semipermanent state of sleep, in the course of which her dreams appeared to center on a single theme: "the Bolsheviks." The year was 1930, and one of the fears of the upper classes—of which she was a member —was the rise of communism in France. When she awoke, she described her nightmares as though they had actually happened, crying that the Bolsheviks were about to take over France. It was then that the illness took a turn for the worse and she became catatonic.

The story did not surprise me. For years I had been interested in the intestinal coliforms and their possible effects. One man, Professor Hyacinthe Vincent, of Val-de-Grâce Hospital, had studied them for some time. On several occasions I had gone to see him and he had shown me his work on the bacteriology of the colon bacillus. In his opinion, two toxins were secreted, one affecting the liver and the intestines, the other the nervous system. His experiments, however, were concentrated on the spinal cord, where the bacillus caused eventual paralysis, and he was not much interested in mental disorders.

Then I learned to manufacture the neurotropic toxin, so that I could inject it into a number of animals: snakes, lizards, birds, monkeys, and cats. Each time I made such an injection the result was the same: The animals would fall asleep, then become catatonic. The effects of the toxin were even more marked than those of bulbocapnine, with which I had experimented earlier.

The neurotropic toxin's effect on higher animals was the most impressive. Under its influence the sleep of a cat seemed to be troubled by hideous nightmares. It would turn somersaults, go into convulsions, and gasp in agony. In fact, the disorder from which it suffered strangely resembled that of my patient.

I asked Professor Vincent to treat her with his serum against coliform infection, and he agreed to do so. We then transferred her to a mental hospital and placed her under the care of Dr. Devaux, a student of Babinski. She recovered within three weeks. When the cure was complete, I asked if she remembered what had happened, if she could describe her dreams. Not only did she reply in the affirmative, but she offered to write a little memoir, which Devaux and I later published. That true story of an invisible, unsuspected, unexplored world, told by an intelligent and sensitive woman, remains a precious document for the science of psychiatry.

What follows are significant extracts from her memoir, starting with a description of the onset of her disorder, that is to say, the moment when she felt that her reason was tottering.

"The first mental trouble I noticed," she wrote, "was what I think of as the mirror. Everything I did seemed to be disconnected; I could see myself acting and thinking. Somehow synthesis never took place. The normal present that we know, made up of past and future, had disappeared; the three stages were separate; nothing was direct any more. The marvelous human machine seemed to be slowing down and falling to pieces. I became aware of my muscles whenever I moved; whenever I did anything at all I was obsessed with the mirror. It was totally exhausting! Then the visual illusions started. The outlines of objects began to stretch out of shape. At the same time, my hearing became terribly acute."

She could not describe exactly how her nightmare came about. In this phase, she hadn't yet become bedridden but still went about her normal occupations and even made a short trip, about which she could not remember one single thing. She experienced the first physical symptoms of the coliform infection: chills, fever, drowsiness.

"I must have known that something was wrong," she wrote, "because I asked for the Last Rites. At least they tell me I did, though I don't remember that at all."

When the toxins went to work in earnest, she began to have nightmares. Her husband overheard her say in her sleep: "Everybody is dead; I must kill myself." She was "comatose," in reality catatonic, her arms and legs absolutely rigid.

"During that period," she wrote, "I lived a nightmare straight out of a dime novel. I thought that my room was the cabin of an airplane and that the Russians were taking me to Moscow. They had told me that if I made the slightest movement my husband and everyone I loved would be shot. I had to hold absolutely still to keep from making the slightest compromising gesture."

At the same time, she felt pain in her arms and legs, which coincided with their progressive stiffening. This discomfort appeared in her dream, she believed that she had moved, and she was convinced that because of her those whom she loved had been killed.

"I could see them, but they were no longer alive, merely empty skins. When my husband came into the room, I screamed, 'It's a ghost!' because I believed he was an apparition, that he had been shot. I felt that I had to die too, in atonement for what I had done. Every bit of the nightmare was real to me."

The fact is that her dreams blended perfectly into the events taking place around her, so that real persons fused with the phantoms in her mind. Laporte and I had come to be Russian doctors, while her departure for the mental hospital had metamorphosed into a kidnapping whose object was to take her to the prison where she would be judged and condemned.

"That departure was terrifying," she wrote. "I could hear different members of my family called by name, sentenced, and killed. I could hear the blade of the guillotine, and I could hear them screaming out against me because my name wasn't called out and it was I who had betrayed them all. I remember my husband escaping and coming to me under a false name. . . . I learned that unless I promised not to stir from my bed they were going to fire on me from the four corners of my room. . . . Then the door opened, and a man came in and said, 'Madame, we've come for you.' They put a dressing gown on me. I asked if the prison was far away, because that's where I thought they were taking me."

At the mental clinic where the serum treatment was given, she became aware of her returning lucidity. The following is an important observation she made for us:

"At first I was still involved in the nightmare. The scenes seemed to be taking place right on my bed. I even saw my little girl burned with vitriol. Then I began to notice that I was being bathed and fed.

There were hours of awareness before I would slip back into the life of nightmares.

"One day as I was coming out of one of the nightmares, I suddenly realized that I had only been dreaming. I slowly became conscious of what was really happening around me in the hospital and began to reason with myself, to persuade myself that I was in a clinic, not a prison. . . ."

I can compare the foregoing case to that of another female patient of mine, a devout Jewish woman who was brought to me in a state of utter prostration and severe depression. The diagnosis was softening of the brain, but I immediately recognized catatonia, and examination proved that there had been no organic change in her nervous system. She remained absolutely silent during the entire time that I studied her. Then, at a sudden noise from the staircase, she said:

"I'm worried. There are some nuns out there who are trying to convert me."

She too was suffering from a coliform infection. I treated her by the same method and she too recovered.

Contrary, then, to what appearances might lead us to believe, these patients lead an inner life of great intensity. A world of sensation, sentiment, thought, suffering, or resignation goes on deep in their unconscious, stronger and more dominant than the inner lives of persons in good health. Thick clouds gather both inside and out and need a healing wind to blow them away. This toxin-induced catatonia is a striking example of the synthesis of the somatic and the psychic elements within us.

But how can a simple toxin create such mental havoc? How can it push us toward nightmares that take over our unconscious as if they were the most incredible of realities? How can it make us lose all critical sense and give ourselves up to phantoms?

It is clear that the disease only exacerbates fears which already exist within us but which our reason and logic have kept in check. The industrialist's wife was afraid of the Bolsheviks, a favorite bogey of conservatives at the time, while the Jewish woman was prey to religious terrors.

The mechanism is simple enough. The subject passes from pathological sleep to dreams and nightmares which he at first recognizes as such. Then his hallucinations lead to a confused state in which he becomes delirious and finally catatonic. A great psychiatrist of the last century, one of the true fathers of modern science, Moreau de Tours, has written that man bears within him two lives, one composed of clear thought and action, the other of hopes and dreams. When, for one reason or another, the centers of sleep are interfered with, the latter takes over and causes mental aberration.

Both of Moreau de Tours' lives are necessary to man; neither can be sacrificed. In a healthy individual, a natural discipline keeps each of these lives in its respective place, and one does not impinge on the other. But if for any reason this discipline is altered, as in cases of coliform infection where the disturbing agent is a neurotropic toxin, everything becomes blocked, movement ceases, and dreams turn into delirium.

However, since the mind as well as the body is affected, a simple emotion may suffice to effect a temporary cure, despite the continuation of the toxic problem. This was the case of a man whose sister had brought him to me from Israel.

The patient was in a state of absolute catatonia. He did not speak a word of French. He had been given electroshock therapy (a barbarous, ineffectual, and often dangerous practice of which I intend to speak later) to no avail. Rather than ameliorating his condition, the treatment had sent him into a state of abject terror. From the moment that I spoke to him in Hebrew he became reassured and calm. Since I had seen cases of catatonia in which sudden death had been brought on by emotional shock, I did not admit him to the hospital but allowed his sister to continue caring for him in her apartment, where I visited him often without, however, discovering the origin of his illness.

Since he refused medication, his condition continued unchanged until I received a visit one day from an Israeli nurse in France on a visit. On an off chance, I spoke to her about the sick Israeli and asked her to go to see him.

At first my patient was silent with his visitor, who spoke to him in Hebrew, of course. Then suddenly his face cleared and he became interested in the conversation. Within a few days he was completely recovered from his psychic affliction. He still complained of violent pains in his stomach, however, had bad fits of vomiting, and sometimes coughed up blood, so I took him to Dr. Caroli. On examination, Caroli discovered that the man had large gallstones and that his bile contained toxins which had caused his catatonia. The Israeli nurse's visit had not made the toxins disappear, but it had cleared up their mental symptoms.

And so, thanks to our experiments with bulbocapnine, De Jong and I escaped from the impasse and arrived at an entirely new orientation in psychiatry, creating the rough outline of a new idea of psychoses of toxic origin, a concept that I was to enlarge upon throughout the rest of my life, especially in my laboratory at Charenton.

Now we could understand the extraordinary attitude of catatonic patients. Heretofore it had been impossible to know what went on in their minds, for no one had dreamed of asking them, once they had recovered, whether they remembered their deliriums. Many of them were able to recall and describe the dreams they had experienced, so that we could comprehend in part the incredible behavior we had witnessed.

For instance, a famous Parisian lawyer became catatonic after a bout of pneumonia. His body was arched, stiff, utterly immobile. He was an excitable man by nature, very vain, extremely active and ambitious. He recovered rather quickly from his illness; an abscess formed in a lung, permitting his body to eliminate its toxins. Afterward, he told me what he had seen during his catatonic sleep.

"I thought I was dead. I saw myself lying in a coffin, with my hands and feet clenched (as they were in fact in his catatonic state). They were taking me to be buried at the Panthéon. The president of the republic, the president of the bar, all the most important people in Paris walked behind my bier. They awarded me the Legion of Honor posthumously."

That was no nightmare! On the contrary, he had been delighted to dream that he was receiving such honors. Dreaming that one is dead is common with this type of patient. Some even draw their bed sheets over their heads, as though they were shrouds. But another dream he had was less pleasant.

"I thought that I was enduring a form of Chinese torture. I was in a clearing where there was a dreadful smell, smoke, and wind. There were searchlights everywhere and I was surrounded by horrible faces. They were torturing me with a red-hot iron."

He had been reliving in his dream the pains he had experienced during his pneumonia. Poisons engendered by the illness caused his catatonic sleep. Diagnoses such as these were to revolutionize all of psychiatry, since heretofore catatonics had only been studied externally, classed as cases of dementia praecox, and as a result condemned to limbo for life. It was believed that their disease had left their minds vacant, but the patients' descriptions of their dreams showed how wrong this verdict was. Nothing in their brains had been destroyed; on the contrary, their memories registered and faithfully recorded not only their deliriums but actual events which took place around them. Some of them described to me the minutest details of hospital routine, the changes of interns, and their treatments. One patient described perfectly a room in which he had occasionally been examined and even remembered medical terms that had been spoken in his presence. He was far indeed from fitting into that sinister classification known as dementia praecox.

The discovery of experimental catatonia was to be a wellspring to which I would return throughout my career in order to refresh my spirit with continuing research. For example, once I had succeeded in putting my finger on the importance of the "initiative" factor in the human brain, I became curious to know at what age that factor appears in the infant, and so I persuaded my student, Dr. Launay, to write a thesis on the subject. By following a series of infants from birth to the age of one year, we were able, by recording our results on film, to determine the point at which voluntary movement appears—about eight months, when the baby has mastered his impulses and can coordinate his movements sufficiently to be able to seize the object he desires.

In conclusion, what we have been talking about here is a true revolution in psychiatry, a revolution which did away with the terrifying consequences of what I call "destructive prognoses," and which is therefore of great human value. In decreeing that a patient was suffering from dementia praecox or schizophrenia, the doctors not only ruined his life but often the lives of members of his family as well. Now we know that such diagnoses rested on erroneous and fragile bases. By emphasizing the role of certain toxins, which are, after all, transitory and easily eliminated, I substituted positive judgments for destructive verdicts, demonstrating that the malady was not incurable but amenable to medical treatment, and thus bringing hope to hundreds of patients.

CHAPTER

DISCOVERIES
AT CHARENTON

THE NAME CHARENTON EVOKES IN THE IMAGINATION OF THE AVERAGE
Frenchman a picture—comic in the mind of one man, terrifying in
that of another—of the unknown world which he believes to be madness. For nearly forty years I was the head of this institution located
southeast of Paris and known chiefly for its psychiatric department.
I am proud to have served there, to have succeeded the eminent men
who worked at Charenton before me, and to be able to say today
that, though its name is not a familiar one abroad, in the French
world of science it stands for a will toward research which has contributed to our country's prestige.

I took over there in 1931, after having headed the psychiatric
hospital at Clermont-de-l'Oise, which treats all the patients from the
greater Paris area. My efforts at Clermont were devoted to examining the links between tuberculosis and psychoses, and to studying the
sensitive defense reactions in cases of allergy.

I arrived at Charenton somewhat overwhelmed by its history. Situated just on the outskirts of Paris, between the banks of the Marne
and the Bois de Vincennes, it was founded in 1642 by the Brothers
of Saint-Jean-de-Dieu. One of the first hospitals for mental disorders,
it was closed under the Convention of 1792, then reopened and na-
tionalized, and under Napoleon it became the sole national institution for the study of mental illnesses.

Its history has been marked by numerous discoveries, the primary
one being Bayle's discovery of progressive general paralysis of the
insane, the first mental illness related to cerebral lesions, which shook
the world of psychiatry to its foundations. Then there was the enor-

mous contribution made by Jean-Étienne Esquirol, a student of Pinel's from Toulouse, who compiled a veritable catalogue of mental ailments, describing in masterly fashion mania, depression, delirium, and what he called monomanias, or lucid insanities, as well as disclosing the causes of some of them, such as puerperal psychosis. He also compiled statistics, the first on mental disorders, and took energetic action to better the condition of inmates in lunatic asylums, traveling throughout France in order to see for himself how they fared.

The tone of nineteenth-century psychiatry was set by Esquirol's students. In 1848, Jean-Baptiste Parchappe became state inspector of lunatic asylums and took upon himself the ardent defense of their inhabitants. He discharged the director of one asylum for abusing the inmates, and, most important of all, he fought against the division of mental illness into curable and incurable categories practiced in Germany, a system of classification whose consequences were terrible.

Another of Esquirol's students at Charenton, Jacques-Joseph Moreau de Tours, established the analogy between dreams and madness, foreshadowing the discovery of the effects of toxic substances on mental health.

When I first set foot on those premises, the situation was far from brilliant. Charenton had been transformed into a lying-in hospital for unwed mothers and part of the hospital had been transformed to accommodate these girls, who coexisted with the mental patients. During my first years at Charenton, I was described in the circular announcing my appointment as a "Doctor of the National Lying-In Hospital (Department of the Insane)"! We finally were able to recover the entire premises, expanded considerably, and instituted a program of overall modernization.

At that time, Charenton was merely a way station through which patients passed on their way from the provinces to the Paris hospitals, and most of the doctors attached to it looked upon it as little more than a stepping-stone. An exception to this rule, I decided to stay on and restore to Charenton its lost prestige. I believe that I succeeded.

Those early days at Charenton were undoubtedly the most difficult of my entire career. I discovered that the patients were chained, a restraint that represented a throwback to the period before Pinel, to the darkest days of mental medicine. During my rounds I also noticed that some of the patients were drunk, though the nurses tried to convince me that they were simply delirious. A summary investigation revealed that alcohol was being stored at the hospital and that the nurses and inmates were drinking together.

It was not easy to restore order, for I was interfering with long-standing habits which had become sacrosanct, and I was regarded with a jaundiced eye for freeing the patients of their chains and cutting off the liquor supply. It was evident that my critics were asking themselves why I could not be like my predecessors, who, knowing they would not be staying for long, had shut their eyes and stopped their ears to what was going on around them.

I decided to reorganize the establishment from top to bottom. Fortunately, I found an ally in the person of a high official, Inspector General Raynier, who came to Charenton at my request and spent days touring the establishment. His final report recommending that it be completely renovated received the full attention of the Minister of Health. Raynier was a remarkable man who paved the way for a total reform of French psychiatry. In 1932, he and I drew up plans for an open-ward program which was later put into effect at Charenton.

But Rome was not built in a day, and for weeks and months I strove against almost insurmountable difficulties. I continually had to deal with plots hatched behind the scenes, one of which I shall recount in order to show the climate in which I was forced to struggle.

Among my interns, almost all of whom were loyal to me, one young man, Dr. Cornu, was unusually dedicated. One day, as Cornu was passing through the kitchen, he saw the chef preparing a superb piece of meat for a private luncheon to be given by the hospital's administrative director.

"Well," Cornu remarked, "the director certainly doesn't mind spoiling himself, does he? That's a gorgeous piece of meat!"

This observation, which he had made without thinking, was immediately reported to the director by a curious personage with whom I had to deal for several years, a male nurse who was well thought of by higher authorities in the Ministry of Health because, I believed, he was an informer who retailed all the gossip at Charenton to several of the Ministry's bureau chiefs. At that time he was also secretary of his union, a post he eventually lost when his comrades realized that he was using his position solely to advance his own personal interests.

In my opinion, he was slightly deranged, for he was paranoiacally arrogant and utterly convinced that he was capable of directing the entire establishment. It had been he who had organized the drinking parties, and he often boasted of being the "chief of the alcoholics." It was obvious that he detested me and that he had informed the director of Cornu's remark solely to do me harm, since Cornu was my protégé. The director exploded, telling me that Cornu was a bastard, a scoundrel, a rotter, and that he must be punished. I asked what Cornu had done, but he cut me short and refused to say any more than that the young intern was a "bastard."

I investigated the incident, sensing something amiss, and soon, of course, the truth surfaced; I had never doubted Cornu's integrity. But the director was not finished with us. He telephoned Cornu at any hour of the day or night to make sure that he was on duty, made minute inquiries into how he employed his time, was on the alert for him to make the slightest misstep. He harassed the young intern to such a point that the other interns rallied around their persecuted colleague and staged a demonstration on his behalf in the courtyard. The director interpreted this as a riot and hastened to notify the Ministry that a revolution was in progress at Charenton.

An inspector arrived from the Ministry. I was accused of not being able to control my interns, who were described as dangerous agitators. The director did not even permit me to explain what had happened. The inspector announced that all the interns would be discharged.

The officials whom I went to see on their behalf listened politely but replied that the inspector was the supreme arbiter. Just as I was on the verge of giving up, the Minister, a remarkable man named Lafont, protested the order to dismiss the interns when it appeared on his desk for signature. I was summoned to his office and gave him my version of the incident. When I had finished speaking, he picked up the paper lying in front of him, tore it in two and threw the pieces into his wastebasket, saying, "The matter is closed, Dr. Baruk. You can forget about it."

Not only the moral but the material side of the hospital needed to be refurbished, and I quickly began the physical restoration recommended by Inspector General Raynier. Sprucing up the buildings would, I knew, produce only an illusory improvement unless I took the personnel and patients, of whom there were about three hundred, very firmly in hand. I could count on only two interns and did not see how we would have one minute to spare during our long days.

It has always been my practice to know each one of my patients personally, and so every morning I would set out down the long corridors to look in on a certain number of inmates. For those who were almost mute, lost in their inner dreams, a few seconds sufficed; but one never knows if the presence of a doctor who is interested in them is not a comfort and an imperceptible factor in their recovery. Others would launch into endless repetitious speeches as soon as they caught sight of me. My colleagues and I had to be armed with infinite patience to weigh what we heard, to know how to give affectionate advice, and to be sincere interlocutors, tirelessly and impartially in search of the truth to which patients, doctors, and staff alike must bow. In my opinion, such painstaking care constitutes the very key to psychiatry, a golden key which opens the most hidden doors and finally reveals the secrets of afflicted minds.

I had to restore order within the staff and dispel the rather strange atmosphere that reigned in the hospital. One fact quickly became clear to me: The uneasy feeling saturating the place was the result of gossip carried to an extraordinary degree. Rumors crept along the walls, insinuated themselves everywhere, spared no one, gave rise to the most insane tales, seemed indeed to have become the chief occupation of every employee, every nurse, and led to incessant sub rosa warfare.

Employees came to see me daily, reporting the most shocking stories, dishonesty being the least of the sins they disclosed. My first move was to institute a drastic reform. Heretofore, conversations between employees and their chief had been secret. The victim was figuratively stabbed in the back and could never guess the reason for his downfall, except that he might remember that he himself had done the same to someone else at another time. I put into effect a system of public inquiry. Every alleged incident had to be described openly and the accused given the opportunity to defend himself. I became a sort of inquisitor who examined each complaint minutely.

If the source of the tale was a patient, I did not settle for his testimony alone but called in whatever members of his family were responsible for his welfare and asked their opinions. I resorted to unexpected checks, collected statements from every possible source, compared them, and confronted their authors. It was tedious work, but clearly necessary.

As it turned out, what I uncovered was not, after all, too terrifying. At least it did not fit the descriptions of other psychiatric hospitals of the period, which were sometimes likened to seasons in hell. There were times when the patients lied; for example, the brother of one patient complained to me that the latter had been beaten by the nurses. I made an immediate inquiry, questioning the aides and the patient himself. At the end of three hours I was absolutely convinced that the patient had been untruthful. The personnel, perceiving that no complaint, whether justified or unjustified, was neglected, tended to watch their steps, and the number of abuses lessened considerably.

There were, of course, plenty of investigations which brought to light revolting practices. There was a poor old man whom the nurses would lock up in a coal bin and amuse themselves listening to his cries. The ill brother of an intern was tormented by members of the staff who taunted him during the night and prevented him from sleeping; they would insult him, then laugh at his wild reaction. I asked the patient when such scenes took place, waited a few days, then burst into the room. Of course the nurses were taken aback, and the fact of discovery was enough to bring the culprits into line.

It took me three years to transform Charenton. It was a joy to me to observe the improved attitude on the part of the staff, to see that aides and nurses alike agreed that my methods were worthwhile. They began to take a serious interest in the welfare of the patients and to consider them as human beings who, like everyone else, needed to feel warm contact with those around them.

Once all the difficulties had been surmounted, I decided to take up the study of psychiatry again. I had a marvelous library, founded by Esquirol, at my disposal at Charenton, and I received many specialists from all over the world there. Alas, that invaluable athenaeum came to the attention of the Curator of Libraries in France, and after I left Charenton it was altered, with an eye to its budget, and installed in an old office ornamented with busts of Pinel and Esquirol, but locked, so that no one ever works there anymore.

That marvelous library allowed me to peruse the whole history of psychology and psychiatry. It was there that I reached an understanding of an essential point relevant to the treatment of the mentally ill: the close relationship between justice and peace of mind. I became convinced that the most troubled mind requires justice, or else its owner cannot recover his inner serenity. This fact would seem to be obvious, but the evolution of psychiatry has caused the moral aspect to be neglected in favor of purely technical solutions, which I consider to be a great error, as it is my aim to demonstrate in this book. Psychiatry is an essentially moral discipline. If today it no longer provides the answers sought by a troubled world, that is because it has ignored this fundamental precept.

At that time I only glimpsed the above truth. I was still experimenting, and now, after a long interruption, I was able to return to my studies of animals, which thus far had led me to define catatonia. In 1934, with the help of the Rockefeller Foundation, I founded the laboratory of experimental psychiatry to do research on animals.

I hasten to reassure the tenderhearted that I have always sought to spare animals any suffering. My experiments involved no painful procedures, and the only sensation that my cats and monkeys experienced was for the most part a temporary numbness from which they completely recovered. My assistant was a male nurse named Delcros, who loved animals as much as I and saw to it that they were treated with gentleness. Unlike the staffs of some laboratories today, my staff and I worked together on an equal footing, united not only by friendship but by mutual professional esteem. I look back on those days with considerable affection.

Since my retirement, the laboratory has disappeared. It functioned for nearly thirty-five years and had its imitators, especially in the United States, where a center like mine operates today in New York. Primates are studied there, and it also includes a neurosurgical unit. In the institute bearing my name in Israel an identical laboratory has been proposed to continue the studies which I began.

Interest in experimental research of this kind on animals is considerable and has led to the creation and development of the science of psychopharmacology, which is the treatment of mental illness by chemical means. It is the rule in all branches of medicine today to experiment widely with new drugs on animals before using them on human beings. This was the work that occupied me in 1935.

The laboratory possessed twenty-five to thirty monkeys of different kinds. I had invented a special table, which bears my name, to perform craniocerebral operations on these animals. I also observed their behavior and mimicry very closely.

The study of animals has taught me much on the purely psychiatric level. One of my students, Dr. Guilhot, who is today a professor of psychology on the faculty at Rouen, and I published a work on the social life of monkeys. Their mimetic activity showed us that among creatures which are not highly organized emotions are demonstrated in the lower part of the face, that is, the mouth and the nose, and that only among the more evolved monkeys does mimicry include the use of the eyes and the upper part of the face.

The trait that struck me most in these primates was their extraordinary solidarity. The moment we took a monkey out of his cage to give him an injection, all his comrades became profoundly upset, leaping and squealing as though they wished to defend him.

I did not limit my research to monkeys; indeed, it is a common error to content oneself with trying out a product on only one animal. In lectures or in speaking with my colleagues, I have always insisted that one cannot be sure of a product's immunity until it has been tried on all sorts of animals, that is, on the entire spectrum of vertebrates. One of the best examples of how important this can be is the history of Imipramine.

When this medication was launched on the market, accompanied by an enthusiastic prospectus, it had been tested only on mice. We, however, were experimenting in our usual way with *all the vertebrates,* and we observed that while certain animals, especially mice, were insensitive to this drug (whence had come its reputation for absolute innocuousness), other animals, primarily monkeys, suffered from toxic side effects, a minimum dose of thirty milligrams per kilo causing epilepsy and a dose of forty milligrams endangering their lives. I used this example in October of 1974 in a speech before the International Congress on Experimental Medicine at Tel Aviv over which I was presiding. A professor of pharmacology had brought up the subject of experimentation on animals and on man, and I cited the regrettable cases of human epilepsy caused by the premature use of Imipramine, which might have been avoided if experiments with animals had been carried further.

Uniting my research efforts with those made at the center headed by Professor Ivan Bertrand at Salpêtrière, as well as with those of Professor Bosque of the Faculty of Medicine of Valladolid in Spain and of Dr. Palomo Salas of Madrid, I studied lesions caused by strong doses of Imipramine. Large quantities of this drug can affect the brain and lead to anatomical disorders that interfere with the sense of equilibrium. Such undesirable consequences of the use of a product too hastily launched on the market were already appearing among patients under treatment. We advised the Swiss laboratory which was manufacturing this drug of our findings, and they changed their recommendations for use of the medication in their prospectus. This is only one instance among many in which man has benefited from experimentation on animals.

I have always insisted that the clinician must spend a great deal of time in his laboratory. For instance, I opposed the passage of a law which would have called for psychopharmacological experimentation to be performed by a technician rather than a clinician. I have never believed that a pure technician, who has no knowledge of psychiatry and thus no ability to interpret the psychic reaction of animals, could address himself adequately to experimental animal psychopharmacology.

Research conducted along with Drs. J. Launay and J. Bergès led me to the discovery of an important law relating to "psycho-organic states," pertaining to the fact that drugs in small or moderate doses affect the psyche, whereas in large amounts their consequences go beyond that and bring about changes in the neurological system and the structural design of the brain, and lead to paralyses, contractions, or epilepsy. For example, as I have already pointed out, in small doses bulbocapnine induces sleep, in larger amounts brings on catatonia, and in very strong doses may cause epilepsy or involuntary rigidity.

PATIENTS ARE PEOPLE LIKE US

Such data acquired through animal research are of primary importance, for some doctors appear to believe that in order to obtain a therapeutic effect with pharmacodynamic drugs it is necessary to use large amounts of them, thus producing a Parkinsonian state, or considerable affection of movement, so that we see an increasing number of patients whose psychic and motor reactions are frozen. They make another even more serious error, prolonging the therapy indefinitely and using psychotropic drugs to treat cases of mental illness in the same way that insulin injections are given daily to diabetics. Such treatment amounts to actual cultivation of the malady and makes patients who might otherwise be completely cured invalids for life.

Until World War II, the laboratory functioned to capacity and I continued my work on catatonia. I would often bring home at lunchtime cats, mice, or pigeons in a state of drug-induced suspended animation, and during my meal I would observe them sitting as if turned utterly to stone on the sill of an open window. Afterward, I would take them back to the laboratory to wait for the effects of the substance to wear off, for the bird to come to life again and fly, the cat to regain its supple and lazy walk, the mouse to resume its scampering. They were eloquent illustrations of the disease which in man exhibits the same mysterious automatism.

Another exciting branch of my research in those days had to do with sex hormones, in particular the follicle-stimulating hormone in female animals. This work helped me to cure a certain number of patients as well as to acquire a better understanding of human nature and to arrive at the overall concept of mankind to which I subscribe today.

In speaking about follicle-stimulating hormones, I should like to begin at the beginning, that is, with the mystery a doctor faces when he finds himself confronting a patient suffering from an illness for which he can find no clue. I am going to describe what was surely the most typical case of hyperfollicular psychosis that I have ever observed—that of a young woman who fell in love with her dentist. At first there seemed to be nothing very surprising about her infatuation. The strangeness of the case lay not in the patient's sentiments but in the form her delirium took and, most important, in the cause of her illness, which on the face of it appeared to be merely psychological.

She was forty years old, married, and had always behaved irreproachably. The first signs of her disorder were a vague feeling of depression and, at the same time, symptoms of erotomania which took the form of passionate love for her dentist. Now the latter had never given his patient any encouragement by word or gesture. Though infatuated, my patient kept her emotions in check at the start, and restrained her feeling out of the deep affection she felt for her husband and which he reciprocated.

The second stage of her illness seemed to be the reverse of the first. Her repressed passion for the dentist turned into hostility. He was Jewish and she began to accuse him of all the sins of Israel. She would declare that he was horrible, that he had designs on her virtue. Hers was a classic example of guilt transference, of rationalizing a temptation too strongly felt by accusing the other person.

A real battle was raging inside the woman, as though she were in fact possessed and struggling against her inner demon. Her condition worsened from month to month, the figments of her delirious imagination became increasingly oppressive and numerous, and her state of mind steadily deteriorated.

She believed herself to be persecuted by the dentist, then by her servants, her friends, her family. In the process, she became rabidly anti-Semitic, declaring, for instance: "Those dirty Jews think they can take advantage of a decent woman!" She became increasingly violent and abusive, and I must confess that her doctor, Professor de Gennes, and I felt lost in the beginning since we could find nothing physically wrong with her.

Then it occurred to me that perhaps I should examine the patient's level of folliculin, recalling a case of hyperfollicular psychosis that Dr. Hamburger, one of the most distinguished doctors working in the Paris hospitals before the war, had brought to my attention. Such disorders were not much understood at that time, and so I had decided to look into them by experimenting on my animals. I had soon discovered that under the effects of an excess of the follicle-stimulating hormone most female animals became very combative, and, that, contrary to the widely held view at the time, in animals such an excess of this female hormone caused not sexual excitement but rather hostility and a special aggressiveness toward the male.

We witnessed some extraordinary sights during our experiments, for example a fight to the death among a group of mice that had been given the hormone, and an enraged pigeon trampling her own eggs in a singular access of belligerence.

When, however, we further increased the hormonal doses, the clinical picture altered: The animal grew enormously fat, fell into a kind of apathy, and suffered from uterine leukorrhea, a colorless watery discharge indicating a severe imbalance of the endocrine system, in particular the pituitary gland.

How does the follicle-stimulating hormone act on the body and on the mind? Our experiments disclosed that its effect on the circulation of the brain was considerable. Thanks to the work done by Luys, we had been aware that states of excitement are accompanied by an increase of blood in the brain, and that conversely, depressions are marked by a reduction in circulation, a condition then called cerebral anemia.

Along with two great neurosurgeons who came to work in our laboratory, Professors David and Puech, I discovered that an excess of the follicle-stimulating hormone definitely augmented the quantity of blood not only in the large vessels of the brain but also in the smallest ones, causing extreme vasodilation. We conducted a biopsy on the cerebral tissue of a monkey, before and after the action of the hormone, and analyzed it under a microscope from the histological point of view. Thanks to Picksworth's method, we learned that even the capillaries were affected by the increase in circulation resulting from the action of the follicle-stimulating hormone.

Thus we arrived at the explanation for hyperfollicular psychosis and delirium, whose practical manifestations in animals led to cruel battles waged against other members of their species and in human patients, in particular women, gave rise to a marked, but short-lived eroticism followed by antagonism, then depression, delirium, and delusions of persecution.

The sole difference between the form the disorder takes in animals and the course it takes in human beings lies in the rate of escalation. The animals react rapidly and directly, their aggressiveness being triggered with split-second suddenness. In the human brain, on the other hand, the evolution of the disorder is complicated by reversals, feelings of repentance, dissimulation, and above all complex feelings of guilt. If the agitation is of a sexual nature, it is disguised and hidden; in order to escape judgment, the patient becomes angry and accusing. One can recognize here the derivation of many of mankind's and society's ills, one of which is anti-Semitism, which represents a clear transference of feelings of inner culpability to victims selected as scapegoats.

To return to my young woman patient, examination showed clear evidence of an excess of the follicle-stimulating hormone, and once the trouble was discovered it was easily remedied. When her hormone level returned to normal, we witnessed an impressive improvement. The only vestige of my patient's crisis that remained was a vague and lingering anti-Semitism.

We had proved that the sole cause of this impressive erotic crisis had been due to a clinical agent: folliculin.

Another patient of mine had a similar history. During certain periods in her menstrual cycle, at the moment when she was experiencing the greatest effect of hyperfollicular activity, she espoused Hitlerism, with its attendant anti-Semitism, and boldly advocated the extermination of the Jews.

When the level of the follicle-stimulating hormone returned to normal, she regretted her excesses, was critical of her behavior and apologized.

"It's like putting on a filthy coat," she explained. "I want to get rid of it but it sticks to me."

Such disturbances are now very well understood, and studies made by such researchers as Professor de Gennes, Dr. Herschberg, Dr. Labonnelie, Dr. Veziris of Athens, and many others have confirmed the role of hormones in mental illnesses. More recently, at the International Endocrinopsychiatric Congress in London in 1973, I reviewed this subject and went on to describe the effects of another hormone, ACTH, which is used chiefly in the treatment of rheumatism. ACTH can cause cerebral edema by blocking the returning flow of blood in the venous system, and catatonia ensues. The experiments with ACTH confirmed theories advanced by Etoc Demazy, who more than a century ago was the first to suspect the existence of cerebral edema.

As for the male hormone, it produces the same effects but in a much less pronounced fashion. It also leads to disorders of the liver, accompanied by secondary jaundice. Dr. Eduard Brown-Séquard, who was the first to experiment in this field, administered glandular extracts from testicles to himself when he had reached an advanced age. The adverse effects were negligible, and Dr. Brown-Séquard observed in himself a renewal of his sexual powers and youthful strength.

At the same time that I was studying hormones, several worrisome cases in my practice led me to look into malfunctions of the pituitary gland, which is situated at the base of the skull. I was convinced that pituitary disorders had a definitive influence on mental functioning; the personalities of such patients seemed to depend utterly on that gland.

A boy of fifteen was brought to me because he was afflicted by cyclical troubles. He was chubby, even somewhat obese; at birth he had weighed nine pounds. Unstable, unruly, and with a certain tendency to kleptomania, he had never been able to submit to the slightest discipline. Work was, of course, foreign to him; the only occupations he consented to indulge in were sports and games.

He did not, however, lack certain intellectual qualities. His memory was good, he had a quick understanding, and he liked to read, preferring works of the imagination, such as fairy tales and stories about the supernatural. He also liked to cook, a job he always took charge of when he went camping with the Boy Scouts.

He was very affectionate toward his parents and seemed to care deeply for them. What he utterly lacked was strength of character. He spent his days doing nothing, sleeping at odd hours, dozing through entire afternoons. He was, obviously, unable to remain for long in any school because of his indolence and lack of discipline, which had a disturbing influence on the other students. His father, who was deaf and a highly nervous man, suffered because of his son's problems and berated the boy continually. The lives of the entire family were affected.

I immediately diagnosed a pituitary imbalance and prescribed injections of gland extracts. When the boy returned home for vacation, his mother observed the change in him with joy. He had acquired a taste for activity and for the first time offered to help her around the house. In school the transformation was spectacular. The problem boy had become a fine student and from the bottom of his class he moved to among the top five. Even his physical appearance had changed. He was no longer pudgy as he had been since infancy. The only trait that lingered was his tendency to sleep.

When, for various reasons, his treatment was interrupted, his old problems returned. Work ceased, discipline vanished, laziness became the rule, he was sent home from school again. The scenes with his father resumed where they had left off, more violent than ever, since the period of calm had led to hope of a permanent cure. He began to run away from time to time, and so his parents committed him to my care.

This time I had the greatest difficulty taking him in hand. He refused all advice, was stubborn, hostile, and often malicious. After a considerable struggle, I managed to bring him around enough to resume treatment.

Once again the change was very marked. My patient's character improved, he became pleasant once more, his interest in work returned, and I was even able to rid him of his tendency to oversleep.

This boy's history represents an especially clear-cut example of the effects of pituitary imbalance. Since his ill humor and lack of aptitude for work returned when his treatment was interrupted, and he improved when the injections were given again, like other patients of this type he had to receive treatment throughout his life.

The birth of the new science of psychopharmacology led to the founding of the Moreau de Tours Society. In order to fill in the picture of the fruitful years I spent at Charenton, it is important to mention the discoveries I made in that establishment's prodigious archives, where I came across the works of a brilliant predecessor of mine named Moreau de Tours (1804–1884). At that time his works were hardly known, though they are now celebrated throughout the world.

Moreau was a student of the renowned Esquirol, one of the founders of modern psychiatry, and he had the good fortune to be selected by his teacher to accompany a very rich patient on a tour of the Middle East, where he visited Egypt, Palestine, Syria, and Asia Minor. In his travels he observed the Arabs using hashish and decided to try it himself in order to know its effects at first hand, an experiment which taught him the nature of dreams and delirium and decided the orientation of his future work.

"One of the first appreciable effects of the action of hashish," he wrote, "is the gradual weakening of our power to direct our actions. . . . We feel ourselves brimming with strange ideas on which we want to fix our attention. These ideas, which we have not consciously evoked and which surge up in our mind we know not why or how, become increasingly numerous, more vivid, more overwhelming. If, by an effort of will, we regain the interrupted thread of our thoughts, those ideas that we have just pushed aside still linger in our mind, but as though they were memories of an already distant past, possessing the fleeting vaporous form of half-remembered dreams when we waken from a restless night."

In that last sentence lies the essence of Moreau de Tours' discovery, a notion familiar to everyone today: the pronounced resemblance between dreams and delirium. I was to come upon this later when I brought to light the toxic dream which explains the extraordinary attitude of catatonic patients.

But more important still was the discovery of the role of toxic substances in psychiatry. All my experiments until that time had pointed in this direction, and that is why I got in touch with certain descendants of Moreau de Tours, notably M. Deros de Sarjas, in order to delve more deeply into the study of his life and works. For the die was cast; I was prepared to go beyond Charcot, who saw in mental illnesses only the effect of cerebral lesions, and show that the personality could be changed by biological and chemical means.

A still more valuable conclusion we reached was that the dreams varied according to the toxic substances involved, which meant that a patient could be treated with a whole spectrum of specific medications.

As for the effect of toxic substances on the patient's psychology, this notion was stressed by the fine clinician and psychiatrist Gaetan de Clérambault.

I knew him well; he was an admirable man who, like Charcot, believed in the cerebral causes of mental illnesses, but on a very different plane. He believed that delirium had as its origin small, irritating thorns, often of toxic origin, which left scars on the tissues of the brain. Modern psychiatry is based on his work regarding hallucinations.

Studies of toxic substances led to the experimental catatonia of which I wrote above. For in order to discover whether a substance will or will not be effective in the treatment of psychoses, it is necessary to establish whether in high doses it will cause catatonia in animals. If so, it will be useful to human beings. Today, in every pharmacological laboratory all new drugs are subjected to this test.

My admiration for Moreau de Tours led J. Launay and me to found a society in 1958 bearing the name of the celebrated psychiatrist. Aimed initially at the study of psychopharmacology, it was broadened to cover work in psychiatry, psychology, and sociology. The records of the Moreau de Tours Society now fill five heavy volumes, published by Presses universitaires de France.

Charenton brought me into close contact with hundreds of patients whose ills represented the whole spectrum of psychiatry, gave me full, exciting days, and provided me with the opportunity to pursue my work and perfect my skills in that science which has been my career. Until World War II, I concentrated on the reorganization of the institution, on the care and treatment of my patients, and on my personal studies; and I participated in the great era of psychiatry which was unfolding throughout the world. This many-faceted and often trying work gave me great satisfaction.

Paradoxically, I was beginning then to glimpse what was later on to be taken for granted as obvious: the absolute integrality of man. I say paradoxically because I arrived at this conception of the world by observing creatures who appeared to have suffered the most violent of ruptures not only in their relationships with others but within their own inner being. It was through studying man's major mental illnesses that I arrived at what today I believe to be the profound truth about human nature.

CHAPTER

IV

CURING
THE INCURABLE

THE PATIENT WAS SCHIZOPHRENIC, THEREFORE INCURABLE. ALL THE important doctors who had examined him agreed that he would never get well. He had been at Charenton for years in a state of flexion and intense contraction, from which he would emerge only to burst without warning from his room and assault anyone who had the misfortune to be passing in the corridor. His brief expedition over, he would return to his bed and take up his former attitude, curled into the fetal position, apparently indifferent to everything, rigid as if turned to stone, his eyes blank, his sudden burst of activity apparently forgotten. In short, a lunatic of the most classic, definitive, incurable type, the sort of case before which doctors felt powerless and which they believed could be cured only by death.

I visited him regularly, as I did all my patients. He never spoke to me, never once looked in my direction. I would remain for a few moments at his bedside and, just in case, address a few words of comfort to him. I had the impression that I was talking to myself. I had exhausted every avenue of treatment available at the time and was close to accepting the verdict of my colleagues, who considered him to be a case of dementia praecox, which meant that there was no hope whatever for him.

I was in the habit of leaving my patients, even those so unpromising as this man appeared to be, illustrated papers or magazines on their night tables. One day, after I had put down a stack of old tabloids at this patient's bedside and was about to leave the room, I turned and saw him raise himself up with the greatest ease, take the newspapers and begin to read. Until that moment, he had

((69))

given the impression that he was incapable of the slightest ordinary movement. I started in surprise and the sick man, as if caught out in some guilty pastime, threw himself down on the bed and resumed his attitude of complete rigidity. I first wondered if he were not a faker, but soon dismissed that idea. I examined him again, carrying my tests as far as our knowledge at the time allowed, and discovered that the original diagnosis had been incorrect. He was not suffering from schizophrenia but simply from periodic catatonia. I must confess that I never discovered its cause in this man and that nature did not give me time to treat him successfully, since, astonishing as it may seem, he recovered without any medical intervention. He did describe to me a bit of what he had felt during his illness.

"I was in a sort of dream, a kind of delirium. I believed that I had to do the things I did, to stop living, that is, and then God would tell me when to lash out. The truth is that I don't really know why I acted that way."

Twenty years after the events I have described, this man was still leading a normal life, managing a huge agricultural business, without having suffered any relapse. He came to see me once when he was in Paris. The only vestige of his illness was a contracted or "catatonic" hand, a remnant of the intense flexion to which the hand had been subjected for so many years.

I had another famous case: a woman who had become catatonic after her father's death. She had married within several months, and felt guilty at not having observed mourning for a long enough period. One day she was found in the state I have described for the preceding patient, as rigid as a statue. Schizophrenia, her doctors declared, and sent her to me at Charenton, where I had her under observation for ten years. Then, she suddenly recovered, spontaneously and definitively. So nature sometimes contradicts the arrogant judgments made by men.

I have never ceased to take issue with the idea that schizophrenia is incurable. There are certain words which are fashionable, and schizophrenia is one of them. It is such a catchall word that it has passed into popular language. One often hears in conversations that so-and-so is a "bit schizo" or that he is "completely schizoid." The word has replaced the epithet "crazy," because it has a scientific coloration which appeals to our snobbish instincts. If you ask those who use it what it really means, it is unlikely that they will be capable of answering with any precision.

It is unimportant that laymen use the word too freely. The fad will pass, as have many others. But some of my colleagues continue to use it in such a way that one wonders if they know of any other mental disease. We are in a state of linguistic confusion that authorizes every excess, the most serious being the categorical stand taken by some doctors when they declare that schizophrenia is incurable and that all hope must be given up for those suffering from it, which means the majority of their mental patients.

Why does this diagnostic confusion exist? Here I must fill in with a little background, for this state of affairs is not understandable without going back to the man who was chiefly responsible for it, the German psychiatrist Emil Kraepelin (1856–1926). At a time when French science preferred to describe symptoms without attempting to interpret them systematically, Kraepelin undertook to classify mental illnesses according to the prognosis that could be made for them. This might have been a worthwhile procedure if it had been conducted with any flexibility at all, but that was not the case.

Kraepelin believed that psychiatry consisted of two branches, one that concerned itself with curable illnesses and one that could only describe the definitive character of certain (incurable) maladies. He believed that he had found the common denominator of the latter in dementia praecox.

This illness had been studied by French scholars, especially by Bénédict Morel, and popularly dubbed "stupidity." Individuals suffering from it appeared to be inhibited, incapable of either movement or speech, their intelligences completely obscured. Now, Morel had observed that certain cases recovered while others became progressively worse. He invented the name "dementia praecox" (literally, premature dementia) because its victims were mostly quite young.

Morel had never treated that term as more than a clinical description and did not believe that it necessarily pointed to a hopeless prognosis. Kraepelin, however, did not show such prudence. Arriving on the scene at a time when attempts were being made to create order in the science of psychiatry, he began a rigid regrouping of symptoms to serve as a blueprint for mental medicine.

To this end, he ranged under the rubric of dementia praecox a certain number of illnesses which had been described before his time such as catatonia, hebephrenia (a kind of schizophrenia suffered by the young during puberty), and a whole series of irrational states which he had so far considered to be chronic and incurable. In the preface to his work, he declared that the chief aim of psychiatry was not to cure the patient but to forecast his future, that is, to determine whether or not he could be cured.

The method had an advantage in that it was simple. It reduced all psychoses to only two types: dementia praecox, in the presence of which one could merely sadly bow one's head; and periodic psychosis, which consisted of short-lived crises and for which one could extend a degree of hope.

Unfortunately, Kraepelin was taken seriously and his thesis enjoyed a success throughout the world. The worst damage was done in the Anglo-Saxon countries, England in particular, where textbooks were published in which all psychiatry was reduced to a single mental illness: dementia praecox.

It was at this time that Bleuler, a Swiss disciple of Freud, coined the word *schizophrenia*. And it was in the light of Freud's teachings that he studied cases of dementia praecox. He described extremely well those persons "divided" or "separated" not only from the world of their fellowmen but within their own minds, where a real fracture takes place, so that they are totally self-absorbed, lost within dreams and ruminations, morbidly withdrawn from the world, oscillating between an exaggerated sensitivity and a complete anesthesia of feeling, their association of ideas profoundly disturbed. It is unfortunate that Bleuler lumped together schizophrenia and dementia praecox as conceived of by Kraepelin. And so schizophrenia took over psychiatry, inundating every nook and cranny of the discipline, leaving no place for other disorders, and assuming the incurable character given to dementia praecox. We have not yet recovered from this confusion.

This circumstance would not be of grave importance if only scholarly discussions among specialists were involved. But it concerns men and women who are condemned without appeal on the basis of a particularly ill-advised diagnosis. They become lepers, are declared unable to work or to pursue any activity, and are sent to institutions where brutal therapy awaits them. If a slight improvement is glimpsed, even if they seem in fact to recover, they are still not regarded as "safe." The reputation of having been a schizophrenic clings to them; the taint of being someone who from one day to the next may yet become dangerous and who will never really recover remains to haunt their lives.

I too must plead guilty and confess that I have made mistakes. Certainly it is often difficult to distinguish schizophrenia from periodic psychosis. But it is of paramount importance to resist the temptation to indulge in hasty diagnosis and to resign oneself to the painstaking but worthwhile task of studying the subject over a long period, requiring of him the same patience that you demand of yourself. Of course there exist gravely ill individuals whose organic injuries are irreparable and chronic affections which keep recurring. It is extremely difficult to recognize which among these will respond to treatment. Diagnosis is never absolutely foolproof.

I erred in the case of a young man in whom the signs of schizophrenia seemed obvious. He lay rigidly curled up on his bed, making only a few stereotyped gestures and muttering incomprehensibly. He contemplated visitors with a face devoid of expression and was the perfect picture of schizophrenia as it is illustrated in psychiatric treatises. That was the diagnosis I made. Afterward, I lost sight of him. In any case, I was convinced that there was nothing I could do for him.

Several years later, I gave a public lecture in Paris. As soon as I had finished speaking, a young man in the audience leaped to his feet and denounced me with incredible vehemence. The energy of his delivery, his hostility, his animation were in themselves remarkable. With a mastery and a knowledge of the subject which astounded me, he undertook a critique of my lecture. He attacked me so savagely that the presiding officer of the meeting was obliged to call him to order. My detractor's face seemed familiar to me and I was soon able to place him—he was the patient whom I had believed lost forever in the mists of dementia praecox.

Two or three days later he came to see in my office, considerably calmer than at the lecture, though still quite tense. After we had talked, I was able to make an exact diagnosis. His was a case of a classic depressive state in which the patient passes from prostration to aggressive, even destructive, excitement. In reality he was not suffering from schizophrenia but from periodic psychosis, alternately depressive and manic. It is the most common of mental illnesses and, alas, too often goes unrecognized.

I succeeded in restoring the young man to health. His chosen field was education. After he passed his examinations, and he did brilliantly, he became a teacher in the secondary-school system. As you can see, nothing is more dangerous for a psychiatrist than haste. The consequences can be dramatic, especially since these depressive states most often affect young persons whose entire lives lie before them.

I do not lack for examples. A twenty-year-old boy, who was undoubtedly a little retarded in his intellectual development, found a position in a shop after a period in a special school. He worked satisfactorily at simple tasks which assured him a sufficient wage, led a normal life, lived with his parents, loved the movies, and declared that he was completely satisfied with his lot.

Unfortunately for him, his parents listened to friends who advised them to have a psychiatric evaluation made of their son. He was given tests that very strongly brought out his mental insufficiencies. He emerged from the experience with his morale greatly impaired, humiliated and angry.

Ever badly advised, his parents agreed to commit him to a psychiatric hospital, where he found himself among gravely ill persons. Soon his case was assimilated to theirs and it was decided that he was schizophrenic. He was psychoanalyzed, and became resentful of his parents, whom he considered responsible for his incarceration. He also became convinced that he was an inferior being who would never be able to lead a normal life, and turned into a creature with raw nerves who nursed an unremitting bitterness against the entire world.

He was brought to me an utter ruin. At first he was so full of distrust and hatred that he refused to listen to anything I said. I finally persuaded him that he was not incurably ill, not the failure he now believed himself to be, and that his parents loved him but had been misguided.

The most difficult part of all came after the boy's recovery, when I had to find him a job. Coming out of a psychiatric hospital is like coming out of prison. A former mental patient is looked upon as a person who has served time and is always suspect. The doctor must often use all his influence to persuade employers that the certificate of good health is evidence of a real cure.

Errors of diagnosis sometimes rest on the most feeble grounds. Twenty-odd years ago I knew a young man who had been slightly deaf from birth and afflicted besides with quite poor eyesight. He was understandably depressed by this double infirmity and so his mother took him to a psychiatrist, whose verdict was implacable: "There's no hope for your son; he's schizophrenic."

The boy was sent to a mental hospital, and there he would have remained for the rest of his life if his family doctor had not been a good friend of mine. He had been astonished by the psychiatrist's diagnosis and had advised the boy's mother to consult me. I examined her son and soon realized that he was not schizophrenic. Released from the hospital, today he has a fine job, is married, and, despite occasional bouts of depression, is quite happy.

Not every example has such a happy ending. I recall a young artist who was married, the father of a family, and beginning to attain a certain celebrity when suddenly, as the result of overwork, he fell into a state of acute depression. The doctor who examined him pronounced the fatal word *schizophrenia,* adding that he could foresee no possible recovery. He advised the young wife to remake her life.

Since her husband had not been committed, divorce was possible under French law. The young woman followed the doctor's advice, then met another man and married him. The false diagnosis had destroyed the artist's marriage, and later, even though cured, his life was ruined by sorrow at his loss.

How is it possible to distinguish true schizophrenia from periodic psychosis? What symptoms can be relied upon to avoid the irreparable harm occasioned by a mistaken diagnosis? The task is complicated by the fact that as far as periodic psychosis is concerned the diagnosis can vary depending on the phase the patient is in at the time of his first psychiatric examination. This is the reason why the clinical examination, which is so little understood today, is indispensable.

Dr. Séglas, a physician who was an accomplished clinician, wrote that if, in spite of his apparent incoherence, the patient's expression is alert and if he is capable of performing certain tasks, one should suspect hypomania and eliminate schizophrenia. These instructions would seem easy, in principle, but the fact is that they are not.

For decades I have followed a patient whom I knew at Charenton. He had arrived there in an indescribable state, grimacing continuously and uncontrollably. We were able to do nothing to help him for two years, but Professor Moreau of the Academy of Medicine was interested in his case and thought it would be useful as an example to his students of typical schizophrenia. I agreed with him, for the patient had all the clinical signs of that malady.

One day, without warning, the patient recovered! He returned to his job and worked at it successfully for over forty years, with only one recent remission, a depression from which he also recovered. Therefore, we now know that he suffered from a periodic psychosis and not from schizophrenia. It is evident from this example that one must learn to be humble when practicing psychiatry.

It is essential never to pronounce a final diagnosis and always to leave a possibility open for review, even in those cases which seem to be completely hopeless. To my mind that is one of the most sacred rules for the psychiatrist to follow. I refuse to consider any patient as being beyond the help of medicine, doomed without hope. I look on the inmates I cared for at Charenton and on my patients today as human beings afflicted by illnesses whose causes I cannot always discern. But even when I find no answer, I keep my mind open to the possibility that one day I shall stumble upon one.

In some cases it is difficult to extend such hope. There are always patients who appear to be so affected that they will possibly never emerge from the shadows. There was an inmate at Charenton who gave me a great deal of trouble. He believed that he ran the service and seemed to consider me as some vaguely useful employee who was at his disposal.

He was possessed of the most extraordinary energy and took a categorical stand on everything; he formulated lightning diagnoses on the condition of his fellow inmates and ordered everyone around as though they were his slaves. He had a certain gift for playing the role of sovereign with his subjects, now proud and overbearing, now threatening and sarcastic, now suave, now outraged. He exerted a real domination over his fellow inmates, and even the nurses hesitated to fight back when he made cutting remarks about or to them.

From one day to the next this patient was capable of casting out his demon. Then he would be found on his bed, lying there limp as a rag, terrified, fallen from the role of sovereign to that of the most abject slave. He would seem to have touched the very depths of despair. Just as suddenly, the dashing bully would return with the old fierce exuberance. These fantastic personality transformations were accompanied by corresponding changes in the patient's physiological state.

Another patient, who throughout a long life had vacillated between periods of excitement and depression, found himself at an advanced age madly in love with the queen of England. He was convinced that his passion was returned, so he went to London and presented himself at Buckingham Palace. He was, of course, sent immediately to a psychiatric hospital and then returned to France, where he was placed in my care.

He told me that he was descended from the Plantagenets and thus related to the queen, a fact which he was convinced upset the people in power very much because they feared that he might claim part of the royal fortune. He wrote "his" queen several poems a day and planned a trip to the château at Angers, the Plantagenets' old home.

Then the form of his delusion changed and he believed that he was descended from the line of Louis XIV. He remained quite cheerful at the apogee of his crisis, and he was so amusing that we wondered if he really took himself seriously. He then became arrogant and aggressive, and literally believed that he was the king of Charenton. From this stage he became utterly incoherent and lapsed abruptly into a state of prostration, accompanied by the sudden realization that he had been living a mad dream. He kept telling me that it had all existed in his imagination.

Did this mean that he had recovered? Not at all; he had merely gone from one extreme to the other. This man, who had lived in a marvelous world of fantasy, complete with childish and aberrant dreams, had now lost all his creative spirit. He no longer dreamed, no longer spoke, ate sparingly, was scarcely able to digest his meager meals. He began to waste away, to become emaciated. He was so dispirited and exhausted that we had to force-feed him.

Too many psychiatrists are literally staggered by the word *delirium*. As soon as they utter that word they believe that they are confronted by a grave and incurable psychosis. They forget the temporary delusions of melancholiacs so well described by Séglas. Above all they lose sight of the fact that delirium is not meaningless but represents feelings and thoughts which have to do with man's innermost being.

If the doctor listens with only half an ear, the patient suffering from delirium seems to be talking mere nonsense with no possible logical meaning. But, if he gives his close attention to searching for the thread which links this seeming incoherence to the deep nature of the illness, he may end by understanding its structure, traveling through a deep tunnel to the original source, to the philosophical significance of what is happening.

I shall illustrate my remarks with one of the most startling case histories that I have had the opportunity to observe, that of a young officer, a native of Brittany, who was sent to me with the vague diagnosis of schizophrenic delirium.

He was about thirty, pleasant looking, and at first sight gave no indication of being mentally deranged. I installed him in a small room adjoining a garden and began to observe him. I did not open his medical record, because I felt that it would be full of words that might distort the reality. I still prefer to see for myself, to look, to listen, to think for myself.

The nurse finally notified me that the new patient was having a crisis. I posted myself in the corridor outside his room and heard shouts, screams, obscene epithets, the sound of the patient jumping, stamping his feet, beating on the floor with his shoes, kicking the furniture and the walls. I also heard God's name endlessly repeated.

When the noises stopped, I entered the room. The patient did not see me, but his verbal and physical violence began again. When I asked for an explanation, he did not reply. Red-faced, his eyes starting from his head, he vented his rage against mysterious enemies. I left him alone and told the nurses that he was not to be disturbed.

His crisis lasted for several days. When I was informed that he had become calm I went to see him again. He lay exhausted on his bed, a wholly different man, eager to talk with me. He did not, however, confide in me, but remained reticent, explaining only: "It's a force that gets hold of me." He refused to elaborate, and I did not insist but went on to other subjects.

Since his great interests were philosophy and theology, we had long discussions on those subjects, and little by little he began to accept me as a friend. With dogged persistence I broke open the armor that held him prisoner. During our entire dialogue, which extended over a period of several weeks, his crises continued, each one lasting several days. I would always wait until he was calm again before resuming our talks.

One day he confided, "That force I told you about is awful. There's nothing I can do to fight it. It's stronger than I am."

I asked him where it came from and he replied, "It's the implacable justice of the only true God. The justice I'm talking about is inhuman, it's absolute, awful, like iron. It makes me violent. It's true that sometimes the Lord becomes a God of love, compassionate and loving, and then I feel like that. He's then embodied in the eternal feminine, in the charm, gentleness, and affection that women possess."

That was the key to the strange personality of my patient. He told me that he had been born in Brittany and reared very religiously, his life full of constraints and restrictions. After brilliant work in school, he had become an officer. Then he had fallen in love with a girl who did not belong to his social background. His parents, though not enchanted with the prospect of such a marriage, did not actually oppose it. The young officer himself broke off the engagement, having decided that they had too little in common.

That decision, taken on his own, occasioned a great emotional shock. He left the Army and entered a Dominican monastery. However, he doubted his vocation, and seeing no possible answer to his dilemma, he became desperate. It was then that he had his first crisis, which took the form of bizarre manifestations, and he warned his companions to beware of his terrible impulses. Shut in his room at the monastery, he began to shout, stamp, and beat on the walls. Since he was still considered to belong to the military, he was sent to the Val-de-Grâce Army hospital and then on to me at Charenton.

It became obvious that he had retained from his religious upbringing the idea that woman is an instrument of sin. Renan in his memoirs of his youth tells how his teachers compared woman to a loaded revolver which must be avoided as dangerous. The idea of woman as a symbol both of original sin and of shared love was comparable to my patient's vision of the God of love and the God of wrath, the duality which was tearing him to pieces.

I tried to reason with him, explaining that justice and love were not irreconcilable, but on the contrary symbolized the very unity of the world. And I told him about the Hebrew word *tsedek,* which conveys the idea of justice and love simultaneously, as Moses intended in the famous verse, "Love thy neighbor as thyself," by which he meant a true identification with the needs of others.

The young officer did not immediately accept my vision of the world, which he felt was not the realistic view that God had intended. He insisted on distinguishing between justice, which was in his eyes harsh and unyielding, and love, which he believed to be complete gentleness. This was the source of his perpetual conflict.

At that time we had none of the medications which exist today to help modify psychological behavior. Therefore, I embarked on a course of pure psychotherapy, consisting of long conversations, intimate talks in the course of which the patient felt that he was with a friend and not a doctor.

My treatment had nothing to do with straight psychoanalysis, which would not have worked in this case and might even have been dangerous. An analysis of that kind would have necessitated an attempt to destroy his religious convictions, since the boy was of a strong moral turn and utterly under the influence of an education received in the strictest of Catholic families. Believing that if he were liberated in that sense, he might merely have run from woman to woman, and perhaps thus cause even more harm to his psyche, since the conflict still would not have been solved, I never once fought against his beliefs but rather tried to preserve them. I felt that it was important to create for him a moral climate in which his beliefs and his daily life could be brought into harmony, to suppress the contradiction in him, to efface the conflict by unifying the elements of his personality that were at war with each other.

This considerable task would have been impossible without his total confidence, which I did obtain. The work took time, but I would remind myself that the illness from which he was suffering had been considered chronic, or virtually incurable. A change began to take place little by little.

"I think too much," he stated one day. "There's a gap in my education. I spend too much time thinking about philosophy and religion. I ought to learn to do something practical."

Then he met an engineer in the ward, a gifted physicist, and asked me if they could start a laboratory together. Of course I gave my permission. He had discovered on his own an important principle: the transformation and neutralization of obsessive ideas through physical activity, the defusing of a mania by way of work which has nothing to do with it. I was especially pleased because his idea fitted in with my own notion of making our hospital into a place in which I could encourage spontaneous initiative wherever it might be compatible with the efficient running of our services.

I assigned the two patients a spacious room overlooking a peaceful garden, and they were extraordinarily ingenious in fitting out their laboratory very cheaply, making their own furniture and constructing their own equipment out of odds and ends. At last the former officer was able to begin work on practical studies. This was the beginning of the light at the end of the tunnel for him as well as for his friend.

His crises did not, however, miraculously disappear. We were at war at the time, and his recurring deliriums were now accompanied by dark prophecies. His preoccupation with theology led him to announce the end of the world, for example. But curiously enough he exempted our hospital from this dire forecast. He stated that it was a haven, a privileged spot which would escape destruction.

Woman, with her double aspect of salvation and damnation, had remained his obsession. Because of the mobilization of men to fight, plus the imprisonment of innumerable Frenchmen by the Germans, we were now obliged to use female nurses. One morning as I was making my rounds, a bit earlier than usual, I opened the door to his room and found him in bed with a night nurse. He was extremely alarmed and apologized profusely. I reassured him and severely reprimanded the nurse. I have never believed in the sort of cures offered in those so-called avant-garde establishments in which patients are encouraged blithely to rid themselves of their inhibitions privately or in the company of their fellow inmates.

The influence of two young women interns who were working under me contributed much more constructively to my patient's welfare. Both were cultivated and intelligent young women, full of charm and grace. The comradely ties that grew up among the three of them accustomed my patient to consider women in a different light from "loaded revolvers." He understood for the first time in his life that he could share with women an intellectual attraction that excluded the sterile idea of sin.

We had come far from the diagnosis of incurable schizophrenia pronounced at the Army hospital. My patient not only recovered, but he became an example to the other patients, who began to build their own workshops. Even if the results of these enterprises were mediocre, or in some cases nonexistent, such undertakings could not help benefiting the mental state of their promoters.

My patient was finally able to remake his life, a handsome achievement of which I cannot help being proud. When I suggested that he might leave the hospital, he was afraid of a life of freedom, but I convinced him to take things slowly. At first he took short leaves, which later became longer, and he visited his family. He enjoyed seeing his nephews, and his ties with Charenton were gradually relaxed. After he left Charenton for good, he married, found work, and was happy, having succeeded in reconciling his ideas of justice and love. His case remains for me the finest example of the successful application of that mutual trust and respect which must be present between the doctor and his patient.

In today's hospitals, the chief of service does very little visiting, leaving this work to his students. The method is a poor one, because students and interns lack sufficient experience to build up the very full and intense relationship with patients which is indispensable to treating them successfully. The ability to discern the truth lying hidden behind the thick fog of a disturbed person's visions presupposes skills of exploration which can be acquired only with years of experience.

Also, when one begins to understand, or to believe that one does, another temptation must be guarded against. The doctor must not force his view on the patient. A moral attitude cannot be imposed upon a mind which has long been lost. It is necessary to identify with the patient, to be humble, and to shepherd him gradually toward a new conception rather than oppose him.

Often the psychiatrist must contend not only with the patient and his illness but also with those near to him, such as parents, wife or husband, employers; and it is not enough to extirpate his deliriums, but this must sometimes be accompanied by the act of convincing those around the patient that he has indeed recovered.

I had this problem concerning a patient sent to me from another mental hospital, an engineer who had been working in a highly responsible position with an industrial firm and had become depressed when his wife and children had left him to take a long holiday. Paradoxically, he gave the appearance of being a bon vivant, scarcely likely to succumb to melancholia, a habitué of pleasant restaurants who loved ample meals accompanied by quantities of wine. Although he was not an alcoholic, he did drink too much. Such continuous excesses, rather than having an exhilarating effect, finally produce in certain temperaments a feeling of fatigue leading to a confused sadness that has no apparent cause.

At first this patient was placed in a sanatorium, where he was forced to rest and to abstain from drinking in order to restore his lost energy, for the diagnosis had been overwork. When his condition showed no signs of improvement, he was sent to another hospital, where the surveillance was stricter and the treatments harsher. The medical director of this latter hospital regarded his patients rather as though they were inhabitants of a zoo. He was prone to rather cruel jokes, which terrorized them. His patients had no feeling of being supported or helped.

The engineer felt that he had been trapped. The mental aggression inflicted upon him made his condition worse. From depression he went into a state of pure and simple delirium. He told me later that he had believed the doctor was determined to destroy him. His fears soon took the form of auditory hallucinations in which he heard the doctor threatening him.

When I first saw him at Charenton, he transferred his fear to me, and despite my attempts to reassure him he continued to tremble in my presence. He was convinced for a time that the doctor from the other hospital had followed him to Charenton. When I showed him that this was impossible, he said that the doctor had sent a henchman, who was hiding in the water system.

I saw that it was going to be difficult to get a grip on this man. His irrational statements had no bearing on reality, for his mind no longer had any control over them. I wondered if his affliction were not a chronic delusion of persecution. Nevertheless, since the tests I had made on him showed an enlarged liver and hepatic insufficiency, I began a vigorous course of treatment to correct the consequences of intemperance; alcohol alone could possibly be the root of his problem.

The liver condition improved with treatment, and the patient's delusions subsided to some extent. But he still feared his persecutor, and it took little to bring back his hallucinations. Realizing then that alcohol poisoning was not the only cause of his trouble, I began to search for the psychological reason. I stepped up my contacts with my patient, engaging him in long discussions in which at first I attacked his irrational fear. It took me long weeks to dispel his anxiety and to make him admit that his fears were groundless. At this point his delusions left him and he seemed to have recovered. However, I knew that I had not got to the root of his disorder, which meant that it could reappear.

The next step was to discover what, besides his excesses at table, had had the force to disorient a man who had been described as clearheaded in his work and little given to fancy. The day came at last when he trusted me enough to unburden himself completely. During his wife's absence, he had become involved with his secretary. It had amounted to nothing more than a flirtation, but, a practicing Catholic who loved his wife, he believed that he had committed a great sin and broken his marriage vows. He had also been clumsy about hiding his "affair" and had overheard some of his colleagues making ironic comments about his behavior. It had taken no more than these minor matters to bring on the depression from which all his troubles proceeded.

His confession made, the delirium dispelled, apparently recovered, he still had a horror of his sin and its consequences and continued to rehash it endlessly, the only difference being that rather than brooding over his remorse in solitude he now did so in my company. I pointed out to him that the sin was not particularly shocking, that his remorse was enough for his religion to forgive him. He came back with the comment that even his boss must think pretty badly of him.

It seemed impossible to stop him from going around and around in his whirlwind of obsessions, from wallowing in his guilt. Seeing that I was getting nowhere, I appealed to the head of his engineering firm. That fine man understood me immediately when I told him that only his intervention could help my patient. He came to Charenton and told him that he had the greatest respect for him and wanted him back on the job as soon as possible.

That meeting did more for the recovery of my patient than all the hours we had spent together. Though his delusion had not yet been entirely eradicated, his high spirits returned. He now wished to recover and take his place once more in society. When he seemed to me completely cured, I called his employer and told him that I was sending my man back to work.

Alas, I had also to notify my patient's wife, whose signature was required for her husband's release. I was most surprised to see her face darken when I announced that her husband had recovered. She looked at me with hostility: "They told me that he was schizophrenic!"

When I asserted that that was not the case, the young woman bridled as if she had been grossly duped. She replied, "But I've arranged my life around his schizophrenia!"

Needless to say, I was horrified. It was obvious that I had upset her plans by curing her husband. She was living with another man, having believed that her husband's malady was incurable. She then refused to sign the papers. I found myself in a delicate situation because the rules for voluntary commitment at that time required the wife's signature on the release papers. I was also aware that if her husband did not leave Charenton within a relatively short time his condition would start to deteriorate. I decided to bluff and was assisted by the administrative director of the hospital, whom I had taken into my confidence.

The wife, impressed with our threatening attitudes, finally became intimidated and agreed to sign. But victory was not yet final. A few days later I learned from the manager of the firm that my patient's wife had not merely planned to replace him in her affection, but had also taken over his job and was now refusing to give it up. I described to the couple's employer the scene that had taken place at Charenton, and he replied that he would fire the wife and reinstate the husband.

The story did not end there. After the inevitable divorce, my patient's religious scruples prevented him from remarrying, alas, and his personal life remained forever shattered. A long time after his recovery, he began drinking again and died of cirrhosis of the liver, without, however, any recurrence of his mental troubles.

The idea of incurability has lost ground today. A number of us throughout the world have fought to make it disappear. Of course I do not believe that schizophrenia is an empty concept; as a psychological description I find it most interesting. It is the assumptions that have been made regarding it that seem to me erroneous and dangerous. For example, such assumptions have led in Germany to the construction of mental hospitals which have pavilions for patients who are considered to be curable and others for those who cannot be expected ever to recover. The sole fact of having been sent to one of the latter condemns a person for life.

This view carried to its extreme resulted in Hitler's massacre of the mentally ill. On a trip to Poland, where I had been sent by the French government to treat an important person in Warsaw, I met Professor Stanislas Batavia, who wrote about the massacre of the "incurably" insane in Germany and Poland. From 1940 to the end of August 1941, 70,273 "unproductive persons" were killed in order to "disinfect the population" and for reasons of economic necessity.

I felt exceedingly ill when I read a passage from Batavia's book describing the slaughter of 450 patients (304 men, 128 women, 18 children) at the Chelmo psychiatric hospital near Lublin:

> The soldiers began to herd the inmates out of Building Number Two, pushing them toward the front door where machine guns had been set up. The guns opened fire and the patients, driven from the building, were shot on the threshold, where the pile of bodies grew

higher and higher. The Germans pursued the terrified men and women through the rooms and threw them out of second- and third-story windows. Some managed to break through the circle of soldiers, and then a wild chase through the hospital began, ending always in the death of the mental patients. The Germans' most difficult job was to catch the children, who had hidden under chests and beds. But they were all found and shot.

That was a massacre of the innocents in every sense of the word. If only in memory of that atrocity, psychiatrists should hesitate to condemn a man or a woman with one sentence because it is the easiest thing to do.

My trips throughout the world in recent years have proved to me that there has definitely been a change for the better. Even in Germany, the birthplace of schizophrenia, doctors are showing signs of reconsidering the question. I went to Heidelberg a few years ago to see what remained of Kraepelin's system and was told by my colleagues there that his concept was considered to be out of date. Professor Poliakov, one of the most important specialists in Germany and holder of the chair in psychiatry at the University of Münster, came to Paris several years ago. In the course of a commemorative speech, he declared:

"We must make amends for our past. Kraepelin's concept of dementia praecox has often been misinterpreted. . . . The most important mental illness is actually periodic psychosis."

I was pleased to have the support of so eminent a man. In my opinion, periodic psychosis can take every possible and imaginable form, not only psychological but also purely physical. There exist periodic paralyses, disorders involving the autonomic nervous system, or organic disorders of a cyclic nature which affect digestion, sleep, and sexual activity. Their study is of the utmost importance and covers an enormous terrain which includes mental illness, heredity, acquired causes, and the multiple kinds of violence and aggression to which we are all subjected in our era—in short, disturbances suffered throughout an entire lifetime.

((89))

Statistics have also provided me with an interesting argument against the idea that schizophrenia is incurable. I collected data on eleven hundred patients of both sexes whom the most highly qualified specialists had diagnosed as schizophrenic and whose cases had been followed for over twenty years, and was able to count a rather impressive number of total recoveries or definite improvements. And this was before we doctors had recourse to the efficacious pharmaceutical weapons used in modern treatment.

I base my observations on equally obvious facts when I qualify as "destructive" those diagnoses which are still too often delivered against young patients, who are thus stigmatized for the remainder of their lives, a tragic mistake which makes me heartsick. In order to distinguish between schizophrenia and periodic psychoses, it is necessary to follow the cases for many years. It is in this way alone that a doctor can fulfill his mission, which is to keep safe the patient entrusted to him.

I am aware that there are some gravely ill persons who will never recover because they suffer from chronic psychoses. But that diagnosis cannot be made until the day that death intervenes. No doctor should forget the trite saying: "Where there's life, there's hope." But it is a sad fact that a whole school of psychiatrists exists which turns its back on this idea. A physician is not a god; therefore, he cannot command the future and sacrifice human beings in the name of an entirely hypothetical science. We have all witnessed unexpected and unforeseeable resurrections from various forms of such cyclic psychoses. Such recoveries may even come at an advanced age. I have seen old men, apparently so lost that one thought immediately of senile dementia, rise up suddenly and resume their activities with an energy that astonished their acquaintances.

What is the origin of this "periodic" disposition which may be inherited and which is a factor in these periodic psychoses? The fundamental trait of such individuals is that they "vibrate" to reality more strongly than the average man. It is erroneous to believe that this hyperreactive temperament affects only the mind, for it affects every activity of the organism, not excepting a single organ. Reactions can include hammering of the heart or intestinal spasms. It can lead to artistic or scientific genius, to evil, perversion, or crime. Where then do we draw the line between what I shall call beneficial deliriums, those which are creative, and harmful deliriums, those which are not? Many causes—biological, social, familial—can serve as criteria. And here we touch on the problem of moral conscience, which to me is of supreme importance.

Life goes on in the body and soul following a pattern which in spite of everything remains mysterious. That is why throughout my career I have protested so vehemently against those who decree that life has lost its force in a mentally ill person. What do they know about it, and who are they to proclaim after a few examinations that its vigor will never return?

I have always fought not only against schizophrenia but also against the abuse of the word, and above all against the peremptory "labeling" of patients without sufficient evidence. I hope that even in the minds of laymen I have succeeded in dispelling confusion. We must keep in mind the essential fact that it is not true that men affected by insanity for transient reasons—fatigue, overwork, sorrow, stresses of all kinds—are of necessity schizophrenics; not true that persons who pass from a state of excessive excitement to one of complete prostration are lost forever to their families or their professions; not true that mental illness is incurable and in every instance sure to reappear some day.

Such myths harm not only patients and their families but the whole social body. These legends endure, nourished by ignorance and the mystery surrounding the world of psychosis. It is unfortunate that some men of science themselves persist in such notions, despite available evidence to the contrary.

Perhaps logicians resent nature's less implacable judgments, and that is why they refuse to accept her wisdom.

MISTAKEN DIAGNOSES
OF PARANOIA

Paranoia IS ANOTHER WORD WHICH, LIKE SCHIZOPHRENIA, IS USED TOO
loosely and causes the same kind of damage, such a diagnosis also
being irreversible, a condemnation without appeal. The effects are
even more serious because the public believes that a "paranoiac"
is even more dangerous than a "schizophrenic." If one can believe
the man in the street, the schizophrenic might be said to be harm-
lessly insane, while paranoia represents the threatening madness of
despots and murderers.

It is true that there are dangerous and harmful paranoiacs, but
their existence does not justify the current amalgam which includes
a multitude of perfectly inoffensive men and women who, though
their troubles have nothing at all to do with paranoia, and who may
even be victims of slander, have their lives ruined by having acquired a reputation which they in no way deserve. It is up to us
psychiatrists to look deeply into the hearts and minds not only of our
patients but also of those friends and relatives who surround them.

I became responsible for the fate of an eminent colleague of mine
who was in charge of research in chemical biology in a laboratory of
the Faculty of Medicine, and who other psychiatrists had decided
was paranoid. I would certainly never have succeeded in saving him,
although he was perfectly sane, without the help of some of his
friends. My role in this adventure won me the lasting enmity of
several of my fellow physicians, and for some time my career suffered. Needless to say, I am proud of having been victorious over
envy, jealousy, and simple laziness.

Dr. Y's position on the faculty was that of researcher into the effects of cyanic substances on cancerous cells. In his work he used daily, as reagents, and this fact is important, deadly cyanides. He was about fifty years old, married, and the father of a son when the affair broke out.

His wife had been operated on successfully for cancer of the breast, but soon afterward she began to suffer from psychological problems. Her doctor determined that a metastasis of her cancer had reached her brain, and he sent her to a hospital specializing in the treatment of this terrible affliction. It was there that the remark which led to the scandal became public.

"My husband tried to kill me with cyanide," she told the doctor who was treating her. "I will always have to live with that danger."

The doctor took this accusation at its face value. I have asked myself time and again why he didn't attempt to verify such an assertion, why he had been so confident that his patient was telling the truth. He then proceeded to commit a highly imprudent act: He addressed a strong letter to the police, in which he faithfully repeated and corroborated Mme. Y's story.

"Though he is a physician," he wrote, "it seems to me that there may indeed be cause to suspect him and that it might be well to take precautions before it is too late. I would advise that he be required to submit to a psychiatric examination."

He next got in touch with Mme. Y's regular doctor, who assured the cancer specialist that his patient had already confided such fears to him. This man also wrote to the police, adding his personal impressions of Dr. Y. Today when I reread this letter, which was included in Dr. Y's record, I continue to be amazed at the casualness with which the man was denounced, and at the pitiless judgment that was pronounced on him.

"First of all," wrote this doctor, "I must say that Dr. Y's pleasant manner and conspicuously attractive appearance win one's sympathy at first glance. Unfortunately, I know him intimately and feel that it is my duty to inform you of the fact that these external characteristics hide a nature which is completely despicable. It is obvious that Dr. Y possesses no moral sense whatsoever. I have checked on certain information which has come to me and am convinced that he married his wife not for love but out of necessity. He has lived with her, and continues to live with her, as though she were a servant to whom he owes nothing. The couple's present situation comes as no surprise to me.

"What I have written should be sufficient to indicate the mentality of the man in question and should convince you that he can be dangerous. I believe that he considers himself the object of persecution, and in my opinion he is a typical paranoid."

This terrible denunciation was not likely to leave the police indifferent. It was reminiscent of the opening of a chilling novel, with the madman in his most menacing form, a paranoid whose job it is to handle deadly poisons every day. I can understand the reaction of the police to all this, but not the one-way direction the investigation was to take. The main idea seemed to be to get rid of Dr. Y at any cost, since he came to be considered, a priori, a dangerous lunatic.

The police discovered that Dr. Y was in the habit of keeping bottles of cyanide at home. When asked why he did not leave them at the laboratory, he replied that his associate had died, there had been a change in the staff, and he had thought it safer to keep an eye on the poisons. His explanation was not believed, and the bottles were used as circumstantial evidence.

Of course, colleagues, co-workers, and employees of the faculty were questioned. Their depositions varied greatly, some being admiring, some much less so, some strongly critical. But what body of men would unanimously support a man about whom such terrifying rumors were circulating?

The most impressive testimony came from a schoolteacher who gave private French lessons to the accused man's child. She confirmed the accusations in the letters written by the two doctors.

"I remember one day, when Mme. Y didn't realize that I was present," she confided to a police officer. "She flew into a terrible temper and refused to drink a glass of champagne that her husband had given her and accused him of trying to poison her with it. Some time after that, he had a fit of rage and stormed at his wife most cruelly over some small thing or other. He lost control of himself completely and ended by declaring that one of them must go!"

Dr. Y was conducted to the special police infirmary and several days later he was transferred to Sainte-Anne, the hospital for so-called incurably mad patients. It was believed that a man like him might be capable of inflicting terrible harm, was obviously not responsible for his actions, and had to be put where he could not endanger his fellowmen.

My associates at Sainte-Anne were extremely embarrassed. They could see no striking signs of paranoia in their colleague, and they were relieved when it was suggested that Dr. Y be sent on to Charenton. That is how I found in my office the man whom many others wished to consider a paranoid poisoner.

I gave him a most complete examination, using every means at my disposal. I put him through a gamut of tests and talked to him at length, asking him to describe as frankly as possible his relations with his wife. He replied that, except for the unimportant rough spots that are part of every marriage, he considered the marriage to be a good one. When I asked if he hated her, he replied, "Not at all."

"But she has accused you of trying to kill her, and because of that you have been committed to this mental institution," I insisted.

"Yes, that is very painful," he answered. "She is sick; I'm afraid that she will never recover."

How different these remarks were from the ones that had been attributed to him! And I was convinced that he was not faking, since thoughts can be dissimulated for only a short time when one is under constant surveillance. It was evident to me that Dr. Y was sincerely distressed at his wife's behavior and condition.

In the case history which lay open on my desk, I read that he had wished to give the impression that he had won the Nobel Prize, an unlikely claim which would fit well with the clinical picture of a paranoiac. When I asked him about this, he was astonished and asked where I had got that idea. I showed him the record, and he shrugged his shoulders in discouragement.

"They've falsified one of my statements," he explained. "I published an important article on biochemistry in a scientific review edited by a winner of the Nobel Prize."

That was quite different from what was written in his record. It illustrates how Dr. Y's remarks, the daily incidents of his life, the history of his career had been systematically distorted.

The most striking example of this appeared in the French tutor's testimony. I asked her to come to my office, since I had been intrigued by what she had reported.

"Yes, it's true," she told me. "A police officer questioned me, and I was so upset that I didn't even reread my deposition. But I do remember that I told him that Dr. Y seemed to me to be a gentle and patient man, incapable of murdering anyone."

I read her the testimony from the record.

She was indignant: "But that's just the opposite of what I said. Actually, I was in the hall, and Dr. Y was about to take me home. I heard his wife shouting that her husband was trying to poison her. I was shocked, and the doctor looked at me sadly as he said, 'You see the cross I have to bear.' Then he added the sentence that has been distorted by the police: 'There's one too many of us in the apartment.' But the words he used were a simple statement of a fact, an incompatibility so great that I even thought about looking for an apartment for Dr. Y so that he could live apart from his wife."

Outraged by the way her remarks had been misrepresented, she decided to register a complaint against the police officer who had questioned her. Meanwhile, I began a counterinterrogation of Dr. Y's friends and colleagues, in the course of which an entirely different story came to light. One of Dr. Y's most salient characteristics was a naiveté which does not exist in the true paranoiac, who is always excessively suspicious and reticent, who keeps minute control over his words and gestures, who complains continually about everything, and who transfers his own mistakes to others. But even under his present stress, Dr. Y retained a completely ungrudging attitude toward his fellowmen, including those who had accused him.

I did not succeed in eliciting from him a single word which might betray resentment toward his wife, however much he had suffered from her hostility. In fact, he wished that she would write to him.

Then one day he received the long-awaited letter. It contained only invective, and he was very upset by it. This time, I told myself, he would not be able to hide his rancor. However, he merely greeted me with a sad smile and told me that her illness had changed her character. He was worried about her treatments because if he were to stay in the hospital much longer he would lose his job and be unable to pay for them. He claimed that she was not responsible; he was troubled about his son.

In the course of our conversations, he returned often to the first years of his marriage. They had been blissfully happy, and it gave him pleasure to recall them. He was certain that only his wife's illness could have turned their shared passion to hate. He clung desperately to this interpretation, and no argument could dissuade him from it.

This excessive optimism, this blind goodwill which made up Dr. Y's basic nature, partly explained the difficulty in which he found himself. A study of his dossier with its collected testimonies on his character convinced me of this.

Here is what a professor on the Faculty of Medicine had to say about him:

> He possesses a degree of knowledge which should not be undervalued, and he has enormous enthusiasm, which is a rare quality in a research scientist. His only fault lies in the fact that though not an Einstein, he has a tendency to overestimate himself. This sometimes leads him to lose his temper and appear conceited. However, given the working conditions of a researcher, and the slenderness of the means put at the disposal of scientific research, such an attitude can be easily understood.

I found a similar comment in the deposition of the laboratory director at the Faculty of Sciences:

> He is in love with research, really a bit cracked, but harmlessly so, on the subject. I admit that he possesses great qualities, but he lacks the final drive which would enable him to bring his projects to a truly successful conclusion.

A professor of medicine went a little further:

> He attracts attention for reasons which are not always to his disadvantage. Looked at against the somewhat rarefied atmosphere in which the research scientist works, he might, of course, be viewed as an unstable person, a crackpot. This may indeed be so, but the explanation must not be connected with his work; otherwise, all his comrades would have to be placed in the same category. It is merely possible to describe him as being more excessive than others, but this can hardly be pointed to as a sign of insanity.

A chemist friend of Dr. Y wrote as follows:

> I maintain that despite his eccentric manner, grandiose ideas, and notorious short temper, he should not be considered a paranoiac. I was surprised that the psychiatrists who asked for my opinion did not seem to wish to listen to what I had to say.

I began to perceive Dr. Y's personality more clearly and to understand why there were so many contradictory judgments about him. He was one of those men of some talent whose problem is that they believe that they are more gifted than they really are. Because they feel that their talent is not truly recognized, they react by being sarcastic and overbearing. These are traits which may seem similar to those of a paranoiac, especially when accompanied by an enthusiastic and dynamic temperament. The fact was that Dr. Y had been a victim of his too open and frank nature, of his innocent ambitions, and of his excessive belief in himself. A man may believe that he is a genius, but that does not make him a paranoiac. Dr. Y aimed too high, but that was neither a crime nor a sign of insanity.

After a month and a half of scrutinizing my patient, I prepared a report which included the following remarks:

> Dr. Y's behavior while at Charenton and the results of numerous psychiatric examinations permit us to eliminate not only paranoia and schizophrenic psychosis but also disorders of affect and personality as possible maladies.
>
> Dr. Y shows none of the typical syndromes of paranoia, especially the arrogance stemming from suspicion, which is its chief trait.
>
> Because of his optimism and naiveté, he makes no bones about his scientific accomplishments. Unaware of jealousy and meanness, he neglects to take the precautions necessary to avoid injuring his colleagues' vanity. He does not suffer from excessive pride but rather has an innocent self-esteem, an open and unsuspicious attitude which is the exact opposite to that of the true paranoiac.
>
> Because his affective behavior has remained intact and unchanged, I have put aside the possibility of schizophrenia. Dr. Y seems to be highly emotional and demonstrative. These qualities explain his sometimes excessive enthusiasm for hypotheses, an enthusiasm which was not always checked by the discipline of testing, as noted by his superiors in scientific research. However, such zeal is also a positive quality in a researcher.
>
> Moreover, no sign of insanity, hallucination, disturbance of speech or of thought, nor any psychopathic or neuropathic symptom, apart from the psychological peculiarities I have cited, has been found. The psychiatric evaluation of Dr. Y is therefore negative.

One task remained for me, and that was to discover the origin and the mechanism of the conflict between Dr. Y and his wife so that I might attempt to eradicate it.

After having studied his record in such detail, I had a vague inkling of what it might be, for in the course of their depositions Dr. Y's friends and colleagues had given certain information about the couple and the personality of Mme. Y. One colleague had been surprised to hear about Dr. Y's being committed, since he believed that he had loved his wife, even though she had made so much trouble for him. He said:

Two years ago she tried to commit suicide in Y's automobile by swallowing the contents of a vial of barbiturates. And that was only one attempt among many others at moral blackmail.

He kept the poison in his house, along with other substances, when the old faculty was being moved from one building to another. This gave her the idea of accusing him. It is regrettable that the psychiatrists failed to understand what was going on.

Her mental condition caused her to lie as a result of the metastasis in her brain but also as a result of the cortisone treatment she is undergoing. I think that she is abnormal and should have been subjected to a psychiatric evaluation.

A doctor friend of the couple also placed the blame on Mme. Y:

The psychiatrists' findings amazed me. Y has none of the inflexibility that is peculiar to paranoiacs. He is simply a rather eccentric fellow whose reactions have been exaggerated. His only fault is that of having a wife who has always been the strong member of the household, deciding everything without taking into account her husband's opinion. She always regretted that Dr. Y did not earn a great deal of money. He suffered from her lack of understanding and approval, but he loved her deeply. I think that his wife's allegations came from her sense of inferiority after the operation to remove her breast. She felt diminished physically and believed that her husband would be better off without her. After Dr. Y's committal, I went to see his wife.

She seemed very strange to me. I was sure that if a psychiatrist saw her he would have known at once that she was quite abnormal.

I was convinced that I should examine Mme. Y myself. I wanted to get a psychological profile of her, so that I might know her as well as her husband. I obtained permission to do so from the director of the hospital where she was being cared for.

I found myself in the presence of an emaciated woman who, though she preserved a remarkable calm and self-control, showed every evidence of having been gravely stricken both physically and mentally. With her first words, I was able to detect the real delusion of persecution from which she was suffering. When I gave her news of my patient, she seemed hardly to be listening, indifferent to the fate of the husband who, through her offices, had lost his rightful freedom.

She explained to me that the sole matter of interest to her now, apart from her son's future, was the fact that her death was near. She insisted that under no circumstances must her husband be given the care of their son.

"He is an unbalanced idealist, incapable of bringing up a child," she cried.

To this day I remember her voice, filled with scorn. She responded to her husband's abiding love with hatred and suspicion.

Suddenly she made a stunning admission:

"I invented the whole thing in order to get him committed. I want him to be locked up for the rest of his life so that after my death, he won't be in the arms of another woman."

And so she confessed her secret. A savage instinctive jealousy had been the starting point of the whole sad story. I left Mme. Y, profoundly affected by what I had seen and heard, and distressed by my own impotence to repair the harm.

I collected one last bit of testimony, from the couple's housekeeper. She confirmed that Mme. Y had never stopped making completely unjustified complaints and accusations against her husband:

> She was always setting the boy against his father. The things she used to say to her husband were so awful that in spite of his patience and goodness he would often lose his temper. Toward the end, she couldn't have a visitor without telling him that the doctor was trying to poison her.

Dr. Y's wife died not long after his release. He returned to work, took care of his son, and led a normal life.

But I had incurred the strong displeasure of the police for having cast doubt on the tendentious dossier they had mounted.

The first turn of the screw came in the form of a note from police headquarters addressed to every psychiatrist and neurologist working in the Paris hospitals. The method I had used, the counterinvestigation by means of which I had uncovered the truth, was to be formally forbidden. Doctors were ordered to limit themselves to clinical tests, to avoid playing detective, even if the real ones had done their work badly, and not to indulge in critical examinations of testimony, even when it might seem to be biased.

I promptly protested to the Society of Physicians and Psychiatrists, asking if a written document should be considered sacred simply because it bore the seal of police headquarters. My colleagues closed ranks with me and we asked our adversaries how they could so misunderstand the basic tenets of psychiatry, its very method, which requires a personal investigation and not simply the study of written records. We made such a fuss that the police withdrew their note.

A few weeks later, before the same society, I was the object of a particularly savage attack by Professor Heuyer, who reproached me vehemently for having failed to live up to the rules of medical ethics. And this because he considered that I had behaved discourteously in doubting the diagnosis arrived at by the first doctors who had examined Y and had observed definite signs of paranoia.

I answered him point by point. Should a diagnosis be a verdict without appeal? Is it the specialist's job merely to confirm the opinions of his predecessors?

However, my victory with my colleagues was not so clear as it had been with the police. The society was rather shaken by Professor Heuyer's invective, and I soon learned the price I was to pay for the stand I had taken: forfeiture of the presidency of the society, for which I had been slated. But I regretted nothing. It was only much later that I accepted the presidency, after having convinced my colleagues that I had been right in ensuring that Dr. Y be given his freedom.

CHAPTER

VI

DELIVERANCE BY INVESTIGATION —SOME RESCUES

UNLIKE A PATIENT SUFFERING FROM A PHYSICAL ILLNESS, THE MEN-
tally ill patient attracts the ill will, denunciation, and persecution
of his fellows. He is regarded as dangerous, becomes an object of
shame to his family and friends, sometimes even to his entire neighborhood. I have been struck by the fact that a person suffering from
cancer is pitied, but that the person who is not "right in the head"
is regarded with suspicion, often hatred, and that the principal
reaction to him is a wish to be rid of him, to get him out of sight
of his more normal fellowmen.

One of the most complex cases I have ever had to deal with was
that of a thirty-six-year-old woman, a fine musician who ran a shop.
She lived alone and had to contend with innumerable difficulties,
foremost among them being a lack of sympathy on the part of her
fellowmen; indeed her entire neighborhood seemed to be in league
against her. They won out, and she was declared insane, then forcibly
confined.

Before meeting the woman, I made myself familiar with her medical record. It mentioned three different stays in psychiatric hospitals
starting in 1963. A report from the special infirmary of the Paris
police headquarters in December 1968 stated that Mlle. P was a
paranoiac.

The following is an extract from that report:

Aberrant behavior probably due to a hypersensitive personality, and
touched off by actual events occurring since the preceding August.

Lives in a state of fear, keeps a dog which on several occasions has bitten customers. Subject refuses to have dog examined by veterinarian. Latest incident involves investigating officers. Very complicated story going back to 1964. Numerous lawsuits in the course of which subject made veiled insinuations, intuitive guesswork rather than statements of actual fact, such as claiming that things don't happen by chance. At psychiatric hospital displays typical paranoiac reaction; alleges that strangers have daily upset her record albums, even physically assaulted her. Wears cast to correct slipped disk said to be result of assault. Recommend observation in specialized institution.

On the basis of this document Mlle. P was sent to Sainte-Anne, where she spent fifteen days under observation; then a second report was filed:

Behavioral and personality disorders in a hypersensitive personality of the paranoiac type. Hospitalized in psychiatric section of Maison Blanche Clinic in 1960. Break with family after that date. Appears to have formed habit of litigation since 1964. For some time has shown personality problems stemming, it would seem, from events whose reality has yet to be established. Said disorders cause conflicting relations with customers, neighbors, police. An amelioration of symptoms observed since hospitalization, under neuroleptic treatment. However, still shows typically paranoid reactions.

In May 1969, as a result of new incidents, a medicolegal examination was ordered. The experts described the patient as a "hypersensitive personality with paranoiac overtones." They did mitigate their judgment somewhat, in recognition of the fact that the patient had not been at all aggressive in their presence, and stated that she might not be paranoiac in the strict sense of the word. It was she who requested that I examine her, to make a definitive analysis of her case.

In my preliminary interview with the young woman, she seemed to me to be deeply scarred by her experience. It was not clear who bore the responsibility for the multitude of incidents that had occurred in connection with her shop.

"I do get upset sometimes," she acknowledged. "But I have good reason to. Everyone hates me!"

Was this the classic persecution complex which is indeed part of the clinical picture of paranoia?

"Why should they be so unanimously against you?" I asked her.

She shrugged. "That's what I continue to ask myself. I only went into business in order to earn enough money to live peacefully. But that's never been possible."

I proceeded to give her the usual tests, which revealed very little. Apparently Mlle. P, aside from the cast she wore to correct a slipped disk, was in good health. She appeared to be totally unaggressive. On the contrary, she was depressed and despondent, her nervous strength at a low ebb.

I explained how I intended to proceed with her case: She and I would have long interviews in the course of which she would have to talk with me as frankly as possible because I wished to know everything about her.

She had been born of Jewish parents, who separated after the war, and had encountered the hostility of her mother and sister at a very young age. Paradoxically, things took a turn for the worse when it was discovered that Mlle. P had exceptional musical talents. She was accepted at the Stuttgart Conservatory, from which she received her degree. Her ambition was to become a conductor, and a fine future seemed to lie before her.

However, her career was brought to a halt by her family situation and by financial problems. Mlle. P lived in a continuous state of upheaval between an ill and exhausted father, who had very little money and no authority, and a mother and sister whose antagonism toward her never lessened.

In August 1960, she contracted a fungus infection of the feet which prevented her from working. This threw her into such a state of depression that she tried to commit suicide. Instead of comforting her, her mother and sister overwhelmed her with reproaches.

"My sister told me that I was a burden, that in their present circumstances she and my mother had no need of that. They talked to the neighbors to get them on their side. She told me that the only solution they could see was to put me away."

This, in fact, was what they did, and she was sent to the psychiatric hospital, Maison Blanche. I have before me Dr. Minot's report describing the situation at that time:

> Family conflict, neurotic behavior, blame laid on the family, broken home, attempt at an independent life ending in failure, return to mother, violent scenes, attempted suicide . . .

If Mlle. P had been lucky enough to have had psychological care at that point, or enjoyed the understanding of her family, her problems, which did not seem to be serious, could have been easily corrected. She was not so fortunate, however. Her few days of confinement at Maison Blanche earned her the condemnation of both family and neighbors.

This is why, after many stormy scenes, my patient decided to burn her bridges behind her. She bought a shop on the Left Bank, where she put her musical gifts and education to use by selling records. The former owner of the shop had turned over the premises grudgingly because she would have preferred to receive higher payment than she finally got. It may be possible that this initial brush with the ex-proprietor led to mademoiselle's difficulties with the concierge, who was to play a thousand and one rough jokes on her. One day, as she was going down into the cellar, the concierge struck her a blow with her fist. It landed on the nape of her neck, aggravating her back ailment and requiring her to wear a special corset. Mlle. P's complaint against the concierge could not have been without foundation, for the court before which the case appeared fined the latter 2,500 francs in damages, with interest.

The following year, strangers entered my patient's shop, assaulted her, were arrested by the police, and were found guilty. Here too it was clear that she had not lied. Nevertheless, when she decided to get a watchdog, her neighbors, disregarding the fact that she was a fragile woman living alone, considered the presence of the animal a provocation.

At this juncture, it became difficult to sort out the truth. One day, Mlle. P's old enemy, the concierge, complained that she had been bitten by the dog. My patient declared that the concierge had made up the story in order to get her into trouble. However, some customers had also testified that the animal was rough and had chased them from the store. Mlle. P assured me, though, that the animal was not at all dangerous.

After these complaints were filed—a total of five—the police intervened and suggested that she have the dog examined by a veterinarian. She refused on several occasions. She was under a severe nervous strain and one day quarreled violently with her mother and sister when they came to see her. She became so enraged with them that the two women notified a doctor and the police. Without making an extensive investigation, the doctor wrote out an affidavit recommending that Mlle. P be committed. She was taken to the special infirmary at police headquarters and from there to Sainte-Anne.

The investigation was extremely summary. "They simply wouldn't listen to me," she told me. Although she had been committed at the family's request, the latter were never questioned. Fortunately, the doctors who treated her were not entirely convinced that they had an authentic paranoiac on their hands, and at the end of a few weeks she was released.

Mlle. P went back to her record shop, her concierge, her neighbors, her customers, all of whom were aware of where she had been. As clearly as if it were printed on her forehead, she bore the label "former mental patient."

And so the hostility toward her did not lessen; far from it. At every opportunity her concierge threw at her the fact that she was "some kind of nut," an insult suffered in silence by Mlle. P. The neighborhood boys made her the butt of their pranks. Her dog had been removed to the pound during her absence, and destroyed as dangerous. Rumors circulated quickly; within a radius of several blocks, people heard "the lady is a little touched" and were quick to take advantage of the fact. Customers would buy objects, keep them for several days, then return them, saying that they were not satisfied with their purchase. If mademoiselle protested, she was reminded that it would be a simple matter to send her back to Sainte-Anne.

Everyone seemed to hope that she would make a misstep, or a gesture which could be so interpreted. That opportunity was provided when she lodged a complaint. She became the object of ironic comments, and the words *persecution complex* were bandied about. A medicolegal examination was ordered. The results were confusing, since the doctors hesitated to give a truly definitive diagnosis. Mlle. P saved herself by demanding to be examined by me.

Such was the tangled web I found when I first saw Mlle. P. She admitted to me that toward the end she had been living in such a state of agitation that she could not bear the slightest vexation. Since she knew that people were against her, every face looked like an enemy's and she would lose control of herself:

Mlle. P revealed such resilience and sincerity, however, that I could not fit her case into the diagnosis of paranoia. But in such circumstances first impressions must be checked with the facts, so I had to examine the process which had led my patient to her present situation and ascertain whether it was true that the whole neighborhood had really conspired against her.

I called the mother and sister to my office and had long interviews with them. Neither one hid her dislike of my patient, and I believed I understood their reasons. The sister was jealous and the mother irritated by Mlle. P's musical gifts. Because of her talent, she frequented artistic and intellectual circles which were closed to them, so that they retaliated by inventing the myth that she might be unbalanced. I also spoke to the father, a man devoid of any meanness, but so infinitely weak that he had been able to do nothing to help.

I blamed the doctors who had examined my patient for their blindness. The responsibility for the break with her family should never have been laid at her door. It had not been her moral character which had been at fault, but the absence of affection in her own people.

I also interviewed some of my patient's "friendly" customers. They told me stories of seeing young customers breaking things, tearing up record jackets. When Mlle. P became terrified and exasperated, they would make fun of her, also making her drop her glasses. They added that some of these vandals were not afraid to represent themselves as police officers.

She brought me printed, typewritten, and scribbled notes she had received. Most of them contained very coarse insults.

Armed with testimony and material evidence, evidence which proved that mademoiselle's allegations were not the figment of a deranged mind, I telephoned the commissioner, who seemed embarrassed to hear that my patient's complaints were based on truth. He agreed that she was probably not completely unbalanced, but he added that she had complained that the post office was holding up her mail, and that the police had found only one lost letter. He assumed that she was suffering from a persecution complex.

I wrote to the local postmaster and discovered that she had been telling the truth. An employee of the post office, for unknown reasons, had unduly held up her mail, which was now being delivered to her. He promised that the guilty man would be punished.

It was now understandable why she had been accused by the police and the court of not answering summonses, not replying to demands for payment of bills. They had been accumulating in a corner of the post office. And everyone had presumed her guilty because she was thought to be a bit mad.

This was a well-known phenomenon, comparable to what I think of as "poisoning." Once it had been established that Mlle. P was a mental case, most people who had anything to do with her had turned the situation to his or her advantage. Mother and sister had consoled themselves for lacking her talent; concierge and neighbors had hastened to gratify the sadistic instinct which lies buried in so many of us. In order to satisfy its lust for cruelty, mankind must have its wounded creatures. As for Mlle. P, perhaps awkward in her dealings with people, she could only aggravate the psychic injuries she had suffered during her childhood.

In a letter addressed to Mlle. P's regular doctor, I dismissed the diagnosis of paranoia and summarized my conclusions:

> The important question was to find out whether Mlle. P's protests against her committal were or were not well founded. Investigation proved that the incidents she alleged to be true were so in fact, and therefore the medical findings and diagnosis of paranoia, based on these complaints of hers, are invalid, since those complaints were normal.

Today my patient is living more or less peacefully, and no one dares call her paranoiac. Whatever its underlying causes, her case is a classic illustration of the danger of making preconceived judgments in psychiatry.

It is essential to talk personally with the patient where paranoia is concerned. The true paranoiac includes the psychiatrist among those he believes are persecuting him, and the presence of this trait is the clearest indication of the existence of the illness. As you have seen, this characteristic was not present in the case of Mlle. P.

This is not to say that there is no such thing as a hypersensitivity which can lead to neurosis. Kretschmer in Germany gave it the name of "hypersensitive psychosis." Here we have a real confusion of terms which led to a controversy of long standing between the French and the German schools of psychiatry.

Ernst Kretschmer's "hypersensitive psychosis" describes a disturbance affecting persons who are above average on the intellectual and emotional level who have been injured by life, have been victims of traumatizing situations, and as a result endure life with their "nerve ends exposed." Their problem, however, is of a psychological order and not at all psychopathic.

Now, in France Kretschmer's term has been badly mistranslated and misunderstood. A dangerous epithet, "hypersensitive *paranoia*," has been substituted. A word which inspires fear has been used to describe a rather benign disorder. Ordinary physicians and laymen have allowed themselves to be misled by this. There exists an essential difference between true paranoiacs and hypersensitive persons: The former are motivated by irrational ideas which completely obsess them, while the latter react strongly to actual events.

I cannot summarize the situation better than by quoting Kretschmer himself:

> These persons of the hypersensitive type are extremely impressionable and highly sensitive, and show a definite amount of ambition and tenacity. Perfect examples of this type are complicated personalities, highly intelligent, of great worth, of fine and profound sensibility, and scrupulously moral. Their affairs of the heart are marked by great delicacy and an ardor which is turned wholly inward.
>
> They are the predestined victims of life's hardships. They are shut up deeply within themselves, hiding the intensity of their feelings, and have highly developed capacities for introspection and self-criticism. They are very susceptible, extremely opinionated, and particularly capable of love and trust. They have a true notion of their own worth but are timid and insecure when it comes to producing. They are introverted yet open and generous, endowed with ambition and drive, and of great value to society.

In sum, a portrait at the opposite pole from that of the classic paranoiac.

I am reminded of an affair which, in the years before the war, received a great deal of notoriety and was tinged with scandal: the commitment to a mental institution of a high official in the Ministry of the Navy, M. S. He too was "accused"—and the term is not too strong—of paranoia.

M. S discovered that his wife was deceiving him with a well-known Socialist deputy. The former, a southerner and a poet, expansive by nature, conceived the idea of writing a rather caustic little play in which a cuckolded husband ends by killing his rival. He then circulated this work and even sent a copy to his rival. Without a moment's hesitation, the deputy notified the police, assuring them that a crazy paranoiac had threatened to kill him.

Without further ado, M. S was arrested and taken to the special infirmary at police headquarters where Dr. de Clérambault, a fine practitioner and a man of absolute integrity, examined him and found him to be in a hypomanic state. This means simply that the man was rather overexcited, a condition for which one must admit he had good reason.

M. S was then brought to Charenton, where I examined him and arrived at the same conclusions as had Clérambault, having noted a slight excitement, a rather feverish animation, a certain volatility. I was convinced that all these symptoms would disappear after a few days of rest.

However, in order to make a truly accurate diagnosis, I wished to go further and find out whether M. S's jealousy was normal, that is, whether his accusations were well founded or irrational. Therefore, I proceeded with my questioning of the subject's friends, family, colleagues, and, of course, his wife.

His wife openly and unabashedly confessed her guilt. The report which I sent to the police recommended that M. S be set free. I had just sent it off when a formidable campaign on his behalf broke out in the press. I congratulated myself on not having wasted any time, since people could have supposed that I had let myself be influenced and made a convenient diagnosis.

There was an investigation in the Chamber of Deputies in which the government was accused of having ordered an arbitrary sequestration. On April 5, 1933, Léon Blum himself intervened. He alluded to my report and it was read to the deputies. The government made the most of it, to show with what care and diligence patients were examined.

It had been obvious that M. S was no paranoiac. He was given his freedom, and the following year he published a book entitled *The Kings of the Social State,* which enjoyed a great success.

Since the only stories I have told so far in this chapter have been about mistaken diagnoses of paranoia, you may begin to ask yourselves if it is possible that such an illness does not exist. Alas, it is a real enough malady and one of psychiatry's greatest plagues. I would define it this way: fear masked by hatred, a poisonous combination, a sore on the body politic of humanity, which at the international level has led to the most hideous persecutions. The true paranoiac, dangerous in the extreme to all those who approach him, is difficult to recognize.

He is so dangerous because he knows so admirably how to disguise himself. His talent for hypocrisy is infinite. In Molière's *Tartuffe* you have the perfect picture of the paranoiac who gives no outward hint that he is a troublemaker; on the contrary, he is all sweetness and unctuousness, and seems to possess an inexhaustible source of benevolence toward his fellowmen. On the surface he is full of compassion and understanding, his amiable mask winning everyone's sympathy.

Diagnosis is thus extremely difficult, no matter how vigilant the physician may be in conducting his examinations. I have sometimes erred, caught between the fear of condemning a man unjustly and the desire to be certain of not releasing a person who is truly sick.

I came very near to making a mistake about a Belgian of about sixty-five years of age who was living in Paris and was sent to me at Charenton by the police. The administrative decision to commit him to a mental hospital had been made after a series of violent incidents with his neighbors in which he had been involved.

He had been living in one of those early housing units, which were not renowned for comfort. One of the conflicts concerned the laundry facilities. His neighbors, who were Polish, had a habit of spreading out on the landing the linen they had washed at the communal tap. This annoyed the Belgian, who would constantly change the position of their washtub or take down the laundry that was hanging up to dry. His battle with the concierge concerned the placement of a pot of flowers. He would take the concierge's pot from where the latter had placed it and change its location, whereupon the irate concierge would restore it to its original position. Finally my patient quite simply broke the pot, further infuriating its owner.

Incident led to incident, and the resultant recriminations ended in blows. The patient appealed to his embassy, which was able to do nothing about the situation; to the police, who tried in vain to bring peace; to a process server, who soon became a familiar figure in the building; to a doctor, who issued a certificate attesting that his patient had been struck by his neighbors.

One day the concierge went to the police station and reported that there was a "crazy man" in his building. The investigating officers found the Belgian in a state of great overexcitement and sent him to Sainte-Anne, then on to me.

He began by denouncing his enemies, complained of the persecution of which he was the object, and announced that he would take revenge. Eventually he calmed down and became so affable, courteous, and composed that I could see no sign of mental illness and even felt sorry for him.

I called his neighbors and the concierge to my office to hear their side of the story. Those few who consented to come for a preliminary interview had little of significance to tell me. "He was always picking on little things"; "he was arrogant"; "he thought he was better than other people"; "he always wanted to change things," they said.

I wanted to confront them with my patient, but that was not easy. Finally the police forced them to come. But the meeting was not very successful. My patient maintained his composure, answered every question calmly, and was extremely polite. He replied to every accusation with unruffled, sensible answers. It was the witnesses who seemed to be overexcited, and the patient's poised, peaceable manner seemed a scathing repudiation of their accusations.

At Charenton, the man's behavior was irreproachable, and so, when he came to me and asked to be released, I found his request legitimate. I wrote to the police bureau concerned, giving them a favorable report:

> The behavior of M. X while in my care has been excellent. He has not complained, he gets along perfectly with the staff, he is always polite, good-natured, patient. He adapts himself well to hospital discipline and shows no tendency to air grievances or look for trouble. According to previous reports, his behavior was not the same at Sainte-Anne, and thus it would seem that his condition has improved.
>
> On the medical level, it is beyond doubt that his emotional state has improved since his arrival. We have seen no evidence of hallucinations or irrational ideas. His complaints are limited to three or four persons, his neighbors, with whom he had a misunderstanding and who filed a petition against him. He expresses no ideas of persecution either in relation to the residents of his building, the police, or those treating him.
>
> However, in order to determine whether he suffers from a certain impenetrable psychological inflexibility, which would explain his problems with his neighbors, it would be necessary to keep him under medical observation as an outpatient.

The police agreed with me, but on condition that my patient move to another apartment house. This seemed to me a wise precaution because it was obvious that if he found himself once more among his same neighbors, the incidents might begin all over again.

The building where my patient lived belonged to an insurance company which owned others of the same type. I asked the manager to come to my office to arrange matters concerning a new residence for my patient. He arrived, wearing a worried expression, and showed me a letter, signed by my patient. Couched in very vivid terms, it ended on a threatening note: "I shall have no hesitation in pursuing you."

It seemed that the patient had written to the Public Prosecutor to complain about the company that owned the building and the manager himself. I sent for him and asked why he had done so. He denied having written to the Prosecutor and became very angry, shouting: "The company is accusing me falsely, and that's why I wrote a letter of complaint to the manager."

I asked my patient to apologize to the manager, since no matter what the trouble had been, he had not been responsible. The Belgian agreed to this, and I then announced that my visitor and I had found a solution to all his problems: a new apartment in another building. I of course expected a great show of joy and gratitude, but to my surprise he fell into a rage, shouting that it was a terrible plot.

I tried to soothe him, saying, "Many people would like to be the victims of plots that would get them a more comfortable apartment at the same price!"

He pointed to the manager, calling him a fraud, accusing him of siding with those who were out to get him; then turned on me, crying that I too was in on the plot.

I immediately had the man sent back to his room, as I was now convinced that he was truly paranoiac. That same evening, he sent me a letter to inform me that I too had become one of his persecutors and that he wanted to withdraw his apology to the manager, whom he believed to be certainly in league with the police.

I wondered whether his condition was due to a passing access of fury which might subside or was an indication of a deeper crisis. In any case, I did not free the patient, and I notified the police of his sudden change in behavior. It was fortunate that I did so. From one day to the next, his paranoia declared itself with stunning swiftness. His persecution complex, until then disguised, came to include the entire world. He had taken the promise of a new apartment as an attack on him, a slap in the face, and that triggered the surfacing of his illness. If this had not occurred, I might have given a dangerous man his freedom.

I was not able to follow his history much further. He remained in my care for a time, lost in his ravings; then his embassy arranged for his return to Belgium.

It is difficult to be sure of anything in my field. There are temporary states of paranoia that exist within the framework of manic-depressive psychoses. This applies to patients who during an often quite long period of time exhibit all the characteristics of the disorder, but whose symptoms then reverse themselves completely, and still later suddenly reappear. This oscillation of the patient's state sometimes occurs at quite regular intervals. It is necessary to have the patient under observation for a very long time in order to make a true diagnosis.

I once had a case of this type which was remarkable enough to have been made the subject of Dr. Montassut's thesis on the paranoiac personality. Dr. Montassut, however, was able to observe this man only in his paranoiac phase.

He was sixty years old, an immaculately groomed, sharp-eyed martinet who rose early in the morning to make the rounds of the entire area as though he were officially in charge of inspection. Afterward, he would shut himself up in his room and write up his grievances, a behavioral oddity called graphorrhea. He would write incessant requests and memos to everyone—the Minister of Health, the President of the Chamber of Deputies, etc.—complaining of the way the hospital service was run. He criticized, maligned, libeled the doctors, whom he called incompetent, and the nurses, whom he described as lazy and careless. His style oscillated between the legal and the lyrical. Here is an example:

> The doctor [me], in response to the mendacious and erroneous reports given him by his slave drivers and stoolies, came last week to threaten me and inflict new horrors. Enraged because I refused to be intimidated, he threatened to have me transferred; meanwhile, he

sets free humankind's worst characters, who then complain of their right to asylum and support!

With diabolic flair, he sensed which of his fellow patients could be most easily influenced and took control of them. By listening to and exaggerating their dissatisfactions, and by counseling them in the direction of provocation, he set them against each other as well as against the staff. He was never at a loss for false accusations with political, class, or racial overtones.

Since this patient always based his tales on a grain of truth, that is to say, on the daily worries and cares of his companions, he succeeded in stirring up discord in the bosom of the hospital staff. I dealt with him as best I could, but it was impossible for me to take the obvious step and curtail the liberty of this scourge who had become the evil genius of Charenton. I had to play a cat-and-mouse game, to keep one step ahead of him by trying to guess what his next intrigue would be and then to cut the ground from under him.

I suffered his presence for years, never succeeding in defusing his aggressiveness. Then one day he brought about his own downfall. He perfidiously urged a fellow patient to assault his neighbor. His victim refused, my troublemaker insisted vehemently, and as a result the former smashed his bad counselor's nose in a fit of rage at the excessive nagging.

The effect was spectacular, and not only physically. One might almost have said that the poison in his soul drained out along with the blood spurting from his nose. The shock caused all the persecuting personality of our terrible patient to evaporate. He collapsed on his bed in a state of total prostration, acute melancholy succeeding his frenzy.

"I'm such an awful person," he cried, beating his chest penitently. "I beg your forgiveness. I deserve to die."

This man, who had been so dashing, so given to elegant dress and to pampering himself, now neglected his person completely. He did not even trouble to bathe. His very physique altered. He refused to leave his room.

I wondered whether it could have been the shock of the blow alone that had changed him, or if the shock had merely been the agent that revealed an already existing state.

It took me a long time to analyze this case. In fact, this fit that we had observed dated from the very night of his marriage. It had come out as an illness that had progressed over seven years and entailed equal periods of paranoia and depression. The blow which had delivered us from a weighty care had corresponded in fact to the moment of change.

Such patients were very difficult to treat without the precious medication we have at our disposal today, lithium. We now know that these alternations in temperament form a unity, and that the period of excitement is a prelude to the opposite phase of depression. Consequently, the best treatment is to attenuate the period of excitement so that the depression will be less severe, and in this way the balance can be more or less regularized.

But it used to be necessary to proceed with moral and psychological therapy, often over a period of many years. I emphasize this *moral and psychological* and not psychoanalytical, a cold and dry method that treats the patient as if he were a chemical compound. The doctor had to then and must today still bring to his work a spirit of love which will ultimately appeal to the highest principles in his patient. He must set an example, he must keep the promises he makes, he must sometimes overcome the repulsion that will be inspired in him by some of his patient's reasoning. I know that if I had not conformed to these rigorous criteria I would never have succeeded in treating the patient of whom I shall speak next. He was afflicted with a grave paranoia, whose most salient manifestation was an anti-Semitism the equivalent of which I have rarely seen.

M. Mathieu X was forty-two years old and had become depressed following a bout of tuberculosis of the lungs. During his stay in the sanatorium, he had displayed excessive emotional reactions. The sanatorium director, Dr. Guinard, had him placed in a rest home, from which he was sent to Charenton.

PATIENTS ARE PEOPLE LIKE US

When I first saw him, his state of depression had been succeeded by a snarling rage. He was haughty and scornful, and from the outset he made one thing clear: He hated Jews.

On Christmas Eve 1931, he addressed a letter of unprintable grossness to the administrative director of Charenton. Soon afterward, he wrote to the Minister of Health. Here are a few extracts from the latter missive:

> I say to you that there are in this place over a thousand slackers, dregs of humanity, scoundrels, bloodsuckers, swindlers, conceited young pups, degenerates, unspeakable hirelings who earn their livings by secretly and shamefully and criminally sucking the life out of an honest man. I say to you that there are here a thousand loafers wallowing disgracefully in their own filth who do nothing from morning to night and from night to morning but slobber, shit, and piss in their own filth, drunk and rotten as pigs. They haven't the guts to wash themselves, and for two years they've been murdering an honest man in their den of thieves.

He fired off letter after scabrous letter to the Minister, attacking the recipient himself with the vilest words of all. These missives were all signed with a swastika and expressed the most extraordinary savagery:

> Blood must be shed, flesh must be sliced, people must be exterminated, destroyed, tortured to death.

One of his favorite themes was that his doctors—myself in particular—considered him to be a homosexual. This he indeed was, and thus he suffered from feelings of inferiority and guilt. Unable to confess his real emotions, he transformed them into hatred and extreme rebellion.

> I revolt with all my being [he wrote] against an accusation which cannot concern me in any way, shape, or form . . .

He rested from these outbursts by drawing and writing poems which showed incontrovertibly—as did his earlier letters and his past psychological history—homosexual and sadomasochistic tendencies. He made constant efforts to justify himself, claiming that he was not sexually abnormal and had never practiced pederasty.

He regarded his confinement at Charenton as having come about as the result of gossip about his morals. It was, in fact, true that he had never been a practicing homosexual. He had been a rather gentle, serious, hardworking young man in whose peaceful nature there had been no hint of his later extremism. His family had noticed nothing that would lead them to suspect him of homosexual tendencies. At most, during a certain period of his life, his family recalled that he had been excessively attached to a comrade.

It was possible that those real but never acknowledged homosexual tendencies, which he had repressed because they shocked him, had become the starting point for his feelings of guilt, his irrational ideas, then his elaborated reactions of hatred. He used the latter to justify himself. This is a recognized pathological route taken by persons in flight from their real or supposed faults, a process of self-exoneration which is almost invariably accompanied by exaggerated pride. My patient at times believed that one day he would be called on to exercise supreme power over the world. He said that he was God, and he signed his letters "The God of the Jews," "The Holy Spirit."

It goes without saying that his attitude toward me was inseparable from the hatred he bore all Jews. He made a drawing of me covered by a swastika ornamented with drops of blood. I did not let myself worry or be influenced by his savage antagonism, and was careful to see that he be given the best possible treatment. I listened assiduously to his requests and tried to satisfy them whenever possible.

Our first encounters were difficult, sometimes shocking. I never answered his insults, but tried to calm him by advising that he try to compose himself. Even in his most hateful period, he would be capable of remarkable bursts of poetry. My job was to help him to recover his true nature, the one which had been in evidence during his adolescence and young manhood, and which still peeked out from time to time. I treated him over a period of nearly ten years, and finally was able to glimpse a crack in the armor of evil in which he had encased his true self. Once I had gained his confidence, we were able to discuss his problems calmly.

Of course his anti-Semitism and hatred did not melt like snow under the first rays of sunshine. The change took place very slowly. I was able to follow it through his drawings; the representations of homosexuality, the swastikas, the scenes of murder and torture disappeared, to be replaced by country scenes where peace was expressed in a still chaotic fashion.

The moment came when I felt that I could tackle the moral side of the problem and apply myself to helping him rediscover the principle of right and wrong, which had totally vanished during his psychotic period. He did not accept my "lessons" easily, but I felt that we were making slow but sure progress.

With his gradual improvement, his appearance itself altered. He had affected an aggressively untidy appearance, refusing to take proper care of his person. Now his taste for grooming had returned, and his manners became less brusque and churlish.

One day, as I entered his room, he held out a drawing in which two men were depicted shaking hands. He informed me that it represented the reconciliation of the Church and the Synagogue. One of the two figures was Cardinal Verdier, the other myself.

I was not able to follow Mathieu X all the way to his complete recovery, but I believe that it did take place. I know, in any case, that I helped to rescue him from a deep abyss in which he might have remained lost forever.

In my long experience of these most dangerous of all patients, I have learned one lesson: Hidden beneath their delusion of persecution lies a profoundly disturbed moral conscience, which makes them judge others harshly in order to escape being judged, and causes them to transfer their own guilt onto the world around them. Rather than acknowledge their wrongdoing, they repress it, and in that internal alchemy it changes into venomous hate.

This must not be confused with the natural aggressiveness of animals. The wild beast that desires its prey devours it; then, satisfied, it goes to sleep. The man who is guilty, or believes himself to be so, chooses his victim, discharges the full weight of his guilt upon him, shames him, pursues him with his loathing, and is still not satisfied.

This concept is very different from that of psychoanalysis, which holds that the real danger in this particular illness lies in the repression of an unsatisfied and hidden desire. Psychoanalysts do not admit the importance of the existence of moral conscience, which is the foundation of my entire conception of psychology. I do not believe that it is desire that is pushed into the inner being but rather a feeling of guilt that a person wants to deny and ignore. I also believe that it is important to look such feelings in the face, as lucidly as possible, in order to efface them. I maintain that the goal of psychiatry is to bring into harmony instinctual desires and moral law, two needs which inhabit man equally. Psychoanalysis places too much emphasis on instinct alone, and the treatment insists that morality give way to the sovereign law of desire. This is a fundamental error whose consequences are not only visible on the psychiatric level. If I had used psychoanalysis on the patients I have described, I am sure that I would never have been able to cure them.

VII

HYSTERIA

HYSTERIA IS A MYSTERIOUS AILMENT WHICH HAS CONFOUNDED PSY-
chiatrists over the years. In order to discuss the subject in some
depth, I shall refer to events which took place during the war years
1939 and 1940, events that will show up quite clearly the mistakes
which have been made regarding this affliction. Hysteria was formerly regarded with terror, sometimes in past centuries as a manifestation of the devil, involving spectacular cases of exorcism. And
today the phenomenon is still not well understood.

In 1939, Hitler had just plunged the world into the Second World
War. I was no longer of an age to serve in the front lines, so I ful-
filled my obligation to my country by directing a neuropsychiatric
center at Reims. Soon, many wounded soldiers arrived, and in the
weeks that followed many of them manifested signs of nervous disorders.

I observed with sadness, but also with curiosity, that the state of
mind of those serving in the Army was very different from that I
had known before.

During the First World War, men and officers had been united
by a spirit of brotherhood as they fought side by side to defend
their country and their freedom. In 1939, the reasons for fighting
did not seem so clear, even though subsequent events proved that
if ever a continent, indeed the entire world, had to fight hard if it
were to survive, it was at that moment.

The common soldiers seemed not to understand the real origins
of the war and, blinded by propaganda, failed to recognize Hitler's
true motives, his desire to impose his monstrous conception of human relations upon the entire world. Despite their superior educa-

tion, the officers were even more divided than the men, and many of them who entertained anti-democratic ideas even hoped that the war would bring about a change of regime that would draw France closer to the Fascist ideal.

The moral crisis of those days is important because it had grave psychiatric repercussions which I observed in my daily work as a military doctor. The first of these were "classics" (if I may so describe them)—soldiers who experienced nervous crises some time after they were wounded. During the First World War, I had been in the thick of the fighting and so had not seen such cases. In fact, I had never witnessed such breakdowns, even under the most terrible bombardments.

Now, I recalled what had been said twenty years or so before about hysteria and the influence of the emotions. Some doctors had assured us that hysterical seizures were precipitated by emotional shock. Babinski had been involved in the argument. In order to answer this assertion, which seemed to him inexact, he went so far as to post himself at the morgue in order to watch bereaved families identify their dead. The emotional stress they were enduring did not produce nervous manifestations.

Doubt was cast on the truth of this thesis from another quarter. A famous neurologist, Clunet, was aboard the ship *Provence* when she was torpedoed in the Atlantic by the Germans. He saw not the slightest sign of hysteria among the crew as the ship was hit and sank.

Clovis Vincent, a student of Babinski who was to become a celebrated neurosurgeon, was attached to a battalion in the front lines. He saw not a trace of this illness in the soldiers he was treating, which led Babinski to declare: "When a real emotion shakes the human soul, there is no room left for hysteria."

However, when Vincent was sent in his capacity as neurologist to a reserve center at Tours, he witnessed many cases of hysteria.

Let us return to my own experience in Reims, at the "rear," in Army parlance. I had occasion to observe a collective hysterical crisis which brought to mind Charcot's famous description of patients suffering from this disorder: rigidly arched bodies, heads flung back, impressive somersaults, fantastic contortions, all those manifestations which might lead one to believe that the afflicted persons were indeed inhabited by an evil force.

Many of my patients had suffered a strong emotional reaction to wounds or shocks, and they exhibited symptoms of either depression or disorders of the autonomic nervous system. I used the same methods that I had employed at Charenton: active psychotherapy based on trust, understanding, and friendship, along with assiduous work, and with comparably good results.

However, I was given a ten-day leave, and the care of my patients was handed over to a general practitioner who, though an excellent physician and very scrupulous, was not used to treating nervous disorders. I gave him advice and reassurance, without much success I was to discover later, for he tackled his new duties with a bad case of the jitters. It so happens that patients with nervous disorders are hypersensitive to the moods of those who come near them. From the very first day that their new doctor took over, the atmosphere changed. They became extremely agitated, and some of them relapsed into fresh crises. Nervous disorders which had been minimal and isolated became general and serious; the contagion spread and accelerated.

Upon my return, I witnessed a sight that I shall never forget. I was utterly overwhelmed by the spectacle of collective madness before my eyes, of possessed human beings out of all control. I would never have taken my leave if I could have foreseen the violence of the crisis.

On every floor of the building, patients were bent backward in the shape of arcs, the napes of their necks nearly touching their heels. In this attitude, which they seemed incapable of breaking, and which gave them the strength of a tightly coiled spring, they made stupendous leaps straight from their beds to the ceiling, then fell back heavily to their mattresses, only to bound up once again. This produced an awesome racket throughout the entire hospital.

My poor colleague was beside himself; the staff members were half out of their minds. Soldiers had been brought in several times in an attempt to reassure and calm their comrades, but this had only added to the confusion. The situation was catastrophic.

Fear was at the origin of this collective hysteria, a fear all the more difficult to control because there is no genuine reason for it, because it cannot be discussed, because it is irrational, invisible except in these manifestations. The illness seemed to have no roots. Where could it be attacked?

I knew that an irrational malady must be met with an irrational remedy. The patients had contaminated each other by communicating their fear, and it was my job to counteract their anxiety by suggesting to them that it no longer existed. To this end, I went to work on each patient individually.

I approached the first man and told him who I was and promised that I was going to make him well. I continued to talk to him calmly, reassuring him as though he were a child who had been frightened by a bad dream in the night. I began to massage a spot on his body gently with my finger, explaining that as I touched him all his terror would evaporate. Soon I began to feel the muscles relax, the body lose its rigidity, and then I saw a look of intelligence return to the half-conscious face. In half an hour normality had been restored to the whole ward. My colleague was speechless.

I had not worked a miracle. I had merely put into practice the guiding principles of the method my teachers had taught me. At Charenton I had saved patients by this blend of authority and trust. The power of suggestion can work in two ways: It can, like a contagion, as if the air itself were laden with dangerous vapors, disrupt an entire section of a hospital without a word having been spoken. I borrowed the same method to dissipate these vapors.

But how do these dangerous vapors originate, laying hold of a human body and mind, stirring them to a hysterical frenzy? Science has not yet entirely answered this question, though great progress has been made since the days of Louis XV, when men and women gathered around the tomb of Deacon Pâris in the Saint-Médard cemetery to participate in those scenes of mass convulsions recorded by history.

In the first place, what is the origin of that extraordinary physical strength possessed by persons in a state of hysterical crisis? Such individuals are capable of performing feats comparable to those of the finest acrobats. Hysteria transforms the patient's muscular capacity, giving him a suppleness and a strength which disappear once the attack is over.

In the second place, such disorders do not seem to surface at the moment when the organism and the personality must react to a threat or to a strong emotion, nor are they present in subjects who are completely exhausted. They appear only after a period of rest or reflection, in a second phase, one in which the patient relieves his feelings and the events which led up to them, as though experiencing a dream, while he is safe from danger and is not actually required to defend himself. He surrenders himself utterly to pure emotion, and the "mental image" impressed upon him is thus all the more traumatizing, and he all the more receptive.

This was the case with the patients in Reims, who had all been wounded. After weeks of rest, at the moment when they were beginning to recover, they were stricken with nervous disorders. The trauma they had suffered in battle appeared belatedly, when their bodies and minds no longer had to fight against the effects of the wounds themselves.

There is also the problem of malingering in order to be excused from battle, as soldiers were accused of doing during the First World War. The suspicion is understandable, since certain mental patients, catatonics, for example, often give the impression that they are acting, which they most certainly are not. However, unless the faker happens to be a technical expert, he cannot get very far with any such pretense and is soon caught out.

Hysteria is often confused with another malady, epilepsy, since the dividing line between the two is not always clear. It can be said in general that when the attack is not too violent there are psychic reactions, and when it is more so, organic reactions appear.

However, an essential difference exists between epilepsy and hysteria. In the former, consciousness is completely lost, while in the latter it is merely "clouded over." It is still difficult to distinguish between the two, because the patient may deceive the doctor and himself by imagining that he has actually lost consciousness. Observers have noticed, for example, that such a patient may have been careful not to hurt himself when he fell, or he may remember certain things which were said to him during his attack, which proves that he was at least half-conscious at the time.

On the other hand, the epileptic seizure is marked by amnesia and total unconsciousness, as well as by the suddenness of the onset. This clinical differentiation is of less importance today, since encephalography allows us to make an almost certain diagnosis. I do not say "absolutely" certain since this highly effective technique has produced its share of mistakes. For instance, it is useless to try it on an epileptic a long time after his crisis, for the brain tracing will show no anomaly by then.

It is by the presence or absence of amnesia that one can distinguish epilepsy from hallucinations or somnambulism. The patient suffering from the former disorder remembers nothing; even if he has been an ambulatory epileptic and, in the course of his crisis, taken long or complicated journeys, he will retain no memory at all of his adventures.

I once had a patient who, during an epileptic fit, went to the station, bought a ticket to Le Havre, boarded the train, and came to himself in the streets of that port. He never was able to understand why he chose to go there, what motives had guided his unconscious mind, or what he had done during the trip.

This demonstrates why it is impossible to simulate epilepsy without very special training. One can only imitate the separate disorders that accompany it, a phenomenon on which Babinski cast considerable light. An organic hemiplegia cannot be reproduced consciously and voluntarily, because one muscle is contracted and the other is not. I can make a fist or open my hand, but I cannot single out one muscle and contract it independently of its fellows. In an epileptic seizure, the onset occurs suddenly, the subject has tonic convulsions (consisting of contractions accompanied by rigidity) and clinical convulsions (consisting of rapid muscular contractions producing broad movements). It is no small matter to reproduce both these symptoms at once.

I would define hysteria as follows: a particular form of neurosis in which a psychological idea engenders organic disorders. For centuries it was considered an essentially feminine ill, and the origin of the name comes from a Greek word meaning *uterus* or *womb*. Even its symptoms were linked to troubles of and even displacements of that organ. Charcot put an end to that myth by showing that the malady can affect both sexes.

But where is hysteria situated and what individuals are likely to be afflicted by it?

Here I wish to make one point clear. Hysteria does not consist only of major seizures such as I observed at Reims. It can take far less spectacular forms, such as paralysis or the loss of certain senses. The definition of hysteria does not have to do with symptoms but rather with the origin of the illness, which is purely psychological.

While at Reims, I rejected the diagnosis of hysteria in a twenty-six-year-old soldier who sometimes stamped his feet or rolled on the ground. Before I saw him, it had been assumed that he was either hysteric or epileptic. He did not suffer from any vasomotor disturbance. His seizures occurred most often after vexations which amounted to little more than the disappointments that everyone meets in the course of a day. If many people happened to be present, the spasm became worse. They had only to help and support the boy for his crisis to reach a real paroxysm and beat all records for duration.

In treating him, I tried to eliminate all witnesses, to talk to him calmly during our sessions, to lecture him firmly and reassuringly, so as to impose an air of mastery over him which would inspire his respect.

He calmed down quite soon, and together we tried to find out where his extreme sensitivity to events came from. Of course it was in a certain measure constitutional—he had always been high-strung. He was a small, angry, vulnerable man who lived with his fist clenched and was charged with a dynamism unaccompanied by any self-control. His father was an alcoholic, tyrannical and given to violence. He had rebelled, and sharp conflicts with his parents had arisen. Finally he left home.

Fatigue, insomnia, and alcohol played a determining role in triggering his attacks. The period of stress which had brought him to the hospital had come on the heels of a leave he had spent with his family, with whom he had at last become reconciled. He had overexerted himself, working in the fields, drinking, going to bed late, and sleeping poorly. When he had returned to the Army, he had been at the end of his tether.

Because of the vicissitudes of war, I was not able to follow his case for very long. He needed complex care, including strict physical and mental hygiene, sedation, and a vigorous course of treatment for his liver, the whole crowned by attentive psychotherapy, avoiding excessive solicitude, which would have fostered his condition, but also any humiliation, which would have exacerbated it.

Years ago, at Salpêtrière, I saw a woman who had suffered a complete breakdown after serious family and other problems. First, she had complained of violent headaches, then her right arm had become paralyzed. She was brought to my ward. My professor, Souques, was on vacation, and his replacement, who was not an experienced neurologist, examined her.

Because of her headaches and paralysis, he thought immediately of a cerebral tumor, and mentioned in her presence that she might become blind. A few days later, Souques returned from his vacation.

A consummate neurologist, who always used Babinski's method of thorough clinical examination, he instantly recognized that the patient was suffering from a psychic paralysis with no organic involvement. He administered an electric current, the effect of which was nil except for its power of suggestion on the patient. That same evening, completely recovered, the woman took the train to return to her home in the west of France.

Six years elapsed, during which she enjoyed perfect health. Then several of her children became sick in succession, and she became overtired caring for them. Her headaches began again and then she apparently lost her eyesight. She was taken to me at Sainte-Anne in Paris. When she entered my office, she was walking with a cane, feeling her way around objects, bumping into things like a blind woman not yet accustomed to her infirmity.

I noticed, however, that she kept her eyes completely closed. I lifted her eyelids and saw that her eyeballs were rolled down and to the left, which made me think that her blindness might be voluntarily simulated, because in paralysis of the motor nerves of the eyeball, there is an opposite effect.

I examined her eyes thoroughly and they were perfectly normal. She had lost her sight for purely psychological reasons.

"Do you remember when the doctor who examined me said that I might become blind?" she asked me. "Well, his prediction has become true. He mentioned a brain tumor . . ."

My patient had taken it into her head that Souques had been wrong about her and that his substitute had seen her ailment clearly. She was a perfect illustration of the effects of suggestion as described by Bernheim and later by Babinski.

I treated her with a medication which I was beginning to find efficacious in cases of hysteria: scopochloralose, a combination of scopolamine and chloralose, which brings on a light sleep in which the nervous system relaxes and the patient can hear what the doctor is saying. In this way, a very abbreviated form of psychotherapy can be practiced. As soon as she began to drowse, I spoke in front of her as if I assumed she were deeply asleep and could not hear what I was saying to some intern or nurse:

"She'll recover completely. When she wakes up she'll be able to see as well as you or I."

I continued in this optimistic vein until she opened her eyes to find herself completely recovered from her pseudoblindness. Irrefutably, this woman's malady had been hysterically induced and her hysteria had disappeared by way of pure suggestion.

But this does not mean that impressive cures such as this one are simple if one possesses a little knowledge of psychology, a dash of authority, and a great deal of common sense. Those qualities are necessary, but they are not enough. For if hysteria, once detected, is to be treated successfully, it must be distinguished from other very closely related maladies.

A few years ago I was called in to examine a shopkeeper who lived near me. She had been attacked by a dog which had not hurt her but simply torn her dress. She had been extremely frightened and now suffered violent pains in her legs and her lower back, which made walking very difficult for her.

Her doctors believed that she was suffering from hysteria caused by the emotional shock of her experience. This seemed logical until I made my examinations, following Babinski's method. To my great astonishment, I discovered areas of insensitivity that related to an injury at the base of the spinal column, symptomatic of the existence of tumors, as well as certain defensive reflexes which in my opinion had nothing to do with anything mental.

However, my opinion was ignored and her doctors decided that she should be psychoanalyzed, since she had suffered an emotional trauma. She was placed in a mental hospital and given psychoanalytical therapy, with lamentable results: After several months, she became totally paralyzed and incontinent.

I was again consulted and made another neurological examination, which showed clear signs of pressure on the spinal cord. I succeeded in getting the patient admitted to Salpêtrière, where I recommended her to the care of Drs. Alajouanine and Thurel. Their examinations confirmed the existence of a tumor pressing on the spinal cord. It was removed and the patient recovered, without any subsequent complications.

Quite simply, the emotional trauma relating to the incident with the dog had triggered the symptoms, which in any event would have surfaced sooner or later. Actually, the dog's attack had been a stroke of luck, for it had led to the discovery of the tumor in time to remove it before it had caused irremediable damage.

Such errors can have fearful consequences. The human mind is quick to see supernatural forces at work in phenomena which it finds difficult to explain. The substance of collective madness is then built upon such a foundation, and the necessary scapegoat, some living creature who can be held responsible, is found.

A few years before the war a young girl was brought to me, suffering from nervous attacks which took place most often at nightfall, and which were accompanied by contortions that terrified those who witnessed them. These events took place in a region whose population was quite primitive and where witchcraft was still practiced.

The patient was first subjected to a general consultation at the hospital during which the doctors, in her hearing, uttered the words *hysteria* and *suggestion*. Her parents seized upon the latter word and gave it a very special sense: *bewitched*. They then pointed out that there was a specific man who had cast a spell on her, a nearby farmer who lived alone, refused to mingle with his neighbors, spoke oddly, and dressed strangely.

Priests were consulted, and there was talk of exorcism, then of taking revenge against the devil's emissary. Rumors spread quickly and the troubles they engendered were transmitted by a mental contagion that flowed like a stream. I believe that lynch law is written deep in the hearts of men, unfortunately.

The young girl was sent to me, and it did not take me long to diagnose her problem: encephalitis and the beginnings of Parkinson's disease. Her parents, however, insisted to me that she was not sick but "possessed." They refused to believe that an organic injury could cause the manifestations which they had witnessed, especially the contortions, which seemed to them surely to have been dictated by the devil or his followers. I finally succeeded in making them listen to reason, to "acquit," albeit grudgingly, their neighbor, and to see to it that their daughter was given the necessary medical care for her maladies.

The secrets of hysteria have still not been entirely unraveled. It is true that the term has been stripped of its false trappings: manic-depressive psychosis, delirium, mental imbalance, catatonia, etc. Also, today one rarely sees the spectacular crises such as those Charcot has described. Credit for this must be given to Babinski, who took a stand against Charcot's attribution of the physical and mental manifestations of hysteria to injuries or disturbances of certain zones of the nervous system. I repeat that Babinski proved that under no circumstances were those manifestations linked to localized injuries of the brain.

It is thanks to Babinski that the role of suggestion was proved to be both the cause of and the remedy for the illness. Because of his discovery, and that of Bernheim before him, we see today only rare examples, notably during wartime, of such epidemics of hysteria as I have described.

Apart from hysterical crises, we also have to deal with paralysis and contractures. As Kourilsky and I demonstrated in a case of hysterical contracture, electromyograms can reveal currents of action similar to those which occur during a voluntary contraction. Our patient had a contractured leg; as soon as we began trying to change the flexed position of the leg, violent currents of action appeared on the electromyogram. When the leg was bent back into its previous position, the currents disappeared. The subject's unconscious mind had morbidly willed the leg's contraction, though his conscious mind was unaware of the psychic attitude he had taken. Administration of scopochloralose brought about a rapid recovery.

As I have pointed out earlier, a great deal of neurological and psychiatric experience is required for the successful treatment of hysteria. Generally it will give way before the powerful effect of instantaneous psychotherapy. Although today we seem to have turned away from this form of treatment, preferring objective observation and analysis, I believe that we will be forced to return to it in the future. The fact is that psychiatrists know less about hysteria than they should, since most patients who suffer from it are usually not sent to them but to general practitioners or neurologists.

No progress will be made toward understanding hysteria unless the pernicious separation of psychiatry and neurology into two distinct fields is abandoned. The mystery of hysteria—for it is still a mystery, despite what some would have us believe—will only be solved by the closest collaboration between the neurologist and the psychiatrist.

Today, when the physician cannot decipher a given set of symptoms and all his tests show negative results, he says that the problem is "functional," or "hysterical," two formulas which cover a vast gulf of ignorance. Such a dangerous attitude in the old days led to the classification of Parkinson's disease as "hysteria," until, one day, the disease's characteristic lesions, which had nothing whatever to do with hysteria, were discovered.

I think that I can state that the frequency of diagnoses of hysteria is inversely proportional to the competence of the doctor. Even in recent years there has been an enormous amount of fantasy bandied about on this subject. We have seen a cerebral tumor, or even a tumor which pressed on the spinal cord, diagnosed as hysteria. Multiple sclerosis cases have also been tagged with this catchall word. It is true that the latter disease sometimes begins with manifestations that appear to be of hysterical origin, so such a diagnosis might be understandable. However, a man skilled in making neurological examinations could never make such an error. I do not mean to imply that there are not many cases of hysterical paralysis, since I cured in one afternoon, by the use of suggestion, a patient who had been immobilized for months with the malady.

It is true too that hysteria, with its violent effect on the body and on behavior, possesses elements that can well baffle the little-informed observer or the practitioner who has had little opportunity to study a real case. But its mystery should spur the puzzled physician to further effort rather than to concocting a snap judgment. Psychiatry will have taken an important leap forward when it solves this enigma.

The problem of *hypnosis* is related to that of hysteria and catatonia. I studied clinical and psychological hypnosis with Pierre Janet, who was a great friend of mine and whom I often invited to lecture when I succeeded Professor Delay as director of the psychiatric clinic of the faculty at Sainte-Anne.

Janet was a brilliant and captivating speaker and one of our great clinicians, a marvelously gifted and warmly humanitarian man, rare in every sense of the word. At Sainte-Anne, he showed us the technique of hypnosis by fixation on a brilliant object. We, of course, realized that one could only hypnotize those who wished to be, or whose personality had been weakened in its resistance to outside forces, as is the case in catalepsy.

This symptom belongs in the category of catatonia, but may also exist alone in the form of cataleptic crises, reminiscent of hysterical sleep and somnambulism. Such cataleptic crises, which Professor Claude and I have called "cataleptic sleep," may last for a few hours, a few days, a few months, or several years. The patient is as motionless as Sleeping Beauty, the eyelids fluttering, able to hold every position imposed upon him, as if he were an articulated doll.

Years ago I had the opportunity to observe a young girl who had been in this state for five years and had recovered. Such patients remember everything that occurred during the time of their illness and even the words people around them uttered, though their own initiative had been suspended. They can neither speak nor move, not because they are paralyzed but their will to do so is inhibited.

It is still necessary to be careful to distinguish such states from the pathological sleep linked to organic injury of the sleep center of the brain. Many examples of this pathological organic sleep were seen at the time of the famous outbreak of encephalitis lethargica (sleeping sickness), which reached such a peak after the First World War and left in its wake so many survivors maimed by Parkinson's disease. Fortunately, that scourge is rare today. In pathological organic sleep, the patient sleeps exactly as in normal sleep, his eyes shut, but without retaining imposed positions, for such subjects awaken very easily.

Cataleptic sleep is not real sleep, but an inhibition of the will, in which consciousness is retained but is passive and powerless. The personality's independence disappears, which is exactly what happens in hypnosis. The only difference lies in the fact that in cataleptic sleep the disorder appears spontaneously, either as premonitory symptoms of catatonia or, in milder cases, as the result of strong emotion or suggestion. We saw an example of this in a woman who on learning of her daughter's death fell into a cataleptic sleep which lasted for twenty-four hours and was accompanied by a significant slowing down of the pulse rate. She was brought out of it by psychotherapeutic means. Such cases may be called "hysterical catalepsy."

Hypnosis produces artificially the same syndrome, either through visual fatigue or by suggestion. In Paris on the Rue Saint-André-des-Arts years ago, I watched the celebrated Bérillon put to sleep a group of subjects who were seated in a circle, repeating as he stroked their eyelids one after the other, "Sleep, sleep, my friends." More recently I observed the same method used in the conference on hypnosis organized by Dr. Paterson in London.

The anesthetic and analgesic effects of hypnosis were made famous in the Cloquet case, which was reported to the Academy of Medicine, in which a young woman operated on for cancer of the breast under hypnosis not only felt nothing but remembered nothing afterward. Lassner has described how chemical anesthesia, especially ether, was later developed in Boston as an alternative to "mesmerism." The famous Mesmer may be said to be the originator of all methods of this type, which are offshoots of his creation—"animal magnetism." This subject has been taken up again recently in France by Barrucand and Chertok, and in England by Stephen Black and Paterson.

Hypnosis, to describe it briefly, temporarily deprives a subject of volition and puts him under the influence of another person. Advocates of hypnosis use it to make therapeutic suggestions to patients, particularly those suffering from hysteria. This was very popular in Bernheim's day in the famous school in Nancy, and in Paris with Charcot and his followers. After the craze subsided, hypnosis was discredited in France, only to become the order of the day in Anglo-Saxon countries.

At the invitation of the Academy of Sciences, I made a report on hypnosis in which I emphasized the dangers of subjecting a personality to the will of another, even if the latter has all the good intentions in the world. I cited the disturbing reflections on this subject made by Henri Ey and by Brisset.

I myself have given up hypnosis for moral reasons, far preferring the method proposed to me by a pharmacist in the Gironde, M. Pascal Brotteaux, who wrote to me in 1931 to tell me about a combination of scopolamine and chloralose which he had used to induce a state of "medicinal hypnosis." My students and I made a long experimental study of those two substances on animals, and later studied them in our clinic. We found that large amounts of scopolamine and chloralose do indeed produce a state of hypnosis, but that weaker doses induce only a light sleep identical to normal sleep, producing both a psychological relaxation, a relaxation of the autonomic nervous system with a slowing of the pulse rate, a slight lowering of arterial pressure, and diminution of all vascular erethism (abnormal irritability).

Sleep induced by scopochloralose is extremely useful in treating hysterical manifestations quickly and safely, and I have substituted this new therapy for the old, brutally painful, even inhumane, electroshock treatments.

I shall describe later the role of these drugs in the treatment of certain obsessions.

CHAPTER

VIII

WEARING
THE YELLOW STAR

THE INVASION OF FRANCE AND THE ARMISTICE IN JUNE 1940 MEANT
the capture of all the levers of power by the Germans or their min-
ions, bringing with it racial laws and, worst of all, the hatred and
intolerance carried by the Nazis in their impedimenta.

I had to decide what to do in order to work and survive. Because
of my military service in the First World War, I was permitted to
keep my job on condition that I wear the yellow star, which all
Jews were obliged to do. I had no illusions and was well aware that
a mortal danger hung over our heads.

After the armistice, when I had been demobilized in the free zone,
the Rockefeller Foundation proposed to help me settle in America.
The temptation was great now to take them up on that offer, but I
did not want to abandon my country, which I loved so well. I knew
many other Jews who made the same choice I did.

The Ministry of Health at Vichy, where I had many friends who
were worried about me, offered to get me an appointment to a hospital located in the free zone, either at Toulouse or in the Midi, but
I refused, not wishing to accept any favors from the Vichy government. Instead, I returned to my old hospital, Charenton, and the
memory of the welcome I received there fills me with gratitude even
now.

I wore the yellow star during almost the entire Occupation, even
when I made my rounds. Some of my patients were surprised to see
that emblem in the center of which was written the word *Jew*. Far
from clothing me with the humiliation which its promoters meant
it to, it seemed to confer on me an added respect, like homage
rendered to an unjustly persecuted people.

This was true on the hospital grounds and among my colleagues, but outside things were different. It was a shock to see even telephone booths lettered with the warning: "Forbidden to Jews and to dogs." One day I forgot that the parks were subject to the same regulation and took a stroll in the Bois de Vincennes. At first I came upon a German officer on horseback who looked at me but said nothing. Then a guard hurried up to me and told me that I was in danger, that I needn't be afraid of him, but that one never knew who one was going to meet, and that I had better get out of the park quickly. I was saddened at the thought that such things could happen in a country that loved freedom so much.

One night the doorbell of my apartment rang loudly. I leaped bolt upright, my first thought being that I was about to be arrested. I was just considering jumping out the window when the telephone rang. It was my good and courageous concierge, a member of the Resistance, who was calling to tell me not to be afraid. It seemed that my laboratory assistant had suffered a gastric hemorrhage and wanted me to go to see him.

I reacted to the virulent anti-Semitism that arose with the advent of the Occupation by taking up again my study of the Old Testament and post-Biblical texts. These studies have played an important role in shaping me professionally, and helped me better to understand man and the world he lives in.

Shortly before the war I had received a visit from a man to whom I am deeply indebted, a former headmaster of a Hebrew school in the Ukraine. M. Kontorcyski had been giving lessons in Hebrew since his arrival in France. During the course of our conversation, I remarked that I had noticed a similarity between my philosophic method of treating patients and certain psalms in the Bible. He told me that I should learn Hebrew in order to understand the nuances and subtleties of the sacred texts.

Soon M. Kontorcyski was skillfully guiding me past the usual traps of grammar and usage. I arose every morning at six to study

Hebrew before I went to Charenton at eight. I met with my teacher once a week, and before long he had me transcribing Biblical texts.

Then the war came along, followed by the Occupation. I continued to begin each day by studying Hebrew, the circumstances giving the work a bittersweet flavor of revenge and hope. I mastered the art of writing Hebrew fairly well, and by now it is as natural for me to write in that language as in French.

I have never ceased to pursue this exciting study. Through it immense horizons have opened before me, and in these texts I found a mirror of my own experience. In a section of the Talmud entitled "The Sanhedrin," which is devoted to the organization of justice, I found described exactly the sort of examination of witnesses that I had been practicing for years at Charenton. What I read seemed to me so impressive, so precise, so scientific, so moving that I longed to translate the texts into French. I did so later on with the help of a M. Weisengrun.

I was taking the opposite path from the one my father had taken before me. He, a Talmudist from childhood, had left Eastern Europe and Hebraic culture to become assimilated to the West. In my youth he had spent long hours giving me the benefit of his knowledge of the Greco-Latin and French cultures, and this only to find his Western-born and -educated son discover Hebrew culture as an adult! I was making the trip back—and under what historical circumstances!

I made a vow that my first trip after the Nazi nightmare was over, if I were still alive, would be to Jerusalem. One day my father and mother appeared at Charenton. The Germans had driven them out of their house in Angers, after beating up my father. The three of us lived in mortal fear from then on.

During that period of despair, when we were not only horrified at the Nazi villainy but astonished at the cowardice of so many of our compatriots, I became obsessed with one idea: to seek out those Jews who were worthy of their history and had the courage to face their dilemma with resolution. Dr. Minkovski told me of a meeting place at Number 36 Rue Amelot where, in a gathering of academics brought together by a wonderfully courageous and energetic former Polish national, M. Jacoubovitch, I would find men of the caliber I had in mind.

The heroic leader of the group was an unforgettable figure named Rappoport, a small, bearded, thickset man with handsome bright eyes. He met with the victims of the Nazis, made the necessary decisions quickly, provided false papers, found hiding places, and with the help of a few remarkable persons, such as the wonderful Mme. Courbet, who was not Jewish, organized the escape of many Jewish children. Rappoport received secret information from the French Resistance revealing that the Germans were engaged in mass killings of the Jews in Poland. When he passed the information on to us, we refused to believe that human beings were being placed in gas chambers and then burned. But he, who knew his sources well, never doubted the truth of such stories.

The discovery of the rue Amelot was of great reassurance to me, for it proved that there still existed Jews worthy of the Patriarchs and the Prophets, truly filled with the fire of Sinai and the light of the Just, ready to defend Jerusalem. Our group shone like a beacon in a Paris crushed under the Occupation.

I was often tired in those terrible years and suffered from painful neuritis and pleurisy. The hospital staff remained faithful to me, with the exception of only one employee, the man whom I described earlier as calling himself the "chief of the alcoholics," who had been a tale-bearer to the Ministry of Health before the war. I had believed that his influence was no longer harmful, but, unhappily, such persons are born to prosper in troubled times.

Denunciation was his passion. He moved like a fish in water during the Occupation, writing more false reports and anonymous letters than ever. I finally became a victim of his machinations when a revolver was found in the possession of an inmate working in the garden. The administrator turned the weapon over to the police, informing them that we had no idea how the patient had acquired the weapon. That should have been the end of it, but the "chief of alcoholics" went to the Germans and declared:

"You should have arrested Dr. Baruk long ago. He's a Jew and he keeps revolvers in his room. He uses them to arm the patients."

Quite soon thereafter, two German policemen presented themselves at my lodgings and promptly shoved me, half-dressed though I was, into an automobile. They announced that they were taking me to be sentenced. At the German headquarters of our area, I found myself in the presence of a German officer who declared:

"You have weapons in your possession; this is a crime. Therefore, you are condemned to death and will be executed in ten minutes."

Fortunately for me the director of Charenton appeared and told the officer how insane the accusations against me really were. The German, who by good luck was not a member of the Gestapo, let himself be convinced of my innocence and replied:

"All right, take your doctor back, but be extra careful from now on."

The incident left its mark on me, and I suddenly realized just how vulnerable I was. My health had also been shaken by the emotional shock of my arrest, and so when friends urged me to go into hiding I followed their advice. A colleague made me welcome at his home in the country, where I stayed until the Liberation.

During my absence, the "chief of alcoholics" ran amok at Charenton, denouncing the best of his fellow workers. Everyone was terrified, including all the nurses and doctors, but no one dared oppose him openly. Besides denouncing the hospital personnel to the Germans, he was responsible for the arrest and deportation of a number of French workers who had attempted to avoid forced labor in Germany. Finally he even attacked functionaries in the Ministry of Health. At the Liberation he barricaded himself in the hospital laundry with a gun and threatened to shoot anyone who came near. But the workers in the town of Charenton, whose comrades he had denounced, ferreted him out and turned him over to the police. He was interned with other collaborators, but a psychiatric expert examined him and declared him to be mentally ill, thus saving him from all punishment. After a few months he was freed. At least we were definitely rid of him for good.

I returned to Charenton after the liberation of Paris and found that almost everything had to be done over. Like the rest of France, the hospital had suffered both morally and materially. However, the staff that I had put together remained more or less intact, so that my task of rebuilding was less difficult than I had feared.

I established the first organized courses for training nurses and hospital workers in the handling of patients, as well as in medicine. The results surpassed my fondest hopes. The following story will illustrate the efficacy of that training.

One morning I received a call from a supervisor, M. Maniotte, who was among the most efficient and devoted members of our staff. He informed me that he was worried about one of his patients. The intern had seen the man and promised to return in an hour, but the supervisor was afraid that might be too late to help.

One look at the patient told me that he had a perforated gastric ulcer and peritonitis. I turned to the supervisor and told him to call an ambulance immediately, as the patient required surgery.

Maniotte replied, "I already have. When I saw that rigid contraction of the stomach, that boardlike abdomen, the first thing I thought of was peritonitis."

I knew that I could work confidently with such men and happily devote myself to my task of making Charenton into a pilot establishment for the study of clinical psychiatry, following in the footsteps of my illustrious predecessors, Esquirol, Calmeil, Foville, Marchand, Mignot.

I now headed the services for both men and women. We received a diverse lot of patients, referred to us not only from the urban sectors but from the government and the armed services. As never before, I adhered scrupulously to the rule laid down by Bayle for our profession at the beginning of the nineteenth century, which decreed that the doctor in charge must see to everything himself and be certain to receive personally the families of his patients. I was never to depart from this method of operation.

In those early postwar years, we received a category of patient which particularly touched me, the former deportees. Though they suffered from the same illnesses as our other patients, their problems had a very special character. Those men and women endured an unbelievably intense degree of atrocious physical suffering and terror. Inside those wasted, rachitic bodies, whose photographs were published all over the world, were ruined minds and souls upon which we had to rebuild normal human beings.

My dear, dead friend, whom I sorely miss, Dr. Dvorjetzki, born in Lithuania and hero of the ghetto uprising in Vilna, has described all the drama of the deportation, the heroic efforts at resistance, and the guilt feelings of those who survived while their comrades died.

I myself have made a number of observations concerning the effects of moral conscience during deportation. Just as occurred in combat, excessive neuropathic reactions were hardly ever observed in the camps themselves, though somatic affections were legion, and general debilitation, whose ravages continued after their liberation, claimed many victims. It was only later that characteristic pathological manifestations were observed among the former internees. The persistence of these manifestations is extraordinary, and what is also characteristic, they occur below the level of consciousness, often appearing in dreams, as though the emotion had been deeply repressed. Such disorders have lasted in deportees up to the present time.

Today still, many former deportees relive their experiences at night, and their anguish may be such that their screams wake several floors of an apartment building. Such nightmares sometimes drive them so deeply into sleep that the sleep takes on a cataleptic character and it becomes necessary to use violent means to bring the dreamer back to consciousness. These persons generally remember their dreams, which are always scenes they themselves have lived through or have witnessed.

One of my patients had escaped from Auschwitz, but his wife had perished in a gas chamber. One day, walking near the Gare d'Austerlitz, which name reminded him of Auschwitz in Poland, he recalled his past in all its horror. In suddenly hallucinating images, he saw his wife walking to her death. Without warning, there in the crowded street, he began to scream on and on. The passersby called the police, who took the unfortunate man to the hospital.

Besides such hallucinations, there are other psychic holdovers from deportation that may be lumped together under the rubric of "jumpy nerves": excessive irritability, oversensitivity and impatience, sudden violent anger. Medically speaking, one notes in these persons disturbances of the autonomic nervous system such as aerophagia (swallowing of air), spasmodic colitis, disorders of the cardiac system, gastric or duodenal ulcers. There is rarely a survivor of the camps who is free from one or another of these afflictions.

To all this is added the loneliness of those who are the sole survivors of their families; those who feel remorse at having survived while the people they loved died; those who suffer from a conscious or unconscious fear of new persecutions. I have also observed cases of extremely serious neurosis which were directly caused by deportation—especially catatonia.

At Charenton, I treated a man who had escaped from extermination in Poland, hiding in forests and eating like an animal during an amazing odyssey across a good part of Europe, before he managed to reach safety. When I first saw him, he was typically catatonic, his body totally flexed and rigid, exhibiting panic and anxiety to the point of paroxysm if one went near him. He obviously believed that we were enemies who wished to recapture him.

Such patients cannot be treated in the same manner as others. They have been flayed alive, in a very real sense. Treatment may bring on death, unless it is done with the greatest care and gentleness. Day after day they must be convinced anew that the world is not totally cruel and barbaric. After many long hours in this patient's company, I had the great joy of rescuing him from his despair.

Some deportees tried to combat their sickness by marrying other survivors of the camps, but such marriages did not always bring about the hoped-for results. And young deportees suffered from having their education cut short, often forever, thus being obliged to accept inferior jobs when, had things been different, they might have expected brilliant careers. This disappointment too cast its shadow over their lives.

All of these elements made up what might be called the philosophical syndrome of many deportees. The heinous deeds they had witnessed had killed their confidence in mankind, robbing them of the very sense of life. It has often been observed, and I myself can corroborate this, that former inmates of concentration camps who live in Israel have better morale than do their comrades in other countries. Their faith has been restored by the fact that they are helping to resurrect their adopted country and are building a future.

On the scientific level, the observations I made while treating these men and women support what I saw during the two wars regarding the role of mental images in the resurrection of past emotions. Their effect proved once again to have an unbelievable power in moments of relaxation when the body and the mind are unprepared to defend themselves and are taken unawares. The pathological disorder, encountering no barrier, can develop freely, and the person whose forces had been mobilized against the initial emotion can no longer struggle against its ghost.

Cases of hysteria such as these could not be treated by measures that succeed with ordinary patients, for the wound goes much deeper in survivors of the camps. Their memories cannot really be effaced since they have forever scarred their minds and bodies. They could only be helped by good living conditions, peaceful surroundings, personal therapy tailored to their specific form of nervous disorder, and medical help for their physical ailments. Deportees are much more vulnerable than other people to physical problems, and easily subject to nervous disorders because of them.

Despite the enormous work load involved in putting Charenton back into running order and transforming it into a model establishment, I sometimes dreamed of continuing my university career. When Professor Jean Delay was appointed to the senior professorship at Sainte-Anne, he telephoned to ask if I would come to see him.

He informed me that a post for a full professor was opening up at Sainte-Anne, and that he wished to support my candidacy for it. If he was to succeed in renovating Sainte-Anne, he said, he would need someone to help him with teaching.

I had to tell him that I hesitated to accept his offer because I did not see eye to eye with him on the new therapy. By this I meant new methods of treatment such as lobotomy, to which I was bitterly opposed.

"The result," I explained, "would be that two men sharing the same professorship would disagree over truly vital points. We would be teaching conflicting theories."

This amounted to a refusal, but Professor Delay was not daunted and promised that I would have complete freedom to teach as I wished. He asserted that two different schools of thought within the same professorship would only enrich the teaching, because the students would then see all sides of the problem instead of just one.

I asked for time to think it over, then accepted Professor Delay's generous proposal at the end of the week. And so I shared the teaching load with him for nine years, spending my mornings at Sainte-Anne and my afternoons at Charenton. When Professor Delay left for a visit of several months to the United States, my schedule became even more demanding. In his absence, I was asked by the Minister of Health to fill the chair at Sainte-Anne and to carry out the functions of professor in the clinic. I assumed those duties each time that Delay was absent.

Those were rich and rewarding years for me, during which I helped to create the degree in neuropsychiatry and became head of a clinical course associated with the university. This conferred a flattering distinction upon Charenton, since it was the second psychiatric clinic I was directing in Paris. As a result, the Faculty elected me a roving professor. Then, when I retired, they gave me an honorary degree and included my clinics at Charenton and Sainte-Anne among the university psychiatric clinics of Paris.

Despite my endlessly growing weight of responsibilities, I did not forget the vow I had made during the Occupation: to visit Jerusalem. I wanted to study Judaism at its source, and to find out why the Jewish race had been so persecuted through the centuries. I also wished to know the Holy Land, the cradle of the ideas toward which certain practical experiences in psychiatry had led me.

A rather banal incident gave me much food for thought at the time. One afternoon, when I returned to Charenton, the concierge advised me that a patient had staged a revolt in one of the dormitories. He had torn out some pipes and was threatening the nurses who tried to approach him.

At the entrance to the dormitory I found the administrator, the housekeeper, the supervisor, and several nurses. The patient stood inside, brandishing his improvised weapons and shouting threats. The administrator whispered that they intended to use a lasso to catch the man. I bridled at this and refused to permit such a tactic. Instead, I sent everyone away, except for one nurse. Then I approached the sick man and gently asked him what was wrong.

"This morning you promised to let me walk in the garden!"

"That's right, so I did," I replied.

"And you didn't change your mind?"

"Of course not."

"Then why wouldn't they let me go out there when I asked?"

"They made a mistake. I'll give orders to let you go now," I promised.

At this the patient dropped his arms and came forward to embrace me, crying, "You're a real brother to me!"

This episode is a perfect illustration of a principle I have always lived by and which has led me to the doctrine that became central to my work: *Tsedek* is its Hebrew name. At this time I had not yet completely formulated this doctrine, but through episodes like the above I had glimpsed it, and that was why I wanted so much to go to Israel. I felt that I held in my hand mysterious threads which, if brought together, would lead me to the truth for which I was searching.

The Hebrew word *tsedek* has no equivalent in other languages. It is commonly translated as *justice*, but its meaning is much broader. In French, the ideas of justice and loving charity are not included in the same word. *Tsedek* brings them together and, what is more important, expresses the love referred to in chapter 19 of Leviticus, in the celebrated verse from the law of Moses: "Thou shalt love thy neighbor as thyself."

Here is a love which implies identification with others, requiring that one ask what he would do in another man's place, what he would like his neighbor to do for him. In this way, through such an effort of the imagination, which is not often easy, words of comfort spring to the lips, kindly acts come to mind and make it possible for one to act as a savior.

If there is no identification with one's neighbor, it is likely that men will forget that they may one day find themselves in their neighbor's situation, so that they may even go so far as to oppress him.

The other face of such identification is the notorious law of "an eye for an eye and a tooth for a tooth," enunciated with such force in the Hebrew text. This law, denounced and often garbled, is, despite appearances, merely the opposite side of the law of love. It calls for punishment of those who do not obey the law, and makes certain that the rule is put into practice in our own lives and not dismissed as an ideal for someone else to live by.

I shall give an example of what I am trying to say, a lesson I was taught by the victims of the deplorable situation that I found when I first arrived at Charenton. The inmates had been mistreated; they had been chained and so brutalized that they complained of their misfortunes in pitiful terms. After I had put an end to those abuses, and protected and lavished affection on the victims, I was dismayed to see them become proud and oppressive in turn, inflicting on their weaker brothers the cruelties and excesses they themselves had suffered.

Moses proclaimed, "Thou shalt not favor the poor unduly," shortly after he had stated that we must help the poor as much as possible. Those two commandments are not contradictory, because to help the poor does not imply that one should enable them to become unjust in turn. Love without justice is an empty word, and *tsedek* represents the fusion of the two.

I had one other reason for making this trip. I wanted to establish ties between French psychiatry and that of a country in the process of gestation. I set about making my preparations with joy and anticipation.

I had been told that my hopes of getting a visa were mad. It was 1946, and the Jewish state had not yet officially been born. Palestine was under British mandate and armed fighting raged between British soldiers and rebellious Jews who had joined together in the Haganah, a clandestine organization. Undeterred by such pessimism, I went to the British consulate in Paris, told my story, and was immediately granted my visa. Before I left, I received a dispatch from some Jewish doctors in Jerusalem urging me to postpone my departure because there was so much fighting still going on. But undismayed, I took my plane on schedule. A first lap put me down in Cairo, where I met with relatives of my father and profited from the stopover to see something of Egypt. When I arrived in Jerusalem, after flying in a small British plane over the Sinai, I was choked with emotion.

The program for my stay included, among other things, lectures which I was to give in Hebrew. I had not yet completely mastered that language, but had managed to write my own texts, which I then submitted to specialists for correction. I recited aloud every morning before I left my room; a chambermaid coming in unexpectedly obviously thought I was mad.

I opened the series of lectures at the University of Jerusalem, on Mount Scopus, the highest peak in Jerusalem, from which the Romans had conquered the city two thousand years before. Even if it had not been haunted by historic memories, the view would have been superb. The air was so clear that we could see, as though it lay directly at our feet, the Dead Sea some forty kilometers away, and the entire country lay spread out before us.

After my lecture, entitled "The Crisis in Psychiatry and Some Remedies," I was invited to talk about *tsedek*. The Consul General of France in Jerusalem, M. de Neuville, a practicing Catholic, was present at one of those informal talks and from the start was captivated by my thesis. He arranged a lecture by me on the subject before the assembled diplomatic corps.

It was impossible to forget that Israel was at war. There was often fighting in the streets of Jerusalem, with bullets flying in every direction. A curfew made it difficult to go about at night. However, I traveled as much as possible and visited many Jewish homes, feeling great love for the land and for the nation in the throes of resurrection.

Today still, the close ties between my professional and intellectual activity and the Holy Land are still strong. I continue to study Hebrew, and, as a member of the administrative board of the temple on the rue Buffault, I follow the office and the liturgy. Holidays such as Yom Kippur, which last twenty-four hours and are accompanied by complete fasting, represent an extraordinary effort of spiritualization, during which the soul, untrammeled by the demands of the body, submits to the holy texts and rises toward the One God.

Upon my return from Israel, I married. I have described how my wife, born in Toulouse of a Sephardic family like my own, and educated in the sciences, was a teacher of physics and pharmacology. With her at my side, I have been able to meet all the demands of a full intellectual and moral life. Our one great sorrow was the death at birth of a little daughter.

THE ERA
OF NEUROSES

IT IS ONLY TOO OBVIOUS THAT OUR ERA IS PROPITIOUS FOR NEUROSES.
The reasons for this are well known. To the aftermath of World
War II and, in Europe, the Occupation have been added the conditions of life itself: its pace and overcrowding, the difficulties caused
by displacement, the loss of security, anxiety about the future, as
well as the failure of morality, the confusion of so many of us as we
face a world without faith.

It is important that we agree on the definition of these neuroses
and their place in psychiatry. There is still a regrettable confusion
regarding illnesses which are highly diverse and of varying degrees
of seriousness. The danger involved in mistaking one for the other
is not only of importance for scientists but can have repercussions
that affect the destinies of the men and women who are suffering
from psychiatric ills.

The word neurosis, which means "nervous disorder," refers to
only minor mental illnesses which were formerly roughly grouped
together under the term *neurasthenia*. Symptoms differed greatly:
headaches, dizziness, aerophagia, stomach troubles, intestinal spasms,
and backaches; but also, on the psychological level, sensations of
fatigue and prostration, insomnia, sexual impotence.

These manifestations had nothing to do with the organic changes
in the body treated by ordinary medicine. They were linked to
problems of the nervous system whose modalities were not very well
understood.

Pierre Janet (1859-1947), the psychologist, observed in great detail
a series of obsessions and described them as no one before him had
ever done, an achievement which led to their classification as neu-

roses. He also gave us our best description of the mental state of obsessed persons, their loss of volition, their doubts, their incessant need to verify facts, their inner agitations. It was Janet who gave the name *psychasthenia* to this genre of illnesses. His idea was that obsession proceeds from a psychic weakness which prevents the subject from controlling spontaneous and irresistible thoughts or impulses.

I have discussed the sometimes destructive role of mental images that can completely disorder an impressionable subject's psychic functioning. Obsessions have the same effect, taking control of the mind and governing its processes. The subject becomes incapable of reasoning or even of discussing the *idée fixe* that holds him in its grip. Obsession is like a mental pulse which regulates the rhythm of thoughts and reactions.

For example, take a man who lives in fear of getting his hands dirty. He is terrified of germs and washes his hands continually. Or we have those persons who shudder at the idea of coming into contact with dust. Or else there is the man described in Georges Duhamel's novel *Life and Adventures of Salavin*, who suddenly takes it into his head to perform some bizarre act, only to spend his days dreaming of it and never taking the vital step to accomplish it. This is known as an "obsessive impulse."

On the other hand, obsession may act as a brake, as with a man who at the moment of sealing a letter which he considers important cannot bring himself to execute that simple gesture. Doubt seizes him; he can no longer remember what he has written. He becomes too upset even to reread the words. He takes the letter out of the envelope over and over again, staring paralyzed at the sentences dancing before his eyes.

That is not alexia, which I have already described as the suspension of the ability to read, with letters and words meaning nothing to the person's mind. In this case, the subject, who is quite capable of reading, becomes a victim of a paralyzing emotion which renders him powerless to concentrate his attention or mobilize his energy enough to reach a decision. This is what Dr. Morel has called "emotional delirium."

Neurosis is not the same as psychosis. It is important to distinguish carefully between the two, for neurosis does not affect social behavior as much as psychosis does. It most often arises from an exaggeration of images. The very sight of an object evokes dangers threatening to the subject; a knife, for example, may cause him to see an act of murder, with its attendant images of blood and death.

Instead of an abstract, cold, impersonal idea, we have a concrete image representing a real scene, actually felt by the person and charged with emotion. It does not, however, go so far as to become a hallucination, which is not to say that it cannot have serious consequences, especially if misunderstood. Can you imagine, for instance, having your entire life ruined simply because you have a horror of meat? That seems unlikely, yet it did happen to an intelligent, gifted, and enthusiastic young medical student who seemed to have a fine career ahead of her.

She had inherited her aversion from her doctor father who, although he sometimes did eat meat, declared it to be dirty and unhygienic. When still very young, Mlle. P had gone beyond this stage and had condemned all flesh, at first from the point of view of eating it herself, then gradually extending her obsession to include an aversion to everything that might at any time have come in contact with meat.

She sought after absolute purity, worrying constantly over whether the vegetarian meal she was consuming might not at some point have had a bit of meat mixed in with it. She would become extremely irritated if her worries were not taken seriously.

When I examined her later on, she told me how she had come by her obsession.

"Though I did eat meat when I was little, I ate it without pleasure because of what my father said about it. I sometimes felt that perhaps I was being slowly poisoned.

"One day, I went shopping with my mother, who bought some

vegetables and fruit in a store where both meat and produce were sold. It suddenly occurred to me that these purchases might have touched the meat displayed beside them. From that moment on I could never again look at a piece of meat. Nothing could force me to set foot in a butcher shop or a delicatessen.

"I stopped eating meat and could not bear to see it on the family table. I started to take my meals by myself during the early afternoon.

"My father disapproved of this, but he couldn't convince me that I was wrong. He offered to send me to Paris to continue my studies."

Mlle. P proved to be a gifted student at the University of Paris, but she was unable to rid herself of her obsession. On the contrary, it seemed to be growing and becoming stronger. Whenever she saw a piece of meat, she was overcome by sickening visions of the animal's death, of rivers of blood and masses of offal. Not only was her diet limited to fish, vegetables, and fruit, but she took endless precautions not to touch any object which had been in contact with the substance she so abhorred. She also washed her hands continually, a habit which could not go for long unnoticed.

Since she was intelligent and in full possession of her faculties, she was under no illusion that her repugnance to meat was normal. Therefore, she went to see a doctor, who confirmed that she was suffering from a neurotic obsession. Hoping to win indulgence for her when she took her examinations, he wrote a detailed report describing her condition and sent it to the university administrative offices. Everyone read it, including her examiners. It had the opposite effect on them from the one its author had intended.

They felt that a student as disturbed as Mlle. P could not possibly become a good doctor, and that her neurosis must surely indicate a much deeper problem. The result was that she failed her examinations and was dropped from the university.

Gears were now set in motion in a rather terrifying fashion, as in a novel by Kafka. Mlle. P had become a serious "mental case" in the eyes of everyone at the university. She was openly given to understand that she was a "lunatic" and as such no longer had a place in "normal" society. As the rumor spread, the word *dangerous* was added to "lunatic."

She reacted strongly to what was happening to her, which is quite understandable. But her arguments, her legitimate anger, her attacks of nerves, for which she should hardly have been blamed, were interpreted as so many signs of her "mental derangement." It was even falsely insinuated that she had spent some time in a mental institution. A human being who was in no way a threat to her fellowmen and who, apart from her obsession about meat, could live and work normally—in any case could have treated patients as well as your average carnivorous doctor—was being driven to her ruin.

It was tragic that she received no support from her family. Her parents also believed her to be crazy, insisted that she needed to be incarcerated, and thought it best that she be left alone to help her understand that she could not get along in normal society.

When I met Mlle. P, I was convinced that a serious mistake had been made. She was lucid, even regarding her own case. Her repugnance for raw flesh stopped at the butcher's shop and did not extend, as can happen in obsessions when all similar materials are classed together, to the human body. I believed it would be a pity to prevent her from following a profession in which she would have served usefully.

Alas, even in a university where, by definition, one should be free from prejudice and superstition, the suspicion of persons said to be mentally ill remains strong. A former dean of the university claimed that she was "insane" and the word was repeated by high officials in the Ministry of National Education.

When I took over the affair, the former dean had died and I insisted that Mlle. P's case be reopened. In the meantime she made a new appeal and even began a lawsuit. Suing the university, however, constituted a crime of lese majesty. Our government functionaries would have been paralyzed if they had set a precedent by admitting that they had made a mistake. Better for a person to die than for an administration to repent!

In putting together all the documents in favor of Mlle. P, I got in touch with the physician who had written the original report, asking him to testify that his sole object had been to attract the goodwill of her examiners. But like everyone else, he had caught the contagion of prudence, fearing that they would only say he had made an error.

Misplaced pride is a terrible curse, making men prepared to sacrifice even another's life if necessary. Through ignorance and negligence, the words *neurosis*, *psychosis*, and *mental derangement* had been confused, and no one wished to go back and correct the mistake.

And so, because of a situation for which she bore no responsibility whatever, Mlle. P lived for years in Paris almost a beggar, subsisting on tea and fruit in wretched lodgings on the miserable sum of 350 francs a month. But despite her poverty, she remained in extraordinary physical condition and her mental acuity never faltered. To occupy her time, she attended many medical courses, for in spite of everything medicine remained her passion. Her parents died and she received a little money, her inheritance enabling her to live in better circumstances.

That woman's exclusion from the medical profession is all the sadder when I think of the fine practitioners I have known who suffered from serious neuroses and even so performed their duties admirably. I remember, for instance, a very great neurologist who felt continually the excruciating need to verify facts. He lived in a state of constant exacerbated doubt.

Of course no doctor is always free of hesitation when he makes a diagnosis and prescribes treatment. Still, the moment does come when he makes his decision and acts. The neurologist I speak of was sometimes incapable of writing a prescription. He would freeze before the blank slip, fearing that he might be mistaken and never succeeding in making a choice from among the possible courses of treatment.

He would, at times, tell his patients to leave their address and he would send them the prescription. This would give him time to check and recheck the contents and value of the doses he had prescribed. Pierre Janet named this well-known neurosis, which exists in all walks of life, "obsessive-compulsive fear of inadequacy" (or paralysis caused by self-doubt). It may start out as a healthy quality, such as worry about a mistake in the wording of an important document. But carried too far, it can lead to total paralysis.

My neurologist was never cured of his obsession. But despite this fact, he had a brilliant career and was celebrated throughout the world. He himself was more troubled by his eccentricity than were his patients, who at least received prescriptions which were of value in curing them, in spite of or because of his delay in writing them out. I wonder whether he would have been dropped like Mlle. P if this disorder had appeared at the time he was about to take the examinations for his degree.

In order to give a rounded picture, I must cite another, less comforting example of a great physician whose mind was subject, if I may so describe it, to irrational spells. Gifted with an incredible memory, he was able to make clinical examinations of such admirable precision that he became a marvel to his fellow physicians. But he would also spend whole days cutting bits of paper, piercing holes in corks, or tearing pages from books. At such times his thoughts would come in such a tumultuous rush that they overwhelmed him completely and he would be unable to practice his profession.

This physician never managed to integrate his personality, for lack of proper treatment. He might perfectly well have been cured since none of his faculties had been destroyed, only clouded by his neurosis. Doctors who are so afflicted generally seek treatment because they know that to do otherwise might destroy them since the obsessions tend to become more extensive.

A striking case of the alarming growth of an untreated obsession can be seen in a patient whom I did not treat personally but whom I knew about. He was a Belgian, M. V, whose father managed a shop in Brussels where artificial flowers were sold. One day, as M. V was passing through the shop, he was suddenly overcome by a horror of the flowers on display.

This might have been merely a passing aversion, but in his case it became a serious phobia. From that moment on he was unable to bear the sight of the family business, went to live in another part of Brussels, and ceased to see his parents. Instead of finding relief, he became worse. The moment he saw any shop where artificial flowers were sold, he would experience a violent emotion and would literally take to his heels. He found that he despised Brussels and went to live in Paris.

Even in the train that took him to France, he carried a feather duster and other objects with which he could clean the seats, in case someone in his compartment had touched artificial flowers. In Paris, he soon became truly haunted. Every time he went out he feared that he might be contaminated by artificial flowers, and so he gave up leaving his lodgings. He began a meticulous toilet every morning at eight o'clock, which was only completed at two in the afternoon. Then and then only did he believe that he had eliminated every possibility of infection.

One day his son, who had remained behind in Brussels with his grandfather, announced that he was coming to visit. Our subject lived in a state of real anxiety until the appointed day because he could not refrain from thinking that perhaps his son had been in contact with the artificial flowers in the shop. When they met at the station, M. V became almost physically ill and, in an indescribable state of nerves, had to be helped home to his apartment.

I never discovered whether M. V recovered from his neurosis. It was, however, a typical case which would have responded very well to treatment, by a combination of both psychological and pharmaceutical methods.

I must say once again that the psychiatrist's course of action must always include personal attention, patience, and vigilance. This technique works especially well with subjects who need to feel cared for, to know that someone understands the profound reason for their troubles and can show them the futility of their disturbed reactions. The physician must sometimes play the role of guardian angel of the patient's conscience, not in order to impose a system of morality, but to make him aware of the value of certain rules so that he may regain his mental health.

I treated a highly intelligent, educated man, a member of a distinguished family, whose illness was seriously disrupting his family life. His personal life was dominated to a pathological degree by problems of a sexual and romantic nature. M. A held an important position in a large insurance company and had been converted from Judaism to Catholicism along with other members of his family.

His first marriage had been to a Catholic girl, who had been an exemplary wife and an excellent mother to their two children; they had seemed perfectly happy. But after several years M. A became bored since he was the type of man who lacks the stability to be permanently faithful to one mate. He had many affairs, which Mme. A accepted, making the best of a bad situation. When he announced his intention to divorce her, she protested, but he insisted and later married a woman somewhat younger than his wife, yet one who resembled her in most respects. He had several more children with his second wife.

Soon he became bored once again and began a liaison with a young, very beautiful, extremely elegant, self-confident, and intelligent secretary. This time, however, he did not get a divorce. He now had two households: At home were his wife and children, while his mistress awaited him in an apartment he had rented for her.

Such a situation is scarcely exceptional. What was unusual here was its consequences, beginning with his wife's reaction. At first, like her predecessor, she accepted the situation; then she decided to make her own life. She took a lover and went to live with him from time to time, a revenge which did not leave M. A indifferent.

His masculine pride suffered an even worse blow when his young mistress began gradually to move away from him. He was fifty and the girl twenty. When she broke the news to him that she wished to leave, telling him gently that it was hardly logical for two persons separated by such a difference in age to consider marriage and that she must think of her future, he admitted that she was right.

Suddenly he saw his world crumbling around him. He had been abandoned by his mistress and was separated from his wife, toward whom he felt guilty. On top of everything else, M. A became ill and had to have an operation. After the comfort in which he had lived, my patient felt that he had failed hopelessly. He became deeply melancholy, then entered a state of depression accompanied by obsessions. He saw himself living alone, of which he had a horror, abandoned by both wife and mistress, loved by no one.

This was when I saw him—a broken, disillusioned man, whose universe had disintegrated. It was apparent to me that I could do nothing for him until his moral values had changed. It was important that he be made to understand that there is one rule in life that cannot be broken: Man must always strike a balance between his instincts and his social and moral obligations.

M. A listened to my arguments without much enthusiasm. What I was saying contradicted all the principles by which he had lived. As a member of the upper class, he had always believed that he could enjoy prerogatives which were forbidden to other men. His neuropathic condition had in fact arisen from this moral weakness. I explained to him that a man of his intelligence should be able to master his feelings. In the end, he began to examine his conscience.

Unfortunately, in this case too I found none of the support from his family that was needed. I discovered that his wife, brother, and mistress were ill-disposed toward my patient. I could understand the rejected wife, who resented being called on to look after a husband who was only turning to her out of fear because her rival had abandoned him; and also she was ill. As for the girl, her lover's illness provided an unhoped-for excuse for her to make a clean break with him and start her life anew with someone else.

M. A was in poor shape, gloomy, weeping continually, presenting a sorry image in considerable contrast to his former dapper self. Everyone, including his brother, proposed that he take a sleep cure. I did what I could to block this move, but I was overridden. M. A was sent to a sanatorium and I ceased to see him, a fact which I regret. I was sure that a sleep cure would do him no good; when it was over, he would be in no better shape than before. But the "elimination reflex" had won out.

Patients afflicted with neuroses are the most difficult of all to handle. One must approach them gently, taking care not to jolt them unnecessarily while guiding them firmly, dinning one's arguments into them by constant repetition, refusing to give in on certain points, refusing to indulge their tendencies. All this must be done in order to avoid precipitating them into an even worse illness, as I learned in my dealings with a young woman with whom I had the greatest difficulty.

Mme. L was a delicately balanced, hypersensitive, oversentimental, and affectionate young woman. She was married to a man who was extremely attached to her. But the early years of their marriage had been difficult, even traumatic. Immediately after the wedding, the couple had gone to live with her husband's mother, who had taken a dislike to her young daughter-in-law. She never ceased humiliating the girl, and the husband, who had always been under his mother's thumb, refused to move away with his wife.

The mother-in-law, encouraged by her son's silence, proceeded imperceptibly from reproaches to threats, then to real persecution. Mme. L lived in daily fear, profoundly disturbed because of her extremely sensitive nature. Her husband, instead of helping her, was very severe in his attitude. He sided with his mother and reproached his wife for not being able to get along with her.

Mme. L came to despise her husband for his weakness and withdrew into herself. The accumulation of her unexpressed sufferings

HENRI BARUK

gave rise to obsessions. She began to suffer from various physical ailments: migraine headaches, digestive upsets, and constant fatigue, with an accompanying loss of weight. These troubles provided her mother-in-law with excuses to ridicule her, but they also led her husband, who was not a bad man and loved his wife deeply, to see her in a new light and to recognize the true situation. He understood now that she had not always been wrong, as he had imagined. He became very affectionate once more, sent his mother away, and also instructed her to behave more kindly toward Mme. L.

But the damage had been done. Mme. L was now under the care of a doctor who had an attractive bedside manner. The relations between the doctor and his patient undoubtedly never went very far, but even after she had ceased to be his patient, and he had moved away from the neighborhood, she could not rid herself of her image of him as the ideal man.

Her romanticized memory of him completely invaded Mme. L's mind, leaving not the slightest room for her husband. The more she dwelt on the doctor as a man of great physical attractiveness, the more she took a negative view of her husband's appearance and came to believe that he was ugly, when in fact he was quite handsome. When I questioned her about M. L, she kept telling me over and over again that he was horrible, that he made her sick.

When certain organic conditions made my patient feel tired, her obsession became worse. In addition to the migraines, she had been suffering from a liver condition, as well as chronic attacks of painful rheumatism.

Of course mental and physical health are not always present in the same person. Because one has a sound body it does not follow that one is less likely to have obsessions. A strapping fellow, who appears to be bursting with good health, may be ill mentally if he is not sufficiently developed psychologically, intellectually, and morally. Moreover, the body may affect the mind, or, conversely, the poorly coordinated and insufficiently educated mind may influence the body. This is why it is important for the psychiatrist to be general practitioner, neurologist, psychologist, moralist, and philosopher rolled into one.

In Mme. L's case, the psychological conflict was clear. Some people might have believed that she simply had a secret desire for love affairs with men who were more attractive to her than her husband and would remind her of the absent doctor. But when the head nurse of a hospital where she had been a patient told her that in our day it was perfectly all right to deceive one's husband and that sexual experiences outside marriage could be pleasant and amusing, Mme. L's condition worsened. The remark had revolted her because she was still deeply attached to her husband. Here I should point out that obsessions often represent impulses diametrically opposed to the individual's true personality.

I first set about restoring Mme. L's physical health, as much as this was possible when dealing with such a weakened constitution. At the same time, I treated her psychologically, my main theme being that she had a pathological obsession. This was in direct contradiction to what the head nurse had told her. Assuring a sick woman like Mme. L that it is normal to have affairs is in effect encouraging her in the direction of her obsession, which is thus justified and reinforced; and it aggravates the clash between instinctual desire and duty, which is very common with neuropaths.

The Freudian solution would have been to persuade her to leave her husband, in defense of desire and instinct, and to get to know other men. Such behavior at her age and in her condition would have led only to disappointments and ultimately to her collapse.

In the method that I advocate, one must not, however, plead for duty in its severe, dry form; that would only discourage the patient. Desires do exist and clamor to be satisfied—they must not be denied or taken lightly; but the strength of a weakened personality must be restored by building up its moral reserves.

In short, these neuropathic conflicts consist of a bitter clash between dream and reality, between duty and the spontaneous impulses which exist in all of us. The dream wins out temporarily and crushes all resistance. The subject must be led gently back in the direction of reality and provided with a durable harmony between the two poles that have pulled him asunder.

It is never easy to reach this point, especially when the patient's family is uncooperative or hostile. I struggled for months over a boy who was suffering not only from a certain debility of intellect but even more from lack of judgment and a retarded personality development.

In spite of his deficiencies, Paul B began his education and then met and fell in love with a young girl who was herself handicapped. A cultivated, intelligent, and very kind person, she had a disorder of the spinal column which had left her slightly hunchbacked.

Paul B's mother, an extremely possessive woman, fiercely opposed her son's marriage. She believed him to be incurably ill and weak, a boy who needed to be cared for all his life. She was prepared to have him hospitalized if necessary, in order to keep him under her wing and prevent another woman from having any influence over him.

On this occasion, her son showed a firmness which surprised everyone. He went ahead and married. In the beginning, everything went beautifully. He found a job in a branch of government where he performed satisfactorily, and eventually he became an established civil servant. The couple had a daughter.

Unfortunately, friction developed between the patient's mother and her daughter-in-law. The latter had brought all of her family to live with her, taking advantage of her husband's weakness, impressionability, and tendency to be easily influenced. She may have done this through motives of self-interest because, after all, she was physically handicapped and the presence of her family would be helpful. The boy's mother felt that her daughter-in-law was too hard with her son and did not allow him enough freedom. Companions in his office persuaded him to have affairs, and this too aggravated the ill feeling in the household.

As if this were not enough, dissension appeared on another, unexpected level. The Bs were Jewish, as was the young wife. She was religious, but the young man, completely assimilated into French culture and fearing to be ill thought of at work, played down everything Jewish and tried to give the impression of being a Frenchman par excellence. At home he refused to observe the dietary laws or to respect the Sabbath, which led to incessant quarrels. Rejected by the Army on the grounds of physical unfitness, he regretted not having been able to serve in the military. When I saw him, he would make anti-Semitic remarks and excuses for the Arabs and the Palestinians.

I knew both his and his wife's family and tried to arrange a reconciliation, which was absolutely necessary if Paul B were to regain his fragile equilibrium, but both families ignored me. The young woman had taken refuge with her family, which backed her completely, and his family insisted that everything was the fault of the wife.

At the heart of the fray was a slightly retarded, easily swayed boy, in whom good sense was not an outstanding characteristic, and who without any doubt was approaching a pathological state. One must not forget that persons of weak intellect are easily influenced, and also that their feeling of humiliation sometimes results in an urge to take revenge. I still have not succeeded in restoring peace to the two embittered families, and the boy has not recovered.

An obsessed person resembles a country occupied by an enemy with whom he collaborates, although he suffers and despises the aggressor. While complaining bitterly of his obsession, he does not in fact see its absurdity, and though he appears to criticize it to some degree, he believes in it. It is easy to understand why Morel called this phenomenon "emotional delirium."

The first thing to do in such cases is to convince the subject of the senselessness of his obsession and of the futility of giving into so stupid and arbitrary a master. I call this therapy a "helping hand"; it aims at supporting the patient and not plunging him into his past all over again, as psychoanalysis does, and does not encourage him to blame others. Along with this method I sometimes use scopochloralose, which relaxes the patient and reinforces the effect of the psychotherapy. Such treatment was effective when used on a contractor from the provinces, whose hatred of Arabs had gradually brought him to financial ruin and mental disintegration.

For years he had got along very well with Arabs, whom he employed in large numbers. Most of them were hardworking and honest laborers who had come to France to earn nest eggs with which to set themselves up at home.

One day a strange idea occurred to him. M. R had been in the habit of shaking hands with his workers. He noticed that many of them spat in their palm before approaching him. He did not dare balk at such an ordinary gesture. He began to feel a certain repugnance and to fear contamination from his employees' germs. Torn between fear of offending the men and his horror of contagion, he began to suffer from a real obsession, which quickly assumed unexpected proportions.

M. R appeared less and less at his construction sites and became aloof, avoiding contact with his employees. His phobia began to extend to all Arabs. He could not catch sight of one, even from a distance, without experiencing extraordinary discomfort. Soon he came to fear contamination from every quarter. Not a single object, not a living creature escaped his fear. Germs seemed to be everywhere, invisible, lying in wait for him. He resolved to live out his life shut up indoors and so avoid exposure to the open air, which he believed was swarming with millions of poisoned particles of dust. He fled town, dragging his family along with him, and gave up all work.

Then his wife became included in his phobia. He refused to go near her under any circumstances and insisted on sleeping in a separate bed. She was a charming woman and adored her husband, so she suffered cruelly. M. R did, however, agree to consult doctors, one of whom advised him to see a psychoanalyst. He underwent years of analysis in Paris, but his anxieties became worse than ever.

He spent the entire day at his toilet. Every morning he would wash his body, including his hair, with soap and water, then wipe it thoroughly with alcohol. In the evening he would repeat the procedure, and only at eleven o'clock at night, the hour at which the couple were at last able to dine, did he consider himself purified. He never set foot outside the house, did no work, and worried about his wife when she was absent from home earning their living.

By the time I had this man as a patient, the couple's life had become a torment. Mme. R's nerves were raw; her husband had used so many antiseptic preparations that he had eczema on his hands.

Here was an illness born of a slight feeling of revulsion which M. R had not had the strength to combat, though he had tried to convince himself that his fears were absurd. I must point out that M. R, like most obsessed persons, had excessively delicate nerves, and that his mother too had suffered from an *idée fixe*.

The first thing I did was to give him scopochloralose, which can only be administered at intervals of at least ten days. I obtained good results from the very start. As soon as he began to drowse, I held out a book to him and asked him to read it. Without the drug, he would have refused to touch such an object, which had passed through many hands and might harbor germs. But now he took it into his hands and opened it. I then ordered him to kiss his wife, which he did with great docility.

When he had regained consciousness, I walked with him to his bookcase. As if discovering the volumes for the first time, he began to take them down from the shelves. A first step had been taken, and it was considerable; in the succeeding days, he began to study works about his trade, which he had not looked at for years.

After the next session he consented to set foot outdoors. He did so without enthusiasm and returned inside in a nervous state, which proved that there was still much to be accomplished. I saw that I would have to pursue a very intense psychotherapy with him since he was still convinced that he risked a thousand dangers in the street, the earth symbolizing universal decomposition and germs filling the air.

I took advantage of his artificially induced sleep to preach to him, telling him that he was making a lot of nonsense out of thin air, that if the world were what he thought it was, everyone would be forced to shut himself up in a stove where the germs would be killed. I explained to him that many germs had proved useful, bringing on defensive reactions in the face of disease. And I reminded him that the discovery of streptomycin had come about as the result of a study of the bacterial composition of soil. Bacteria were not, as he believed, an army marching in closed ranks toward the destruction of mankind, but a varied, contradictory world divided within itself, in which some bacteria could be used constructively to combat others.

I lectured M. R untiringly, both in sessions when he was drugged and in the intervals between. When he was awake and clearheaded, I made a point of explaining to him that every obsessed person is a collaborator in the heart of enemy country, tolerates the obsession, believes in it to a degree, and cooperates with it willingly because it gives him pleasure; he can only be delivered of his obsession if he comes to recognize it as an adversary to be thrown back to the frontiers of his being. He must have the same faith and ardor that a nation fighting to expel an invader has, and must beat it off.

Even with the help of drugs, this work takes a great deal of time. Only at the end of several months was M. R able to take the metro, which had been for him an accursed place. Soon afterward he returned to his office, then, little by little, to his construction sites.

Still later he made a further advance by leaving for a vacation in the south with his wife. At last he was able to return to a normal daily schedule and to live as other people do.

Of course, a few inhibitions remained, some aversions which he found it difficult to vanquish. But he had recovered.

Besides treating a patient in the way I cured M. R, it is equally important to track down the origin and significance of the obsession, to determine how, when, and where it began. I treated a woman who could not bear the sight of a dog. Upon entering a restaurant with her husband one day, she had made a scene because they had been followed into the place by a customer accompanied by his pet.

The fact was that her father had died of a hydatid cyst of the liver, a localized infection containing the larvae of tapeworms, which he had contracted from his dog. The woman now had a panicky dread of these animals. Was her fear conscious or unconscious? It is difficult to separate one from the other, nor is it possible to allege with the psychoanalysts that a neurosis can be cured simply by unearthing its cause. Such knowledge is useful, for it indicates the sort of treatment that will be needed, and Freudian analysis can thus serve as a method of investigation—but it should not be used as a treatment.

The psychiatrist must guard against another danger and that is jumping to conclusions too rapidly. He must never decree that the trouble is "something stemming from childhood" or can be laid to an "Oedipus complex," and then leave it at that. Every case needs long study and careful checking; none absolutely resembles another.

Certain obsessions may even disappear of their own accord, as though they had never existed. This occurred with one of my patients, a woman who, like the anti-Arab contractor, was terrified of germs.

Her dread had come upon her as the result of having had tuberculosis of the lungs, which had left her with a certain amount of sclerotic tissue. After a period in a tuberculosis sanatorium, she returned home, only to warn her husband that she would never again have any contact with the earth, which was the source of all contamination. Fear of the earth is a common anxiety in this sort of obsessed person. She proceeded to derive a number of other notions from this *idée fixe* and began to lay down rules for living, which she insisted on imposing upon her husband as well as upon herself. He was a charming man, ready to go to any lengths to please his wife. She made him take off his shoes whenever he entered their apartment; he could wear only socks or slippers in the apartment.

It is true that other slightly demented women exact the same discipline from their husbands. But this one went so far as to wash down the walls and floors completely whenever a stranger had crossed the threshold. As with the contractor, her battle against germs involved continuous cleaning and disinfecting of her home, which ended by occupying her days and her every thought.

During the war her husband put her into a mental hospital for a time, and she came to her senses there. This recovery was not due to any specific treatment, but because she met a doctor on the staff who was for collaboration with the Germans, pro-Vichy, while she was pro-Resistance. They had disagreements of great violence, and she began to spend her days dreaming up arguments to use at their next encounter. Her new preoccupation brought her such comfort that she forgot all about the danger of germs.

The phenomenon illustrated above has been frequently noted in cases of obsession, in which one phobia displaces the other. Upon her return home, she soon fell prey, to a certain extent, to her old anxieties. But her husband died and she was grief-stricken. Then she had to contend with her husband's partner's attempt to take over the business. She defended herself fiercely and with unflagging energy, a quality often possessed by obsessive individuals. The result of this legal confrontation was that she at last truly recovered from her dread of germs, which her genuine enemy had utterly cast into the shadow.

I observed another spectacular recovery from a major obsession in a railway engineer, a highly valued employee who had become an inspector for the French National Railways. The origin of his illness was, as often happens, a conflict with his mother. Because of her he had failed to marry, and he had never recovered from his disappointment at remaining a bachelor.

As the years went by, he began to suffer from two obsessions simultaneously: the fear of germs and an excessive need to verify facts. Although he was highly thought of in his office, and his employers had expected to promote him rapidly, he suddenly became very difficult, refusing to accept accounts presented to him by his subordinates and demanding that they check their figures not once but several times.

His fellow workers were, of course, affronted by his show of mistrust. Paralyzed by his own neurosis and by the disagreeable atmosphere which he himself had created, he sometimes was incapable of entering his office and would spend the day wandering about the streets, even in a driving rain.

I had the opportunity to observe him when he was hospitalized at Charenton in serious condition. From morning to night he would recapitulate all that he had done the day before. The least gap in his memory would cause him senseless anguish, even if what he had forgotten was extremely minor. He was afraid of the whole world and would stand frozen behind a column in the main courtyard, believing that the stone screen "protected" him. He even forgot to eat, became afraid of germs in the food, lost weight, and ended by contracting tuberculosis. He was sent for treatment to another institution, so I lost track of him for years.

I rediscovered him sitting in the front row of my audience as I lectured at a medical school in the provinces. He came up to me after my speech and informed me that he had completely recovered. I asked what treatment had restored his mental health, and he replied, "None. It happened all by itself, after my mother died."

However difficult it may be to explain such an unexpected passage from illness to normality, his news did not surprise me. It was obvious that his mother's death had set him free, since she had been the indirect cause of his troubles. The malady had disappeared along with the factor that had brought it about.

Such obsessions may be of a "periodic" nature as shown in the case of this engineer. The *idée fixe* lasts throughout a period of depression which may extend over months or even years. When the depression ends and the patient regains his former liveliness, the obsession also disappears.

It is understandable that our society is, alas, rich in obsessions and neuroses. Our small, everyday disappointments have multiplied. We live among the crowd, without faith to support us, jostled and distracted by daily problems. Under such conditions, the weaker among us succumb easily and fall prey to the disturbances I have described.

I have been speaking of images which become too deeply rooted in the personality, as in the case of obsessed persons. But there are other men and women in whom the phenomenon is reversed, in whose minds images fade and disappear the moment they are perceived, leaving no trace of their passing.

The subject thus affected loses all notion of time, which no longer has for him a beginning or an end, and finds himself projected into an infinity in which he floats, cut off from any conscious awareness of his surroundings. He may even lose the feeling that he exists at all, overwhelmed by a terrifying sensation of nothingness.

One of my patients told me, "I consider my personality to be dead. I can no longer think, much less act!"

For such persons nothing remains but abstractions. Another told me, "I see the letters I'm reading, but I cannot picture them. They don't mean anything inside me, don't apply to anything with which I am familiar. It's as if my soul had come to a dead stop."

I asked him what he meant by the word *soul,* and he replied, "My mind, my thoughts, my life, which is turned to stone. Everything happens around me, outside me, never inside. I have no place anywhere. I have the feeling that I'm a ghost, an ectoplasm. It's hell!"

These cases in which mental images have disappeared, this anesthesia of the mind which gives the impression that life is absent, are fortunately very rare. I have, however, treated a few, and the most outstanding is that of a woman who is now seventy-eight years old and whom I have cared for during the past twenty years.

Mme. S first came to me a long time after she had started to experience her troubles, but I have been able to put together a complete record of her case, which is rich in information about this disappearance of images.

Since adolescence Mme. S had experienced periods of depression separated by intervals of good health of variable duration. The troubles which concern us here appeared progressively in the course of these different attacks and after 1953 assumed a deeper intensity.

She suffered her first depression when she was sixteen years old, after a simple angina. The second appeared in 1917, at the age of eighteen, as a result of exhaustion from overwork. It had been her job to reeducate men blinded in the war. She began to have some difficulty with the fixation of visual images, was cared for at a clinic, and after a year of treatment recovered.

There then followed a period of remission, until 1928. She had married and borne two children in the meantime and was overtired by prolonged breast-feeding and worried about her husband's infidelities. This was the start of her depersonalization troubles.

"I could see my body coming apart," she was to tell me afterward. "I couldn't picture it as a whole anymore."

She was taken in hand by Drs. Mallet and Séglas. It took two years to clear up her problems. In the meantime, her husband, using her depression as an excuse, asked for a divorce. Mme. S agreed, and though she suffered from this official separation, her unhappiness brought on no relapse.

In 1937, at the age of thirty-eight, Mme. S had her fourth breakdown. Once again it coincided with overfatigue brought on by too much work. She was employed then by the National Insurance Agency and arose every morning at five to care for her household before leaving for the office. She lost a great deal of weight, and her general physical condition was rather poor.

This time her crisis lasted for a long time—a dozen years, during which Mme. S went from one institution to another. When the war broke out, she took refuge in a religious community situated in the countryside. After the war, she was again hospitalized and remained so for seven years.

During this period, Mme. S managed through sheer force of energy to overcome her depression and even to work part-time as a nurse. Though her problems with visual images were becoming more pronounced, she was able to go about her duties. She analyzed her situation very well and felt not the slightest anxiety about it. Deprived of mental images, living only in the present moment, she was extraordinarily lucid about her condition.

"After all," she was to tell me, "the absence of images helped me to get through a painful time. I was Jewish and therefore risked arrest, deportation, the camps, suffering, and death. I couldn't picture any of that, so I escaped the anguish and fear that were the fate of so many people."

"Still, you knew what was happening around you," I remarked.

"Of course. But it had no reality for me. It was an abstract situation, not anything I felt. It didn't concern me."

In April 1953, at the age of fifty-four, she suffered her most painful attack of depersonalization. Her mother, to whom she had been extremely devoted, had just died. Mme. S could not conjure up a mental picture of a face, a place, a landscape, however familiar. Even the features of her own children escaped her. On the eve of her crisis, Mme. S declared that she could no longer see and that she could no longer govern the movements of her body. Since she remained prostrate, without stirring, she was taken to a mental hospital, where I first saw her.

She was a truly pathetic sight. Her tragic face expressed indescribable suffering. She refused to leave her room, even to sit down, as if she feared never to be able to rise to her feet again.

"What I am suffering is unthinkable," she told me. "My consciousness is destroyed. I have a brain that exists physically but not mentally. I can't get hold of anything because there's nothing but a blank behind my eyes. My own self is too sick, it's destroyed. I've no mental sight; I'm here, but I can't see that I am! My feeling has left my head. My head has turned to wood."

She passed in review each one of her senses and her different means of communication.

"I talk, but I have no way of knowing what I am saying. The

others can't realize what it is like to be nothing, to have no consciousness, no awareness. I can't even tell if a second goes by or a year."

She struck her head with clenched hands and began to cry. I did not interrupt, but let her spill it all out. Her words continued to describe exactly what she was feeling: the total emptiness of her personality.

"I have no quantity, no duration. My body isn't attached to my head any longer. Objects have no reality. I see the bed, but I can't tell if I'm going to it or not. Hot and cold are exactly the same to me. Everything I have learned, everything I knew is lost. And at this very second, I can't think about the one that will come after it."

After I had listened to her in silence, I examined her. She knew what was happening to her, continued to describe her mental suffering to me, but the whole structure of her personality had crumbled. She could no longer feel the movements of her body and progressed by slow steps, like a blind woman. She told me that she had given up reading because she would lose track of the letters and fail to understand the text.

There was an incomprehensible rupture between her body, of which she was still aware, and its use. She made this terrible avowal:

"I still have my reason, but it does me no good, since I am surrounded by a void, by emptiness. I simply can't picture myself mentally. Day and night do not exist for me. I feel completely inanimate."

At Sainte-Anne, where I had one of my colleagues do an electroencephalogram on her, she insisted that she knew me but could not recognize me since she had no head, no eyes. My colleague insisted, "But you do have a brain, don't you?" She agreed, but qualified it by claiming that she possessed only a physical brain, not a mental one. She had the same reaction when shown the results of her electroencephalogram, which had given a positive tracing, thus proving that her brain was not dead.

"That's the physical brain, not the thinking one. I have my

reason left, but that's all. My awareness, consciousness, doesn't exist any longer. Even my eyes don't work. Everything that isn't contained within this second doesn't exist for me. All I have left are the words to explain with."

What Mme. S was expressing was that she had not lost the use of her senses, but that what they conveyed to her had no application. She received information, but was incapable of putting it to use. Her brain and its system of registering emptied continuously, as water drains out of a sieve.

For a time I lost track of Mme. S. In the course of a stay in a mental hospital she was given eight electroshock treatments, at the rate of one every two days. From the second session on, improvement could be seen, and she began to leave her room under her own power. By the end of the series, her condition had undergone a great change. Her awareness of things had returned. Contact with the world around her had improved. But she could scarcely have been regarded as cured.

The sensation of emptiness had given way to a depressed state, hypomania which manifested itself in an irrepressible logorrhea, or flood of confused words, and a significant psychomotor agitation. She returned to me for treatment once more. When I gave her chlorpromazine, she became calm, and once again I was able to question her.

She told me that she remembered nothing, could not picture her room in the clinic or the doctors who had examined her.

"My body is incapable of remembering itself. If I take a bath, my skin doesn't retain the impression of the water. I can see other people, but it's like looking at reflections in a pane of glass. I see them without their having any real existence. I shut my eyes, and they disappear, they no longer exist for me."

She then made a rather abstract speech to me, which is interesting to the extent that it reveals the "work" done by Mme. S's mind and also reveals the similarity between her former crisis and the hypomania which succeeded it. It must be understood that what she described was a sensation she actually experienced. Other patients, of other backgrounds or different cultures, who suffer from her disorder express themselves similarly.

"When I do something, I know that I'm doing it, but I don't feel it. I have the intellect, you might say, but no life. I obviously possess intelligence since that consists in explaining words with other words. I know that snow is white and coal is black, but I cannot envision what they mean anymore. They are just words, they represent no image in my mind. My only past is an intellectual one. It isn't suffering in the human sense, because suffering is something you can picture. This simply isn't human!"

I knew that Mme. S's hypomania was inevitably to be succeeded within a short time by a violent crisis. I asked myself first of all whether the suppression of the vital principle of awareness of oneself was of a purely psychological nature, or if I should look for certain disorders of the brain. In order to find the answer, I drew up a detailed clinical picture of the patient.

To begin with, it seemed likely that she had received at birth a hereditary predisposition to her problem. To this had been added an accumulation of allergic reactions: vomiting, marked discomfort before her menstrual periods, hay fever, enterocolitis, and circulatory troubles.

Her electroencephalograms gave some interesting information. Her disorders of consciousness seemed to correspond to cortical changes of a vascular nature. Therefore, the phenomena were not purely psychological but psychophysiological. The dominating factor, however, was the periodic nature of her illness, for, as I write this, she has been in good health for years and in spite of her advanced age enjoys an active life. She was suffering from "psychic blindness" linked with a periodicity. Yet this periodicity creates intense psychological states.

We must be careful to distinguish the visual problems of a psychically or cerebrally blind patient like Mme. S from that special form of blindness called "cortical," in which a lesion of the cortical center of vision in the occipital lobe leads to real blindness, of which the subject is, however, unaware, though the localized cerebral lesion can suppress a sensory phenomenon. (The work of a research scientist like Henschen was undertaken solely in order to discover the location of the sight center in the occipital lobe.) Although blind, the person still knows what vision is, for he can picture objects, but he does behave like a blind man; for example, he continually bumps into things. This is the phenomenon described by Anton and Babinski under the term *anosognosia*.

Mme. S's problem was something else entirely. She could see and knew that she could see, but the images left her immediately afterward, and she retained no memory of what she had just seen. The proof that her trouble was essentially psychic and not due to a cortical disorder lies in the fact that it occasionally disappeared; this would not have occurred had she been suffering from a lesion.

As she described it, all of Mme. S's other senses had been afflicted in the same way. She could hear what was said to her, but the sentences went in one ear and out the other without leaving the slightest trace of their passing on her brain. When she touched an object, her awareness of the contact lasted only the length of time that it actually took place. She experienced sensation but not perception. Aside from what occurred during her crises, the means of information continued their usual circuit and accomplished their work perfectly.

Even Mme. S's physical appearance changed according to whether she was at that time subject to a crisis or free of it. In her blank state, she had an absent, hallucinated expression, as though she were seeing ghosts and completely cut off from life. As soon as her illness passed, she quite literally came to life again.

Many people who saw this most impressive and crushed of patients during her crises spoke of her as "lost." But that was a great mistake! When I saw her again recently after many years, I found her active, energetic, and devoted to her family. One would never guess that she had once been in the condition I have described.

She remembers her crises and has often spoken to me of that "blank," which she says is worse than physical pain. At first sight, the lesson she learned from her experiences seems to be paradoxical: that the most terrible experience a human being can undergo is not to be able to suffer. She has had no further crises, although she did have to have one of her kidneys removed, an operation from which she recovered with no bad side effects. She still to this day, however, has great difficulty in imagining mental pictures.

There is a word in Hebrew for such difficulty in evoking images: *mouchpat*, which means literally "undressed." Reality is stripped of everything which clothes it. Life becomes a void and has nothing in common with the human condition or even with death.

Despite the fact that we have still not been able to reconstruct with exactitude the path by way of which a person arrives at this emptiness, we must continue to try to help.

The normal man or woman is that person who receives neither too violently nor too weakly an impression of images and uses them to guide the course of his life.

CHAPTER

CRIME
AND LOBOTOMY

CAN CRIME BE RANKED AMONG MENTAL ILLNESSES? THIS QUESTION HAS been raised ever since Lombroso developed the thesis that criminal activity was invariably linked to hereditary or constitutional alterations in the brain. The famous Italian even gave us a composite picture of the typical criminal, a person with a terrifying countenance, the prototype of a murderer or a thief.

Alas, the question is not so simple as Lombroso believed. Crime is not due to one cause alone.

Certain cerebral disorders undoubtedly lead to criminal reactions. Encephalitis lethargica, for instance, can bring on antisocial impulses of extreme violence. Cerebral tumors, in particular those which touch the frontal lobes, produce the same effects. The latter have been studied in Germany by Frau Leonora Welt, and she has discovered that they produce total alterations in moral attitudes and behavior. There are also cases such as have been described by the Englishman Pritchard under the heading of "moral insanity." However, only one factor is involved in such cases, while criminology includes many others. We must never limit ourselves to a single idea or explanation if we do not wish to be led astray.

I have been interested in crime from the point of view of medical ethics as they concerned scientific experiments performed on human beings as well as such techniques as lobotomy, which I have always vigorously opposed. Mme. Stanciu, founder of the Society for Defense Against Crime, and I, working within the framework of that organization, have studied the criminological problems involving the mentally ill.

Our early research concerned crimes committed in the course of one of the most fearsome of mental illnesses, which I call delirious hebephrenia. This malady, fortunately rare but always grave and usually leading to criminal acts, appears during puberty, when the personality is not yet fully developed and therefore is the more easily shaken to its foundations. Kahlbaum and his student Hecker have described admirably how the disorder affects young people, leaving them emotionally indifferent, with an attenuation of feeling and an instinctive propensity to perversion and extraordinary cruelty.

Such persons are capable of committing murders whose savagery is stupefying. They often experience hallucinations and suffer from delusions of persecution. Their personality disintegrates easily, since they have not yet acquired the means to limit their dangerous reactions, and so their impulses can also be dangerous.

One of the cases of hebephrenia which most impressed me was that of the son of a fellow physician whom I knew very well. The son had fallen ill in the course of his military service and had been confined at Charenton. His aggressiveness and urge to violence were appalling. He assaulted the attendants constantly and without provocation.

One Sunday morning, having been informed that he was particularly excited, I went to see him. I disregarded his attendant's warning when he cautioned me not to enter the boy's room and had scarcely set foot in it when the boy leaped at me and landed a formidable blow on my forehead, causing a bruise that lasted several weeks. After every effort had been made to control the boy, a decision was made to remove him to another hospital. But the father, blinded by love for his son, did not believe him to be seriously ill and insisted on taking him home. One day, alone in the house with his mother, the boy beat her to death with a hammer.

The most extraordinary example of this type is the case of the "famous mathematician of Charenton." Every day for forty years this man sat at a table in a little corridor leading to the room he occupied at Charenton, never budging from his position, except to take his meals, until evening. He passed his time scribbling algebraic or mathematical signs on bits of paper, or else plunged into reading and annotating books on mathematics whose intellectual level was that of the great specialists in the field.

When I arrived at Charenton, he had already been in residence for thirty years. He was a fat man with a rather gentle expression on his face. As soon as he saw me, he rose, bowed, and introduced himself. As I glanced at some pages he was reading, I realized that I was incapable of assimilating their contents.

Back in my office, I took out his record. He had been sent to Charenton by court decision after the charges against him had been dismissed on grounds of insanity. At the age of twenty-five, he had savagely massacred members of his family sitting around the table at the end of a meal. It was difficult to imagine that such a charming, cultivated, polite man could have committed such an act. He was the model inmate whom everyone in the hospital loved.

His days were regulated to the minute. He rose at eleven and took his time until noon washing and dressing. Then he went in to lunch and ate heartily. As soon as he had finished his meal, he would install himself at his work table and not budge from it, even to greet companions or attendants, until evening. At six-thirty he would close his notebooks and books, dine, then immediately return to his room, fall on his bed and sleep through until the next morning. Not once did he ever vary this schedule by a hair.

While other patients constantly requested that they be given their freedom, he was perfectly happy to study his equations and keep his correspondence up to date. Serenity, equilibrium, and self-control seemed to be his hallmark.

This man's reputation reached beyond the walls of Charenton and not only penetrated French mathematical circles but crossed international frontiers. His papers were read in learned societies and universities and at the Academy, and he came to be considered one of the greatest minds in the field of mathematics. Most of his colleagues were unaware of his mental condition. He gave a postal address next door to the hospital, and when mathematicians asked to meet him, he would write back pleading poor health or some other vague reason for not setting a date, and requesting that the discussion be carried on by correspondence.

From time to time I tried to question him as to the motives which had led him to massacre his family, but he dodged my inquiries. He had no visits from family members, no letters. The survivors of his clan showed no interest in his welfare, and since I did not know them, I could not get any information except from my patient. Then, one day, I had a phone call from his brother, who informed me that he had been living in Mexico but was passing through Paris and would like to see my patient. When I notified my patient about the projected visit, he turned pale and showed no enthusiasm whatsoever.

The meeting took place in my office. I was present and we were surrounded by attendants. The brother appeared to be quite moved when the patient entered. The latter halted at a distance from his visitor, giving no sign of affection or welcome, his manner extremely cold. This man, who had been so courteous, so ready to express his concern for the staff and the other patients, did not even ask his brother for news about his life. In a sense he treated him as a survivor who did not deserve to live, limiting his interview to precise questions about Aunt Y and Cousin Z, etc. He insisted on exact answers, as though putting together an inventory. At last he rose to his feet, casually shook his brother's hand, and returned to his work table.

The next day I asked the mathematician why he had asked his brother questions about other members of the family and none about the brother himself.

He said coldly, "It's a question of mathematical logic. There were mentally ill people in my family, on the maternal side, to be exact. Normally all that branch of the family ought to have been annihilated. I started my job at the time of the famous meal, but never got a chance to finish. I just wanted to know where things stood."

I replied that his ideas were horrifying and that killing people because there had been sick members in the family was completely unscientific, as he should be the first one to see.

"You are speaking emotionally," he told me. "Mathematics and its laws transcend emotion. You know very well that my philosophy is based on pragmatism and rationalism. I followed the example and applied the principles of a famous female mathematician of Alexandria, Hypatia."

That was all I could get out of him. I did not believe that his sister mathematician in antiquity had massacred all or part of her family for love of mathematics. This was, however, the first time that my patient had revealed to me the reason for the crime he had committed: morbid rationalism. He had wished to cut off a branch of his family because it had been "infected" by the presence of a lunatic. Here was a crime of logic, performed in the name of absolute rationalism, as dangerous as any spontaneous passion.

My patient survived for only a little while after his brother's visit. He began to lose weight, became pale, and complained of various disorders. A blood test showed signs of leukemia, from which he finally died. And so was extinguished a mind which had contained not only madness but genius too.

The two cases I have just described show how false is the belief that the only source of violent reactions is excessive emotions, that is, passion. Already in Esquirol's time there was much concentration on the study of the role of passion in mental illness. I do not mean to contend that this view has no truth in it, only that much more serious crimes may result from the total absence of feelings, from indifference and the kind of "morbid rationalism," as Rogues de Fursac and Minkowski have called it, practiced by the mathematician of Charenton.

Reason, then, is not—and this is another commonly held but erroneous notion—the best gauge of socially approved behavior. Those crimes arrived at by way of reason are often more cruel than others, for they are not counterbalanced by feelings which might operate to prevent an act of terrible gravity. This observation applies not only to individuals but also to society. The greatest crimes in history, genocides perpetrated in past centuries and our own, can be partially explained by this monstrous indifference to the fate of others.

Schizophrenia, when it is genuine, can also lead to criminal acts. Those afflicted with this malady have no moral judgment, no feelings to brake their impulses.

Another cause of crime lies in the biological structure of individuals. The manic-depressive constitution is of considerable importance in the genesis of certain antisocial acts. A famous case which took place in Tunisia in the 1960's illustrates this very clearly.

Tahar B, a Tunisian, married and father of several children, became severely depressed, entered a mental hospital, and was sent to me in Paris for treatment. He was a true pessimist, who saw the future only in terms of calamity and had no confidence in the world, in his fellowmen, or even in his family. He had a charming young wife who was devoted to him, and I was able to put him back on his feet and return him to Tunisia.

Five years later he entered a phase which was the complete opposite of the first. His depression was succeeded by an excessive liveliness, a continuous state of excitement and an agitation which was completely artificial. In the course of this new and different crisis, he killed his wife without an instant's reflection or hesitation, after a friend had jokingly hinted that she had been unfaithful.

At the time of his arrest in Tunis, he wrote asking that I send him a medical statement, which I did. I wrote in his defense, stating that he had been in my care five years earlier, suffering from an access of depression. I added that it was possible that he had been manic when he had committed the murder and that his mental condition undoubtedly lay at the root of the crime.

The Tunisian physician who served as the court's medicolegal expert gave another opinion. Basing his deposition on an ancient treatise on psychiatry, he contended that the malady had nothing to do with Tahar's action. My ex-patient was therefore condemned to death. I then brought the case before the French Medicopsychological Society, comparing the Tunisian's crime to other offenses which I knew had been committed during manic states. I stressed that the manic person, suffering from temporary persecution complexes and from momentary paranoia, has a modified sense of right and wrong, what is just and unjust, because of his personality disorder.

After much deliberation, the Society agreed that Tahar's crime was of pathological origin and had arisen from an illness of a periodic nature. These findings were forwarded to the court in Tunis, which revoked its decision and changed the sentence from capital punishment to a prison term, which Tahar served out completely.

After he was set free, Tahar came to Paris to see me. It was clear that nothing had been solved by his conviction and imprisonment, for he was in the midst of a full-blown depression and suffering from the mystical delusion that God often spoke with him. He told me that God was punishing him for his sickness.

The fact that he was once again in a depressive state is irrefutable proof, if such proof be needed, that his case was of the periodic variety. Such alternating states are the surest sign of this disorder.

Crime has many other causes apart from mental illness. There is an abundant literature which deals with the social factors involved. Low-cost mass housing, too rapid industrialization, the galloping growth of our cities, the miserable living conditions of the poor, the mobility of our society, and the lack of roots, all contribute to antisocial acts.

I should also like to emphasize the moral causes of crime. Our age has eliminated every taboo in the name of man's complete liberation. It is not chic to mention the drawbacks of such a policy,

((189   ))

and one risks being called "behind the times" or "repressive," epithets which in today's vocabulary convey the greatest opprobrium.

I have heard my patients say: "Nothing is forbidden, everything is allowed; in our society, we don't have to worry about restraints." At the Moreau de Tours Society, we have discussed the influence of films in which cynicism, violence, indecency, and savage and cruel behavior are exalted into a cult of sadism.

I do not mean to simplify complex situations. It is also evident that there are many crimes that stem from motives which are obscure and often impossible to determine. There are, for example, "altruistic homicides." Those who commit them intend to kill themselves as well as their children or other members of their family, whom they wish to save from their own despair.

The connection between homicide and suicide has been very well analyzed by a Bulgarian scholar, Professor Schipkowenski. He has emphasized the fact that in both cases one finds a dulling of feelings. My student, Bachet, has made philosophical homicides and suicides his province. He has studied many persons who espoused the vague philosophy that since life itself had no meaning one could at will sever the cord without remorse. Obviously "philosophy" has not much to do with all this, and the intellect plays a small role in these cases. The fact is that such ideas are most often expressed by persons whose IQ is very low. Here too the important factor is a moral one. In the absence of faith, beliefs, and principles, life has no further meaning. It becomes only a trial to be suffered, and ending it becomes a simple affair.

Patients who feel this way can be dangerous to a greater or lesser degree, and it is a good idea to keep them under observation. I have never disregarded a person's statement that he is "going to do something." It is criminal to take such people lightly when they threaten to commit an aggressive act.

On the other hand, it would be a gross error to generalize and to decree that all mental patients are dangerous. Certain social laws are based on the principle that all mental patients, without excep-

tion, present a threat to society. This results in oppressive surveillance precautions wherein the "dangerous" ones are taken into custody or their confinement is prolonged beyond the necessary length
of time.

Such abuses only compromise the ill person's treatment by making
him defiant or, worse, afraid and may even cause him to become
dangerous because of exasperation. Shortly after the end of the
Occupation, we received a message from the Ministry of Health
declaring that when mental patients escaped, the psychiatric hospital staffs were to be held responsible for the said escapes and
their consequences and were, indirectly, liable to penalties.

At first glance this arrangement may have seemed logical, but in
actual fact it was deplorable and contrary to good sense. If the staff
of an establishment feel the threat of retribution hanging heavily
over their heads, they will react by putting into effect a fearsome
surveillance. The patients then become like the inmates of a penal
colony, enemies to be mistreated, and instead of being cared for
they will be continuously spied upon. Actually it may even lead to
the likelihood of more escapes, for the patients will try to get away
from such rigorous, persecutory measures.

Of course, it is not necessary to go to the other extreme and proclaim that mental patients are choirboys and in no way dangerous,
that they may be permitted every freedom, and that no precautions
are necessary.

The fact is that mental illnesses are constantly changing, and
this is the most difficult problem that psychiatrists have to deal with.
Some patients may be dangerous at one time, then cease to be, and
vice versa. A person may inspire terror when in a given state and
then be exceedingly inoffensive in succeeding weeks.

The problem of release is often one of conscience. Public opinion
on this subject is very sensitive for completely contradictory reasons:
If a man who seems to have recovered has been kept in a mental
hospital too long, there is indignation; if a former inmate makes the
headlines after having been giving his freedom, there are outraged

cries. What is the answer? Should only one doctor be responsible for the decision, or is there some place to submit cases for an opinion?

The latter procedure may undoubtedly be useful. But it must be well organized, with a small number of persons who are competent and not overwhelmed by the weight of reports to be studied. My father often spoke to me of commissions set up many years ago by Clemenceau at a time when there was much healthy fear of arbitrary commitments. But those review boards were given the task of examining every release from every psychiatric hospital, and the result was heartbreaking. There were no more discharges because when deliberating bodies are made up of too many members responsibility is diluted and it becomes impossible to make a decision.

That is why the fate of committed mental patients depends on one or several persons, who thus bear a heavy responsibility. In deciding whether the inmate is or is not dangerous, whether he does or does not at a given moment represent a threat, it is vital to withhold labels and refrain from definitive prognoses. In psychiatry more than in any other field nothing can be decided "forever."

I should like to speak about medical jurisprudence as it is practiced in criminal and civil cases in the courts. I fully realize that the doctors appointed to fill this function are ethical men, but, even though endowed with the means to accomplish their mission well, the amount of time they are allotted is of utmost importance.

In order to be of indisputable value, forensic expertise must satisfy several fundamental requirements. The examinations must be many and the tests extensive. I have spoken of how long it takes to establish a diagnosis of schizophrenia or of paranoia. At the moment when a verdict is rendered, the psychiatric report will be of paramount importance, and every possible precaution must have been taken.

The reviews and examinations should absolutely include inquiries of the type that I conduct, calling in witnesses and arranging confrontations. The expert or the physician in the psychiatric hospital must personally conduct the examinations and write out his conclusions himself. In no case should the doctor in charge delegate this work to assistants or associates. It is also indispensable to bring in contradictory opinions. The choice of experts by the courts should be widened. Psychiatrists of different schools of thought must be included. The age, experience, and fame of these men are factors to be taken into consideration. Legal expertise requires not only professional but moral qualifications.

These recommendations will, of course, be opposed on the grounds of cost. Justice has a thin purse and keeps her accounts strictly. A reform of this type is expensive, but monetary considerations should not take precedence over the life and the liberty of human beings.

Should criminals be used as subjects for medical experiments? I often hear it said that this would be as good a way as any for them to "pay their debt to society."

The idea of using human beings as experimental animals was introduced by the Nazi doctors in their infamous experiments carried out in the concentration camps. It goes without saying that the strongest protests against this notion, therefore, have come from Jewish scientists.

When I became president of the Hebrew Medical Historical Society, which was founded in Paris by my friend Dr. Isidore Simon, I gave this question precedence in our research. I have had occasion to intervene several times with public agencies on the subject of experimentation on human beings. In October 1974, at an international congress in Tel Aviv, which brought together doctors, scientists, jurists, and religious leaders, this issue was debated. The words used by Dr. Marc Dvorjetzki of Tel Aviv to assail the proponents of this method still ring in my ears.

We cannot, of course, give up biological experimentation, which derives from the work of Claude Bernard and consists of inducing diseases in animals in the hope of discovering their causes in man and how they can best be treated. To give up such experimentation on animals would mean renouncing all medical progress and compromising the health and the future of mankind.

Biological testing must under no circumstances go beyond the use of animals. If prisoners or consenting subjects are used, the risk of abuse is too great, and contempt for man would inevitably result, which was exactly what happened in the camps where the German doctors conducted their criminal experiments.

The only admissible experimentation involving the use of human beings is what is known as therapeutic testing. In a certain number of serious cases, one is obliged to try out new medications which do involve a risk. The best rule is to weigh the dangers against the possible advantages. The objective is to cure the person and save his or her life. The finest example, often cited, of true therapeutic testing is that of Pasteur and rabies. Pasteur inoculated a man, doomed to death, with his vaccine in order to give him a chance to survive, as indeed the patient did. But he did not submit a man in good health to an experiment which might have harmed him.

The views I have espoused, opposing experimentation on human beings, were given concrete form in the Jerusalem Declaration, a document prepared by Dr. Dvorjetzki, Dr. Krieger, and me, and which I read at the International Congress of Jewish Doctors in Jerusalem in August 1952. Several months later, we were overjoyed to hear Pope Pius XII make a statement expressing the same point of view.

I shall quote our document in its entirety, for it is a charter for doctors in our time, in a century which has so often seen such naked savagery that it is imperative to be perpetually on the watch for its resurgence.

The International Congress of Jewish Doctors:
1. Reaffirms its indignation at Nazi crimes, specifically
—the use of medical science for the purpose of exterminating children, the aged, the mentally ill, the incurably sick, and the crippled, to which its perpetrators gave the name "mass euthanasia";

—the enforced sterilization by pharmaceutical, surgical, radio-
logical, or other means, practiced in the camps as a preliminary step
toward transforming European people of all races into slaves capable
of work but not of bearing progeny;

—the physical and moral degradation of human beings by a
methodical, premeditated, and rationally organized system of starva-
tion, thirst, freezing, beatings, humiliation, torture, nakedness, promiscuity, absence of hygiene, and a permanent atmosphere of fear and
desperation calculated to dehumanize its victims;

—the criminal medical experiments in which humans were used
as laboratory animals: inoculations with infectious diseases, the study
of the effects of asphyxiants and different poisons, grafting of tissue,
bone, muscle from one person to another, experiments to determine
the effects of freezing on man, all other projects in which human
beings were used as guinea pigs.

2. Protests not only the forgetting of these crimes but the too frequent indifference to them, which represents a moral complicity with
those doctors who put medical science at the disposal of Hitler's racist
policies, or who were even the instigators of such criminal biological
theories.

3. Is concerned about the possibility of the conscious or unconscious survival of these criminal biological theories in today's medical
and biological sciences.

4. In view of the above, declares that

—no human being has the right to sacrifice another in the interest
of science;

—the medical world must establish specific guidelines defining
the difference between experimental physiology involving the use of
animals and therapeutic testing on men;

—new and very serious problems of medical ethics are posed by
recently introduced techniques which, through anatomical destruction
or by provoking new illnesses or by disorganizing or weakening of the
personality, and under cover of supposed therapeutic goals, obtain
merely palliative effects or even alter human beings;

—the conscience of doctors must be strengthened and defined,
and they must in no case use scientific knowledge in order to destroy
human beings.

There has been a great deal of comment about this text. It has many admirers and some detractors. I do not admit that any objections to it are valid. What has human sacrifice bestowed on science, even on technical and scientific grounds? It has been universally admitted that the Nazi experiments contributed nothing. Most of medicine's great technical advances since Claude Bernard—vaccination, pasteurization, antibiotics, etc.—have come about as the result of experimentation on animals.

I do not condone those experiments conducted by American medical teams who inoculate diseases into volunteers recruited from among prison inmates. I also take strong issue with those who contend that experimentation with animals is not applicable to psychiatry. Psychopharmacological experimentation with animals is an effective prelude to therapeutic testing on man, and I have proof of this in my own work. Psychiatry has no need to violate the Jerusalem Declaration in order to progress.

Among the new procedures capable of causing anatomical destruction is lobotomy, which consists of removing a section of the brain. According to some scientists, by artificially creating lesions in the area of the frontal lobes, one can profoundly modify the personality and do away with aggressive behavior or anxiety. Since this technique has come into vogue, doctors can be found throughout the world who advocate that lobotomies be performed on criminals as a last resort, the idea being that crime is thus eliminated from the brain of the sick person. I have even read articles advocating this procedure on humanitarian grounds, lobotomy presumably being preferable to jail. But I continue to consider this operation barbarous and dangerous, and believe that the criminally insane can be treated solely by the use of scientific data and human compassion.

In the past, it was often considered good therapy to jolt the mentally ill out of their sickness by plunging them into a dangerous situation, if necessary jeopardizing their lives. Doctors believed that at the moment of asphyxiation or coma the patient would suddenly recover his lucidity. One popular method was to place the subject on a small bridge over a pool of icy water. A trap would open and the patient would drop through. This charming practice was called the "surprise bath." The patient would be rescued when on the very verge of drowning.

Another method much used in former times, in fact well into the nineteenth century, was the "whirligig." The patient would be placed in a rotating machine and spun rapidly, with the idea of producing violent dizziness until he lost consciousness or went into a coma.

The human imagination has never been idle in this domain. Only with the arrival of Pinel at the beginning of the last century was war declared against the icy bath, the whirligig, and other such niceties.

"One can only blush at such medical insanity," he declared. "It is far more serious than the madness of the lunatic whose reason it aims at restoring."

Pinel and Esquirol helped psychiatry to look at last to science for its inspiration, and shock treatments disappeared. Alas, they returned after the Second World War. Perfected techniques in physics and chemistry, such as electroshock or Cardiazol, provided new means of inducing coma in the mentally ill.

I knew the inventor of the electroshock treatment, Professor Cerletti, very well. He had got his idea from visiting slaughterhouses in Rome, where, in order to kill animals painlessly, a powerful electric current was first passed through their heads, causing them to lose consciousness.

Electroshock produces a kind of coma. And Cerletti, observing that the passage of the current did not cause death, believed that subjecting the mental patient to this procedure would strengthen his natural defenses and help him to overcome his troubles. He did not, however, introduce his method (which does often lead to sudden and spectacular shortening of melancholic or depressive spells) without a certain apprehension.

The patient generally remembers nothing, for what he has undergone is no more nor less than an electrically induced epileptic seizure. He benefits, if the word *benefit* is applicable here, from the amnesia characteristic of that disorder. But individuals who have been subjected to electroshock become panicky when they are faced with the apparatus, though the usual procedure is to put the subjects to sleep first by intravenous injection so that they cannot be consciously aware of the machinery that has been used on them, and in principle cannot know they have had the treatment. Still, their terror is real and suggests that if fear has not invaded their conscious minds it must at least have penetrated their tissues. Cerletti was very much aware of this phenomenon.

Though electroshock shortens the period of depression, it also favors the return of certain crises. Its violent stimulation causes the patient to veer suddenly from depression to euphoria or agitation, and the increase of the oscillations accelerates the development of crises, especially if they are of a periodic nature. The alternating phases of depression and excitement become shorter but also occur closer together, and thus electroshock aggravates the illness.

Lastly, the jarring effect of electroshock may cause a sudden vasoconstriction of vessels in the brain. In weak patients this may bring on either cerebral hemorrhages or small capillary hemorrhages.

The abuses of electroshock have brought about truly terrible situations, which could have been avoided by the use of more fruitful, more humane, and less dangerous methods.

I once treated an American who had come to Paris with his wife and fallen prey to depression. I recommended a detailed treatment for him and, to be ethically correct, wrote to his regular doctor. When months had passed without news of the man, I telephoned his doctor, who told me that he was getting along nicely. A few days later, I received a letter from the patient, informing me that despite my letter with recommendations for treatment, against his will and with the complicity of his wife, he had been confined in a so-called "progressive" mental hospital and given electroshock therapy. He was completely devastated. I had hardly replied to his letter when word came that he had committed suicide.

Although my stand against such treatments has attracted the hostility of many psychiatrists the world over, I never quarreled with Professor Cerletti. He was an extraordinarily conscientious, courteous man and, contrary to what many believed, was perfectly aware of the drawbacks to his method. He and I often discussed electroshock together, and his point of view and my own were not so very far apart.

When he died, the Academy of Medicine accorded me the job of paying him homage. It was expected that I would use the opportunity to excoriate him for his views. Of course, I did nothing of the sort, and reminded my audience that Professor Cerletti had spent the last years of his life searching for a technique that would replace electroshock.

He had given up using it on human beings and only experimented with it on animals. He would collect the creatures' serum, which he believed to contain defensive properties that would benefit human patients.

Another technique that I have opposed is the insulin coma, invented by Professor Sakel of Vienna, which consists of injecting patients with massive doses of insulin to induce coma, a state considered to be the specific treatment for schizophrenia. I studied this method very closely, using animals in the laboratory I had built at Charenton, and observed that the vessels in the monkeys' brains emptied themselves of blood, somewhat as the water drains out at low tide, and then the coma ensued. The changes in the circulation of blood to the monkeys' brains were dramatic. At the beginning of the crisis, the vessels constricted violently and the brain became paper-white. Then, the brain swelled with the returning flow of blood and turned wine-red, enlarging to such a degree that it erupted out of the trepanned opening in the skull.

It is easy to see why one must be cautious about applying such violent methods to human beings. When patients are asked what they felt, those who have received insulin recall a less painful experience than those who have undergone electroshock. They remember a feeling of being projected into a deep sleep and do not feel in their bones the terror brought on by the application of current. But I am nonetheless opposed to the method because of its devastating effect.

My fiercest battle has been waged against lobotomy. My opposition to this operation dates back to a time before it had actually been invented and put into practice. The idea floated around for quite a while; the man who first spoke to me about it was an excellent friend and scholar, a remarkable man, Dr. Thierry de Martel, whom I have already described as having chosen death rather than see the Germans enter Paris.

He had observed that in cases of cerebral tumors, when the frontal lobe was affected or when changes took place in it, the patient became indifferent and seemed to show no anxiety; on the contrary, he appeared to float in a sort of euphoria. He concluded that by deliberately creating lesions in this area one could transform the depressed into happy confident people.

I answered that I would object to such a procedure on the grounds of the serious mutilation it would cause to the patient's brain and the impossibility of measuring its far-reaching consequences. Experience in neurosurgery and neurology shows that affections of the frontal lobes are often accompanied by problems of moral control, by indifference, and by personality changes which engender serious inferiority feelings.

Thierry de Martel, with his great intelligence and clear vision, immediately understood what a dangerous path he had been about to take, and he gave up his idea. Unfortunately, it was taken up by

Professor Egas Moniz of Lisbon, who perfected lobotomy, an operation which quickly attained great popularity throughout the world.

In the United States, experiments were made on monkeys, which were first trained to accomplish a given task. If they failed, they became troubled and felt obliged to succeed. Once lobotomized, they had no further cares and their indifference to their chore was total.

This change should have put the medical world on its guard, for that indifference in the experimental monkeys would correspond in man to the disappearance of the internal drives that distinguish us from animals. Even though the operation might cure the patient, he would be diminished for the rest of his life.

I was not content with a theoretical analysis, but personally studied the effects of the operation by lobotomizing five monkeys in my laboratory, with the assistance of Professor Puech, a great surgeon. The main thing we observed in following the progress of our animals was the modification of character: First they manifested bursts of impulsiveness and violence, then all became epileptic and died. We concluded that lobotomy can be extremely dangerous. Despite our conclusion, lobotomy has been practiced on a great scale. The observed results of such operations have been unpleasant changes in the moral sense and the personality.

I have cared for lobotomized persons, and I have no hesitation about calling them victims. For instance, a young man came to see me as an outpatient. He arrived in my office wearing a jeering, almost defiant expression. I was surrounded by my students, to whom he turned to make sarcastic remarks, poking fun at me and laughing. To all my questions he replied, "Oh, everything's just a bed of roses."

The next day he returned and confided to my interns that he was depressed. He confessed that he had joked with me the previous day because he knew I was against lobotomy, that he had felt like a monster ever since his operation, "a pig, a disgusting beast." He then revealed that he had betrayed his father to the Internal Revenue people for cheating on his taxes, and that he knew he had lost the faculty for feeling anything and was suffering horribly.

"There's only one thing to do now," he told the interns, "and that's to do an even bigger lobotomy. Then I'll be completely stupid, I'll become exactly like an animal and won't feel guilty anymore about anything."

He wrote me a series of letters in which threats alternated with praise. He explained that he felt the urge to kill me, since he was the living proof that my views against lobotomy were right. He also wrote threatening letters to the surgeon who had performed his operation. Finally, seeing no way out, he committed suicide by throwing himself under a train.

I can give many other examples. There was the lobotomized patient hospitalized at Charenton whose only idea was to lie and to brutalize his companions. The operation had not even taken away his aggressiveness. Later, he regretted his misdeeds profoundly and became aware of his irremediable loss.

Then there was the woman who had been lobotomized to cure her of insane attacks of jealousy. Her husband told me, "She's become completely cynical. She tells me to be unfaithful and suggests inviting prostitutes to the house for me. She does nothing but laugh and has been turned into a pet animal."

The situation is not always so extreme as this, of course. Still, the patient's personality is impaired, a mutilation I deplore, for it is my view that a doctor's first duty is to respect in his entirety the human being who has entrusted his fate to him.

It is always a mistake to attempt to destroy the moral conscience of an individual. We must respect it, care for it, educate and orient it. A truly humane psychiatry must seek to make a man whole physically and mentally. In the early days of lobotomy there was a legitimate desire to combat disorders of the moral conscience. For example, a depressed person often accuses himself of wrongs he has not committed, a situation which can do him great harm and which must be fought. But though lobotomy effectively eliminates this self-accusing mechanism, it does so only by destroying the personality. The remedy is worse than the illness.

I have suffered many assaults and insults because of the struggle I have waged, for quarrels on scientific subjects can often be bitter.

Reading a neurological magazine one day, I was surprised to see a note declaring: "Dr. Baruk has changed his mind; he is now for lobotomy." I had trouble getting the writer to retract his statement. It took a meeting of the Neurological Society and the support of friends before I obtained the necessary apology and admission of error.

The battle over electroshock and lobotomy has gone on for many years, and I have had the pleasure of seeing my point of view and that of my friends triumph almost everywhere in the world. In the Soviet Union, a meeting of the Congress of Physicians stressed the dangers of lobotomy, and it was finally forbidden throughout Eastern Europe. The reason for this ban was made clear in the work of Mme. Chevtchenko, of Moscow, who studied the brains of patients who had died after lobotomies. She showed that the operation was often followed by extensive lesions throughout the entire brain. In Naples Professor Senise and in Geneva Professor Morel fought energetically for my point of view. Happily, lobotomy has only a few faithful adherents left, such as Professor Lazorthes in Toulouse.

Psychopharmacological methods have, of course, contributed to this retreat. Here too there have been abuses. For instance, there is the mixture of various hypnotic drugs whose object is to "potentiate" and which are popularly known as "medicinal cocktails." These are both dangerous and quite inefficacious. They can, in fact, be even more harmful than shock methods; in certain cases they can lead to coma and death.

A young North African girl, in a manic state, was to be transferred to a Paris clinic. In order for her to make the plane trip without incident, she was given a "medicinal cocktail" in strong doses repeated throughout the flight. While still on the plane, she was overcome with vomiting and pain. She had scarcely arrived in Paris when she went into a coma and died in the mental clinic from the toxic effects of the "cocktail."

These are shock methods, techniques calculated to savage nature, to do violence to the human being without measuring the shock waves that are born and that develop in a body and in a mind all of whose mysteries we do not understand. These methods are a sign of great arrogance, whereas psychiatry's position should be one of particular humility and scrupulousness.

CHAPTER

A CLOSE LOOK
AT PSYCHOANALYSIS

AMONG MY MANY BATTLES HAVE BEEN THOSE I LED AGAINST THE abuses of psychoanalysis, some of which I have already mentioned.

I willingly recognize the importance of Sigmund Freud's discoveries in the realm of psychoanalysis, which is an excellent exploratory tool. Also, psychoanalysis emphasizes the significance of affective and instinctive phenomena, a domain too much neglected in classical psychiatry and psychopathology, and has served to break rationalism's stifling hold over civilization, which lasted from the seventeenth century to our day. Freud revolutionized our branch of medicine as well as sociology, and his influence has extended to all the human sciences. In the realm of pure medicine, his works were a sound reaction against the abuse made of Charcot's cerebral localizations, which Freud had studied as Charcot's student. His research shed light on the role of the unconscious and led him to the technique of analyzing dreams and those unexpressed feelings hidden deep in the subconscious.

But Freud's disciples have gone too far. I have had many an occasion to treat persons abandoned as hopeless by psychoanalysts and to observe the harm done to them. I have had to contend not only with their fundamental illnesses, but with the complications superimposed upon them by psychoanalysis.

Psychoanalysis invariably leads the patient back into the past, often to the first years of life, since that early period is considered to be the time when his neurosis was formed as a result of problems he was unable to surmount. Because of those difficulties, the patient suffers from bitter and painful regrets and develops guilt feelings which are usually transferred to his family, the convenient "scapegoat." However, instead of combating this situation, the psycho-analyst magnifies its importance.

I became involved in the case of an extremely intelligent young girl, Mlle. H, who was suffering from disorders involving the autonomic nervous system, which appeared whenever she encountered a setback or was overworked. These disorders consisted of spasms of the gastrointestinal tract, nausea, vomiting, and excessive salivation.

Mlle. H, who was working toward a degree in science at the university, considered herself to be less favored by her parents than her sister. I was to observe later on that her complaints were not unfounded; in fact, when her troubles became evident, her parents were more preoccupied with her sister's marriage than with Mlle. H's problems.

She had a tendency toward obsession and soon came to believe that she had been sacrificed to her sister. A strongly emotional person on whom the least incident had a violent effect, she was overcome at the prospect of taking her examinations. After her sister's marriage, her disorders became worse, and her family doctor sent her to consult a psychoanalyst.

She abandoned her studies, and for several years her days were entirely given over to her analysis. This incessant treatment played an active part in bringing into full bloom her resentment against her parents, whom she regarded as responsible for all her frustrations. She lived for her sessions with the analyst, increasingly obsessed with her past since it was the only thing she thought about. She never ceased blaming others. Week after week the psychoanalyst helped her to rehash her bitterness against her father and others close to her. No constructive thought was given to her future; instead, she became solidly entrenched in her past, a state which intensified her illness.

After several years, when there was no improvement in Mlle. H's condition, the analyst became discouraged and declared that he was ending the analysis. That was when Mlle. H came to see me, and I began the difficult job of "depsychoanalyzing" her.

This involved taking the opposite tack from the one which had been followed during her analysis. I gave her firm support, was always available to help her face her problems; I worked to disentangle her from her habit of blaming others for her difficulties; I tried to restore her lost confidence in herself and in her family, and to help her recover her lost taste for work.

I began with a course of treatment for her physical condition, which helped her somewhat. Then I insisted that she return to the university, where she finally received her degree in science, a feat of which for years she had believed herself incapable.

This did not mean that she had recovered. She still tended to brood over old grievances. But at least the treatment I gave her proved to be more efficacious than psychoanalysis, since she was able to work despite her acrimonious nature.

I did the same sort of work with a young man who had failed to get his high school science diploma and had been disillusioned in love. He was a highly cultivated young man—his parents were serious intellectuals. Terribly depressed by his setbacks, he unfortunately turned to a psychoanalyst for help.

In a short time, Paul D had completely lost his self-confidence, decided that he was incapable of doing anything, quarreled with his father, left his family, and devoted all his time to his analysis. It is that psychological imperialism which I find the most distressing aspect of psychoanalysis. The patient is turned into a kind of slave, with a diminished will and personality and, by extension, an impaired ability to readapt socially. The treatment weakens the patient rather than restoring his moral and intellectual qualities.

This subservient attitude rarely leads the patient to resent the analyst. Human beings tend to give in easily to those who can dominate them; so the patient admires his "master," in a way loves him. Such a frame of mind is called psychoanalytic transference and can lead to dangerous situations.

It may engender confused feelings, even when patient and doctor are of the same sex. This is what happened with Paul D, whose analyst mistakenly formulated a homosexual hypothesis. Paul D was shocked by such suspicions, and the truth was that the homosexual tendency lay in the practitioner himself rather than in the patient.

And so Paul D ended by consulting me. I found that he had no pederastic tendencies whatsoever, but was merely helpless and depressed, which was not astonishing since he could not earn a living without a diploma and could see no way out of his depressed state.

My most important task was to restore his confidence in himself and in his future. I was dealing with an amorphous human being whose lack of desire to act on his own initiative was the direct result of his analysis. One day he told me that he would like to study medicine, since he was enthusiastic about its humanitarian aspect. I had him come to my service at the hospital and to follow me on my rounds. Since he did not have his diploma, I suggested he take an equivalency examination, which he took and passed. Such a form of therapy requires not only that the physician treat the patient but that he concern himself with every detail of the latter's situation. This is a far cry from the passive interviews conducted on the psychoanalyst's couch.

Paul D's energy, which had been dissipated during the years spent with his analyst, had to be restored. My active, reassuring psychotherapy not only got Paul D back to work but led to the full recovery of his normal sexual nature.

The great mistake made by certain of today's practitioners of the Freudian method has been to carry to an extreme some of their master's observations and to profess that man's fundamental need is to satisfy his desires, particularly sexual ones, without regard for other, moral factors. They have thus arrived at a psychology of pure instinct and have drawn some unexpected conclusions from certain of Freud's assertions.

For example, Freud attacked the famous command, "Thou shalt love thy neighbor as thyself," claiming that it was only a *credo quia absurdum*, a paradox without reality. Certain of his disciples have concluded from this that man's enemy is society. They believe that the ideal order would consist of giving man complete freedom to satisfy all his desires without being hindered by social restraints, which in their opinion annoy, paralyze, and stifle him. Freud, who conceived such a society as represented by a couple disporting themselves unrestrainedly on a desert island, recognized that this utopian situation was not applicable in practice. His descendants have forgotten his reservation.

This hedonistic philosophy, this doctrine celebrating the gratification of desire, has had the merit of helping us to understand instinct and the misfortune to make it sovereign. The ensuing indulgence of desire has become the common denominator of every psychological and psychopathological manifestation, leading to such nonsense as the explanation of grief as a repressed wish to see the loved one dead. Equally foolish is the theory, upheld by Mendelsohn and by Ellenberger, which holds that in a social struggle the oppressed have the secret desire to be enslaved by their oppressors. This is a stupid justification of fascism, though most of today's Freudians seem to be unaware of that. An example of this is obvious in the film *The Night Porter,* in which a former concentration camp inmate ecstatically succumbs to torture and death at the hands of an ex-SS officer whom she had known in the camp.

When the satisfaction of one's own desires becomes the criterion of a civilization, a conflict results, the only resolution of which is seen by its proponents as utter satiation, even at the expense of society. This concept has had a strong effect on education and on the shaping of the young. The smashing of constraints has resulted in the abdication of their responsibilities by parents and teachers, and in the proliferation of patients who are capricious, complaining, aggressive, and discontented with themselves, with others, and with the social order. I do not mean to imply that Freudianism has been the only factor here, but it has lent a helping hand in the destruction.

It is curiously paradoxical that Freudianism has shown itself to be a severe, even rigid and accusatory dogma in the long run. It is at bottom a pessimistic doctrine, which condemns man. Seen through its perspective, man appears to be a hypocrite who takes care to dissimulate the most perverse tendencies under a mask of social conformity. One might say that the psychoanalyst believes all men to be unknowingly guilty.

This systematic suspicion which permeates analysis turns it into a policelike method. The patient is a suspect from whom the truth must be extracted, by traps and trickery if necessary. The psychoanalyst does not speak himself, but through his analysis of dreams or of words which escape the patient he extorts confidences which betray the repressed fantasies. This is, in a sense, a rape of the patient's mind.

My own method lies at the opposite pole from the above. It rests on obtaining the patient's confidence. I never force him in any way and refuse to attempt to wrest his secrets from him. If he does not wish to reveal them, I respect his reserve. I do question him carefully, but he knows that I am his friend, not his master, and that I do not wish to dominate him.

I resent above all the fact that psychoanalysis takes its inspiration from the idea of finding a scapegoat, of encouraging the patient to accuse those around him, his intimates, a situation which creates fresh conflicts among those near to him and often disrupts family peace. This had led me to write elsewhere that psychoanalysis is the greatest manufacturer of paranoiacs that the world has ever seen.

When a patient perceives that the physician wishes only to help him and to give him advice, when he knows that he is safe from manipulation, that he can have full confidence, then and only then is he ready to bare his soul. At that point, treatment, facilitated by the climate which has been created, can begin. The psychoanalytic method, on the contrary, humiliates the patient in order to discover his secrets.

It is regrettable that the psychoanalytic method does not work as it should and that the Freudian purists are such extremists, for the great Viennese's technique is based on more than a modicum of truth. He addressed himself first and foremost to neuroses and obsessions, which he thought were the result of repressed desires rising from the unconscious to the surface of the conscious mind in the form of strange, unidentified entities that terrorize the personality.

Freud believed that by analyzing dreams, chance associations, and those matters heretofore unexpressed by the patient, he could, thanks to the resulting relaxation of censorship, disarm the obsession, remove its pathological power, and so effect a cure. Symptoms were no longer described from the outside but explained within their own system of dynamics. What psychoanalysis has always lacked is factual proof.

It has often been declared that psychoanalysis is a religion rather than a science. It has its dogmas, its rites, and above all, an interpretation that is almost mystical—or, in any case, little subject to scientific control. It is the nature of science that the hypothesis must be subjected to verification before it becomes scientific fact. So, in psychoanalysis, the hypothesis, that is, the interpretation furnished by its author, the analyst, should be subject to the control of the therapeutic result.

Now on this point the results have been rather meager. Very few obsessions have been cured by psychoanalysis. The rare successful cases are much less numerous than the positive results achieved by other methods. I do not believe that psychoanalysis has a very good record, in spite of the intensive propaganda campaign waged by its adepts, who are accorded too much credit by persons in no way equipped to have an opinion in the matter.

The advent of psychopharmacology has provided an obstacle to the progress of the Freudian method. For example, in cases of certain types of hysteria, it would seem paradoxical to undertake psychoanalysis when scopochloralose often brings about recovery in a single day.

But, the reader may now ask, are not sexuality and its problems the special preserve of psychoanalysis? Here too I am obliged to observe that the partisans of the Freudian method are behind the times and that their stubbornness only leads to the encouragement of sexual perversions. The happiness of couples may founder for reasons other than sex.

I treated a Mme. A, who was so depressed that she had become incapable of looking after her home and her family. Her husband was indignant at her neglect of her duties, and the children had been sent to a priest friend in the South. Catastrophe seemed imminent and inevitable.

What was to be done? If they were advised to give free rein to indulge their instincts and desires, which would have been an analyst's choice, they would surely have ended up in the divorce court. I chose another way: trying to make peace between them through understanding.

I interviewed the husband, who was very shaken by the situation. He was irritable and exhausted, and drank to excess. I treated him for his physical condition and then, gently, with great care, persuaded him to cut down on his drinking. It was clear from certain things he said that he still loved his wife deeply, but he did insist that he needed a normal woman to count on and that, in any case, he no longer found her sexually interesting since her illness.

I succeeded in finding the source of Mme. A's trouble in vestiges of an old asthma which had left her with allergies that had a definite connection with her depression. Treatment for the allergies brought rapid improvement, whereas medication for her depression had completely failed.

M. A finally became quite understanding during my joint interview with them. They began to live together happily once again, understood each other, and enjoyed good sexual relations. The children were brought home soon thereafter. These results were obtained within a period of a few months.

The Hebrew Bible has never scorned sexual pleasure. The Hebraic doctrine contains no prudery, and in fact certain episodes in the Bible are recounted crudely. But the carnal act is underlined by strong, ardent feelings which impose a morality based on respect for the other person. Not to deceive, not to abandon, not to behave offensively are duties that derive not from abstract morality but from the very existence of the loved one.

I in no way wish to minimize instinct and pleasure, which play a major role in the development and broadening of the human character. Freud was right to restore the importance of the sexual act, which, under the influence of the Church, had come to be misunderstood and even rejected as impure. Pleasure had been more or less condemned in an excess of spiritualization. Freud's contribution, restoring sexual pleasure to its rightful place, was positive. But he gave it too great an importance; by placing normal sex on the same level with perversions, by paring away feelings of tenderness and respect for the other person, he actually led the way from one abuse to another.

We see the results of King Pleasure's sovereignty in the breaking up of homes, which constitutes one of the fundamental crises of our times. In our practices, we doctors often see husbands or wives abandoning sick mates to amuse themselves elsewhere. A society founded on the selfish pursuit of pleasure and total contempt for others is unacceptable.

It is true that sexual perversions exist and that they are difficult to cure. Is that any reason to accept and even glorify them? Carnal pleasure must be made part of a whole, whose motivation remains love.

There is much talk these days about sex education. The problem is very simple. Sex education must not be reduced to the study of a simple biological function; it must explain and then put the accent on the feelings which give the act its nobility. The notion of reciprocity is essential too, all the more so because an overliberated sexuality ends by exhausting itself.

Although it may sometimes be useful to comfort the individual while bringing him face to face with his hidden, repressed thoughts, and advantageous to lead him, through analysis, to an attitude of sincerity, understanding, and truthfulness, it is dangerous to allow him to believe that animal impulses, which arise from the subconscious with no moral or social justification, are right.

Normally, instinctive ideas which well up from the unconscious are filtered, criticized, and adjusted to fit social and moral requirements. This "censorship" or correction of the raw product issuing from the unconscious can lead to difficult problems. Obsessions often make up a part of such material, which is why they shock and frighten the conscious mind, as if an enemy were taking over the personality. Pierre Janet, who was influenced by the psychophysiology of his time, saw in the ungovernable welling up of such uncontrolled notions a weakening or fatigue of the nervous system, that is, of its power to repress or censor. This is why he listed obsessions under the heading of "psychasthenia."

Freud, on the contrary, spoke out against "censoring" and repression of unconscious desires which, buried deep, emerge in dreams and futile acts. There is some validity in his observation because it is certainly true that immoderate repression leads to the magnification of the repressed material, so that it becomes obsessive and all-important. But inversely, too much tolerance as well as subordination to these unconscious and dangerous factors leads man to bestiality.

If man were to base his morality on mere biology, he would no longer know how to be free. Unless he wishes to fall prey to arbitrary and unjust tyrannies, he must submit to elevated social and moral ideas, to moral conscience, which is a keystone in our basic nature. The practice of psychiatry has taught me that there is a close connection between mental health and the sense of right and wrong.

CHAPTER

THE TRUTH OF
THE TSEDEK

IT IS SOMETIMES DIFFICULT TO DISCOVER THE TRACE OR RATHER THE imprint of moral conscience in a man. Whether his sense of right and wrong has caused his troubles or has been obscured or obliterated by illness, its existence cannot be denied. It is responsible for all that has been described under the heading of "guilt complex." In order for the patient suffering from guilt to be able to get at the root of his ailment, he must be aware of the existence of his conscience and must have the courage to acknowledge his burden of real or supposed blame.

Professor Alajouanine and I treated a patient who occupied quite a high position and was suffering from an apparently incurable depression, accompanied by extreme physical debilitation. He told us that he had been in this condition since taking a trip to India and blamed it on an intestinal bug he had probably picked up there.

We put him back on his feet physically, but he remained a prisoner of his depression. I questioned him at length to discover how such a heretofore vigorous, dynamic man could have come to such a pass. He assured me that he had no idea, but I suspected some secret. It was inconceivable that a mind such as his could have foundered for no reason. There appeared to be no problems besetting him in his professional career, and his love life seemed good. He was tired, certainly, and overworked, but the answer did not lie there.

I gradually gained his confidence, and he began to tell me about his life, which seemed to have contained no major trauma. Then he unlocked the mysterious door and revealed his secret. He had been an officer during the First World War. During a terrible bombardment, he had ordered his men to attack. They hesitated, some of them even refused, but he threatened and cajoled them into action. However, he himself panicked and ran for shelter. Almost inaudibly, he concluded, "They were all killed."

This memory had tormented my patient for years; then he had thought that it was forgotten, and his sense of guilt seemed to have disappeared. Thirty years later, when he was extremely tired and weak from his illness, the guilt feeling came violently to life, more powerful than ever. He must, of course, have had a tendency to depression, but this struggle with his moral conscience had aggravated it. Only moral therapy could cure him. I did the best I could to assuage his moral suffering.

World War II gave me the opportunity to observe numerous moral conflicts, which proved to me that moral conscience does finally take precedence over instinct. That war brought on innumerable crises of conscience which, long after hostilities had ended, continued to have their effect on the men and women who lived through it.

A Jewish couple, the man a lawyer, the wife a psychoanalyst, left Warsaw in 1939 for London. They left behind Mr. V's mother and brother, who had not succeeded in procuring passports. Mr. V had demurred at the idea of leaving without them, but his wife persuaded him that life had become cruel, that each man had to save himself, that traditional morality was anachronistic.

After the armistice, in 1945, Mr. V tried to find out what had happened to his mother and brother. He learned that, unable to escape from Poland, they had been killed by the Germans. The remorse he felt caused his entire life to become paralyzed, and led to the loss of his social position and a decline in his physical and mental health. He even gave up practicing law, which might have assured him a comfortable future. Friends reminded Mr. V that it was not a crime to forget, that forgetting was indeed a law of life. But nothing seemed to work out for him.

Whenever something good happened to him, his feeling of guilt would become particularly vivid. If he was served an excellent meal, the mere sight of the dishes would release in him the image of his starving mother and brother. His dreams were filled with hideous visions of his brother, tortured and beaten by the Germans. Any work requiring concentration was impossible for him, so he settled for a modest job, well below his capabilities, in a bank. He was aware of the wreck he had become and began to behave irritably. It was his wife who made all the decisions since he was incapable of doing so.

Eventually his physical health was affected, and in 1954 he was operated on for a cyst of the thyroid gland. One medical problem was succeeded by another. He had a duodenal ulcer, a hernia of the diaphragm, and then the inevitable heart attack. It is interesting to note that this isolated problem with his moral conscience had no effect on this man's intellectual ability, yet it was so deeply rooted in his being that it affected his entire organism.

It is important to distinguish between such a condition and manic-depressive states. The latter often occur as the result of imaginary or disproportionately exaggerated events. Mr. V's conscience had been wounded by actual occurrences, which were unfortunately terribly real.

Another similar case was that of Mrs. J, who, along with her parents, her husband, and her son, was shut up in the Warsaw ghetto. Upon learning that the Germans had decided to exterminate the population, starting with the old people, Mrs. J's aged parents asked her for poison so that they could die by their own hands.

Believing that she would shortly be following her parents to the grave, Mrs. J obeyed, and they died before her eyes. Soon afterward, through a chain of unexpected circumstances, she and her husband and son escaped from the ghetto. After many vicissitudes, they arrived in the United States. Their adjustment took place under the best of circumstances, and happiness seemed truly within reach.

But suddenly Mrs. J became intensely depressed. The doctors, who could not guess the reason for her trouble, treated her for depression, without much success. They declared her to be a "constitutional depressive."

It is certain that Mrs. J's trouble was directly linked to the events she had lived through in Warsaw. When she came to consult me, on the occasion of a trip to France, I advised her to continue work with old people (which she had been doing in the United States) and to identify them consciously and deliberately with her parents, so that she could learn to accept the terrible memory without turning it into an instrument of self-reproach.

These stories show clearly that there does exist in man's heart a profound sense of good and evil, which has nothing to do with social constraint or fear of being caught.

I have treated patients who had tried to stifle their inner voice.

Mathieu R, an important official in a large company, resorted to slander in order to get a fellow employee's job. He succeeded in ousting his rival and obtaining the position. It would seem that he had every reason to be satisfied.

But from that moment on, his personality changed. He became touchy, bristled with authority, insisted on a show of respect from his fellow workers, and was pointlessly aggressive. He was convinced that all the world was against him. In short, he was the prime example of the personality type that believes himself to be persecuted and who persecutes others in turn.

Everyone who knew him, both his superiors and his subordinates, was astonished. They could not understand where such insane authoritarianism, such constant suspiciousness came from. The answer was simple: Softly but stubbornly, the voice from deep inside was reminding him of the unjust act he had committed. He was unconsciously imagining that people were accusing him, and he was revenging himself on them for his inability to be at ease with his inner self.

Mathieu R was not aware of what was happening to him. The invisible accuser was none other than his repressed moral conscience. With people like this, one should not ask why they constantly reproach other people, but rather why they are reproaching themselves. The answer to the latter will lead to a solution for their illness.

A great writer, Ibn-Gabirol, the Spanish-Jewish theologian and grammarian, conceived a beautiful prayer in which he referred to "that God in our entrails," by which he meant the God of conscience.

Man first became aware of conscience through religion. It is the mainstay of monotheism. The wonderful thing is that on this point, as on others, science has supported theology.

Moral conscience is closely linked to mental health. Striking evidence of this can be seen in periodic psychosis, which has alternating periods of excitement and depression. In the periodic phase, the sense of right and wrong is noticeably dulled. The subject is convinced that what he is doing is acceptable, and he may commit the worst misdeeds without feeling the slightest compunction. His scruples are completely anesthetized.

Then, when he is depressed, we see the other side of the coin. He reproaches himself bitterly for acts he has committed and for those he has not. He feels constantly guilty and searches for expiation at any price, punishing himself unmercifully. He may even go so far as to commit suicide.

The other road leads to the pathology of moral conscience. I once treated a man who spent his entire life castigating himself because he believed that he was responsible for the death of Louis XVI. Between the two extremes of real and imaginary guilt one can find an intermediate truth, that is, something that is real but that has been grossly exaggerated.

Another of my patients, who lived with his mother, had a violent disagreement with her and she died that same evening. The son then reproached himself unmercifully, saying that he had killed his mother because of his cruelty. He became so depressed that he was unable to eat. I did what I could for him, but to no avail. Within a few months he died, utterly exhausted both physically and morally.

* * *

One of the arguments put forward by the advocates of frontal lobotomy was precisely that by performing this operation the torment of conscience would be ended, since the procedure would render the individual deaf to the protests of his inner voice.

I have shown that such a notion is not only fallacious but also dangerous. However, it is understandable that lobotomy enjoyed such a long period of popularity, since our era has seen such efforts being made to destroy conscience forever.

The denial of conscience can be seen especially clearly in Freud's renowned Oedipus complex. The son, jealous of his father, kills him, then takes his place in bed with his own mother. Freud's symbolism is simply a misinterpretation of the Greek legend, which refers specifically to a caprice of fate, so that it is in all innocence that Oedipus kills his father and sleeps with his mother.

The Freudian interpretation represents the negation of every authority, the justification of revolt, not only against the father but against any encroachment of society on the individual. Only the superego exists and it takes precedence over every other factor: society, the family, and the father, who is the very image of constraint. By accepting this concept, and setting it up as a sovereign rule by which our lives should be guided, our epoch has taken a truncated view of man, which has been followed by all the consequences that such a mutilation entails.

It is the prominence of the theme of revolt against the father in the education we have given our children for the past two or three decades which has led us to spare our offspring all effort and all obligation, for fear of making them neurotic. But the result has been the opposite of the one hoped for, and there are too many children who have turned on their parents with a morbid aggressiveness, a near-mad rebelliousness.

Several of these children have been my patients, and they reacted well to my energy and use of discipline in handling them. One of them, who returned to school and graduated with honors, told me after his success, "You're the kind of father I should have had."

HENRI BARUK

Alfred Adler (1870–1937), one of Freud's disciples, stressed the social responsibilities of the individual and so came to a parting of the ways with his master. Unfortunately he did not avoid the danger of going to an opposite extreme. He took issue with Freud's egocentricity and egoism and believed that a society needed citizens who would dedicate themselves to their fellowmen. He was a socialist, and his excellent works have been highly esteemed in England, despite their inherent dangers, of which, I believe, my British colleagues have not been sufficiently aware. The diverse branches of Freudianism, torn as they are between the individualism of the master and the socialism of the disciple, lead only to an impasse.

The Swiss thinker Carl Gustav Jung (1875–1961) also parted company with Freud, refusing to concede his master's purely sexual concept. Jung studied the collective unconscious of peoples, that is, the myths of humanity that have lasted throughout our history. Jung attempted to find a meaning, which was often religious, in this body of folk tales and fables. His was a historical and collectivist psychology, which looked to legends for the origins of philosophical ideas. The works of Jung are highly interesting, but they do not solve the problem posed by Freudianism.

Freud's hedonism, which was exalted and amplified by his successors, contributed to the development of the anarchic and demanding tendencies of today's mores. Only one factor might restore harmony: conscience, which could provide mankind with a higher goal than the satisfaction of purely selfish individual desires or the demands of society.

I have put conscience to practical use in psychiatry, in a test that I devised to which I gave the name of *tsedek*, from the Hebrew word expressing both justice and charity. My students and I have used this test to help us in making psychiatric diagnoses. However, it has ramifications that go far beyond psychiatry.

With the help of Mlle. Ribière (who had helped save many lives during the Occupation) and Dr. Bachet, the *tsedek*, composed of fifteen theoretical situations involving the conscience, was perfected.

((221))

Upon giving an answer to the questions, the individual must weigh his feelings against social necessity and moral obligation. Here are the examples:

1. There has been a theft in a barracks, but the guilty man cannot be found. The commanding officer decides to punish one soldier out of every ten. What do you think of his decision?

2. A serious mistake has been made by an employee in a government agency. One man is suspected, without definite proof. He is severely punished on the theory that he will thus serve as an example. What is your opinion about this?

3. A young man wants very much to have another job. He makes malicious remarks about his rival, and the man is fired. What do you think of this conduct?

4. Two candidates are campaigning for election to the same office. One of them spreads slanderous stories about his opponent's personal life on the theory that all's fair in politics. What do you think of this attitude?

5. A captain discovers that his commanding officer has erred in the line of duty. Instead of speaking to him about it, he goes over his head and tells the colonel in charge. What do you say to this behavior?

6. An ill, cold young woman uses a forbidden electric heater to warm herself during wartime restrictions. She is accused of stealing electricity and sent to prison. Do you think her punishment justified?

7. On learning that a hated enemy has had an accident and is without medical help, a doctor refuses to go to his assistance, arguing that in this way, by his refusal, he is having revenge on his old foe. What do you think of his attitude?

8. There are two different wards in a hospital, one for patients who are expected to recover, the other for incurables. Expense is not spared on the first, nothing is spent on the second. What is your opinion regarding this situation?

9. A young man who has a good job and has not concerned him-

self about his mother, learns that in her loneliness and consequent frustration she has committed a petty crime and been sent to jail. He refuses to visit her or to trouble himself about her in any way, declaring that she is, after all, guilty. What do you think about this kind of reaction?

10. A backward child who does not know how to defend himself is bullied by his schoolmates. Those who would like to help are afraid to do so, lest they be bullied in turn. How would you judge them?

11. A dedicated social worker, who often stays longer than the prescribed hours, frequently forgets to sign the register when she arrives at work and when she leaves. Her employer fires her for not obeying the rules. Do you approve?

12. Every year a teacher presents a certain number of students for examination and comments on their work. He gives all pupils, good and bad, high praise, so that the greatest number of candidates will pass and his school will enjoy a good reputation. Do you think that he is right?

13. In a time of emergency, food is in short supply. Rationing is based on the following rules: very large portions for persons in good health who can work and produce, very small rations for the aged or ill who contribute nothing. Is this fair?

14. A shopkeeper with a limited quantity of merchandise keeps it for rich and powerful customers who can do him some service or furnish him with additional goods, while he turns others away. What do you think of his policy?

15. During a period of rationing, it is decided that the best method is to reserve the major share for the country's citizens and to reduce the allotments to foreigners. Is this inequity justified in your opinion?

The manner of administering the test is extremely important. It is essential to avoid giving the person being evaluated the impression that he is required to pass an examination or that he is being forced to have an opinion. He must be approached casually. For example, one could say: "We would like to have your reaction to certain situations which might turn up in real life and might be confusing. We have asked these questions of many people and have collected many different opinions. We would be happy to have yours."

Bachet and I first administered the *tsedek* to more than three hundred people considered to be normal and chosen at random from various strata of the Paris population: students, intellectuals, taxi drivers, waiters, nurses, postmen, workers, etc. We found that from 80 to 90 percent of the subjects had a very clear feeling of the difference between right and wrong. They did not concede that one human being had the right to sacrifice another.

I do not mean to say that those people conducted themselves in life as uprightly as their replies to our questions might lead one to believe. But our results do show that the normal man's heart still harbors feelings of human kindness toward his fellowmen.

We examined the results of the test in order to distinguish the types of judgment. This analysis allowed us to distinguish these categories:

1. The emotional judgment. The subject is outraged at the thought of sacrificing the incurably ill; his answers come straight from the heart, spontaneously and unburdened by subtleties. "That's inhuman," he exclaims. "That's downright revolting. Everybody ought to be taken care of." Or "It's not fair to punish one soldier out of every ten just because they couldn't find the guilty one," he protests.

2. The unjust judgment. This is the opposite of the preceding reaction. The subject is contemptuous of the victim and thinks only in terms of his own self-interest. He does not put himself in the other man's shoes and refuses to trouble himself about his neighbor's fate. Of the merchant who sells only to the rich, he comments scornfully, "Of course he puts his own best interest first; after all, he's a businessman, not a philanthropist!"

3. The judgment based on social utility. Man's interests are secondary. Society takes precedence over the individual, and the situation is evaluated on the basis of its immediate worth to the

community, independently of questions of justice. Apropos the punishment of one soldier out of every ten, this subject comments, "Too bad that the innocent must suffer, but that's necessary if the group profits by it." In reply to question 5 in which the captain denounces his commanding officer, the subject says, "He did the right thing because it was in the interests of the Army." In replying to question 6 about the sick woman sent to prison for using the electric heater, the subject finds that "her punishment was justified because she broke the law." Characteristically, this subject has more respect for the fine points of the criminal code than for the individual.

4. The acknowledgment of a fact. The subject finds the instance of injustice regrettable but bows before reality. In reply to question 4, regarding elections, we received the following answers: "That's life, everybody does it"; "In politics, anything goes."

5. The double judgment. This stresses the duality between the moral law considered as an inaccessible ideal, in all cases impracticable, and ruthless reality. A judge answered question 1, regarding the punishment of one soldier out of ten, with: "Everything depends on your goal. That is the whole point behind making an example. A decision like that offends ideals of individual justice, but it can have a certain value from the social point of view." To question 3, concerning the young man who engages in character assassination against his rival, one answer we received claimed that it was "wrong from the point of view of bourgeois morality, but everybody also has to look out for himself." These persons attempted to strike a balance between the various exigencies contained in each of the cases we had described.

6. The well-rounded, "synthesized" judgment is the one I found the most satisfying. It was given us, generally, by the more educated subjects. Instead of looking at the test situations from a single point of view, or considering what was practical against what was not, these subjects joined heart to intelligence. The answers in this category expressed regret for instances of injustice not only from an emotional viewpoint but because their authors also envisaged the

long-term consequences of the acts. An intern replied to the situation of the one in ten soldiers being punished: "That's a useless and ineffective measure. The reaction would only be one of general discontent; the men would be set against the officers, the group would be divided, and the result would be prejudicial to the whole. Besides, the moral effect on the guilty man would be nil. To question 4, another man declared that character assassination was "a dirty, low political trick and should have no effect on voters endowed with a minimum of intelligence and might even backfire on its author." To question 6, concerning the young woman who was ill and used a heater illegally, one person answered that there was "no reason why society's needs and humanitarian feelings couldn't be served at one and the same time by giving the lady a warning, or obliging her to pay some small fine, rather than sending her to jail."

This test has been of great importance in evaluating the mentally ill. I have discovered that certain mental patients do conserve intact their moral conscience, while in other cases, for example epileptics, or violent but hypersensitive subjects, this conscience is even exaggerated. There is a third category, in which the sense of right and wrong has been profoundly affected or even completely destroyed.

One of the most striking answers that I received came from a schizophrenic. His reply to question 8, regarding the curably and incurably ill, was especially revealing, as it was given by a man whose above-average intelligence had remained intact:

"You have to know whether the people considered to be incurable can still be useful in some way," he wrote. "If they can perform some service or other, or if they are attractive to look at, you could let them live, the way you would a house pet that's ornamental and makes a pleasant addition to your life. But if that is not the case, then I'd have no hesitation about killing the person."

This is a perfect example of a logical decision made without any trace of human feeling. It represents the essence of the schizophrenic mentality. Whenever I have heard patients express themselves in this way, I have never felt the slightest doubt about the diagnosis.

And so I believe that we cannot deny the essential role played by moral conscience in the formation of the human mind, which is why I am terrified by the proposals of certain so-called "thinkers" calling for the abandonment of the rules of right and wrong. When one has seen, as have I, men tormented by remorse, sometimes justified, sometimes not, and has observed the damage it does to the body as well as to the mind; when one knows from experience that one of the most blatant signs of schizophrenia is the total absence of the sense of right and wrong, one feels a deep concern as the tide of injustice rises in the world.

And this is not a matter of a passing ill. A Polish writer, Professor Bjornstein, has formulated a theory which deserves our attention. He believes that all of humanity is gradually becoming affected by schizophrenia. The icy indifference of public opinion, the cruel logic which we use to solve the most pathetic cases, our refusal to recognize evil because to do so would interfere with the easy flow of our lives can only serve as a dire warning.

However, I refuse to submit to the forecast that the universe will be sick forever, just as I have always hesitated to declare a mentally ill patient to be incurable. But who are the doctors who will come to heal such scourges as violence, torture, sadism, injustice, the glorification of the brute instinct, the deliberate indifference to massacres and even genocides? This phenomenon, graver than any mental illness, is perhaps the single major factor which threatens mankind's future.

That is why the *tsedek* remains, in my opinion, a psychiatric tool of primary importance. It has been studied in many countries, and many of my colleagues have used it to diagnose schizophrenia. Perhaps it should one day be employed to evaluate nations. Mankind's tormented history has its origins in social aggressiveness. Perhaps, one day, we shall arrive at a "science of peace," which Pierre Janet declared, on the eve of war, should henceforth be psychology's chief goal.

Why hasn't psychology yet come to grips with the problem? I believe it is because many of its leading figures wish to bar the door to philosophy and limit themselves to aping the methods of the natural sciences, physiology and biology, which in most cases they themselves are ignorant of, and which, in any event, could never wholly account for the phenomena that must be dealt with. It is impossible to understand man unless one understands this essential fact: that man is fundamentally a moral and physical whole, a fully rounded entity in which the body cannot be made exclusively subordinate to the soul, nor the soul to the body.

This notion is truly revolutionary. Those philosophers who emphasize man's spiritual nature maintain that the soul invariably predominates, while materialists claim that sovereignty for the body. I have found the idea of a balanced unity in man to be absent from all scientific and philosophic systems. The fact that this unity exists is the single most striking truth that I have derived from my life and my career.

CHAPTER
XIII

UNWARRANTED COMMITMENTS

PUBLIC OPINION IS HIGHLY SENSITIVE ON THE SUBJECT OF UNWARRANTED commitment to institutions. I can understand this very well, having spent a considerable part of my life fighting such commitments each time a flagrant case has come to my attention. The problem is agonizingly compounded by the fact that certain commitments, while not at all unwarranted, are still illegal.

A touchy problem, indeed, sometimes the public sets up a hue and cry on the strength of misguided investigations into the commitment of genuinely ill persons. In psychiatric hospitals there is no lack of assertive patients who claim they are being detained even though they are in the best physical and mental health. But then our prisons too are full of false innocents.

This is especially distressing since, under pressure from families, unfaithful husbands, impatient sons or daughters, there are a certain number of human beings, weakened by their situation and therefore manifesting disturbing symptoms, who are brought into institutions. It is all too easy to decide that they are affected by an illness justifying a prolonged and excessive confinement. Their life may hang in the balance.

How can such abuses exist? Sometimes it is enough to have the complicity, witting or not, of a doctor. At Charenton a young woman was sent to me on the strength of a certificate issued by a Paris doctor describing her as ill and dangerous.

It did not take me long to observe that Mme. T was in perfect health, suffering only from a certain nervousness which had come about with good reason; my inquiries provided me very quickly with the key to her situation.

Mme. T, it turned out, owned a garage and had married one of her mechanics, an act which had led to a conflict that had quickly assumed serious proportions. In marrying, she had in effect become her husband's boss. She had looked after the business part of running the garage, while he had been in charge of the workshop.

At first M. T had borne his dependence well; but in the long run he had come to feel humiliated. It is not unusual for men who feel inferior to their wives to compensate by reacting aggressively.

Quarrels ensued. M. T demanded to take over the complete running of the garage. Mme. T, who did not have unlimited confidence in her husband's administrative capabilities, refused. The tone of their disagreements became acrimonious. M. T threatened his wife; it is possible that he beat her. Mme. T decided to get a divorce.

Suddenly M. T had visions of himself out in the street, his new prosperity vanished. He became panicky. Among his customers was a doctor who was very cordial toward him, and M. T represented himself to this man as a victim. He assured the doctor that he was suffering terribly at the hands of Mme. T and that she must surely need psychiatric help.

"Write me a certificate, so she can be put into a mental hospital," he asked.

With unbelievable casualness, the doctor delivered an affidavit certifying that Mme. T needed urgent psychiatric care, even though he had never examined her and only knew her by sight.

After I released Mme. T from the hospital, she got her garage back—and her divorce. The doctor was investigated for flagrant malpractice, but I never learned of the outcome.

A similar story comes from the provinces, where a Catholic woman decided to become a Seventh-Day Adventist. Her husband, an uncompromising Catholic, forbade her to do so. She persisted; he made his rounds of the town where they lived claiming that she had gone mad. If proof was wanted, he pointed out that she was trying to change her religion. And in order to become what? An Adventist! Obviously she was insane.

He managed to stir up his friends, family, and others who shared his views. A doctor with whom he was friendly wrote him a certificate declaring that his wife had lost her mind. The poor woman was then thrust into an ambulance and transported to the local psychiatric hospital. The doctor in charge there kept her two weeks, then let her go.

Divorce proceedings were instituted. The court was asked to rule on the husband's contention that his wife was crazy and on his offering in evidence the fact that she wanted to change her religion. In a quite unprecedented move, the judges appointed psychiatric experts belonging to three different faiths—a Protestant, a Catholic, and a Jew—and this was how I happened, along with two of my colleagues, to examine the alleged madwoman.

We reached the unanimous conclusion that she was sane, and the end of this story turned out to be favorable on every count for the plaintiff. She won damages and got her divorce, and the imprudent doctor was censured for his part in the affair.

In the battle against abuses the psychiatrist faces a number of adversaries, the most redoubtable of whom is the family. The family is most often at the heart of the plot, the aim of which is either to be rid of a burdensome relative or to obtain his property. This is a universal evil: In every country doctors find themselves called on to defend the innocent.

One of the fiercest battles I ever fought had a Canadian background. In the face of the most concerted opposition imaginable, I defended a woman who might have spent the rest of her days in an asylum because her husband wished to be rid of her.

Mme. Y came from a devoutly Catholic background in Montreal. She bore eight children, five of whom died, which had a devastating effect on her. Some of her pregnancies had been very difficult, with the result that she was very often ill and needed much rest.

Well educated, she had helped her husband pass his examinations in mathematics and find a teaching position at the university. But gratitude had not been made a handmaiden to love; M. Y resented having a wife who was always sick in bed. He heedlessly forgot that his wife was thus paying off a debt in which he had a part.

While Mme. Y was in the hospital being treated for hemorrhages, M. Y consoled himself with another woman. He fell in love and took it into his head to get a divorce.

In the milieu to which the Ys belonged, divorce was not allowed. In order to conform to the rules of his religion, M. Y resorted to a rather complicated maneuver which would give him his liberty while not breaking with the Church.

First he obtained a civil divorce, then he applied to the archbishop.

"My wife is mentally incompetent and incapable of looking after our children," he pleaded.

To support his claims, he had found a psychiatrist who had written a report in which he described Mme. Y as suffering from a mental inadequacy for which there was no treatment. Misled by this document, and thinking only in terms of the children's interests, the archbishop annulled the marriage.

So there was M. Y, set free with the approval of both civil and ecclesiastical justice. He could remake his life as he pleased. Mme. Y meanwhile was separated from her children, rejected by the community and the world of free men, considered an incompetent of the first order, one might even say a moron, and relegated to the category of hapless souls incapable of the slightest intellectual effort.

Now she happened, as I have indicated, to be an extremely intelligent woman who had once been a fine student, and she had brought up her children very well. Her deep love for them gave her the impetus to fight, however handicapped she might be.

As soon as she had recovered some of her strength, she went straight to France, where two of her uncles lived. The first step in her "rehabilitation" was to try to overturn the judgment based on the psychiatrist's certificate.

She came to see me and I submitted her to a thorough examination, which turned out entirely in her favor. Mentally Mme. Y was perfectly normal, in no way retarded, in fact far above average. I could foresee a bitter struggle ahead and took every precaution, carrying her tests as far as possible. Another psychiatrist, Professor André Soulairac, also subjected her to a meticulous examination at Sainte-Anne. His diagnosis agreed with mine.

Armed with our affidavits, she returned to Montreal and undertook to secure a reversal of the rulings that had been handed down against her. In Montreal, Professor Ellenberger studied our reports, examined Mme. Y, and confirmed our findings. She got in touch with a number of political, religious, and judiciary figures in Montreal, most of whom agreed to help her; it now seemed that she would have no trouble winning her case.

But did she? The answer to this question is no, for in every country justice suffers from the same fault: It refuses to admit that it could have made a mistake or been unjust. Mme. Y did not win her appeal or even manage to see her children, two of whom were sick and suffering from their parents' separation.

When she came back to France she appeared to be desperate and on the verge of giving up. Certainly her predicament was not an easy one. She had against her the decisions of both Church and State. The more serious of the two was, of course, the annulment of her marriage by the Church. She consulted many priests and went to see Cardinal Daniélou, who on reviewing her case was outraged. Though the laws had been changed and the papacy no longer held its former powers, he attempted to intervene on her behalf in Rome. The Vatican replied that it could not easily interfere in an affair which was properly the business of the archbishop of Montreal.

I now took drastic measures. The authority of the Moreau de Tours Society is recognized throughout the world, and I presented Mme. Y's case before a session of this organization, which brought together twenty-nine persons, eight of whom were guests of the

Society—doctors, psychiatrists, jurists, lawyers, magistrates, and ecclesiastics, one of whom was a priest who specialized in problems of canonical law.

The meeting occupied an entire morning. For at least three or four hours the group interviewed Mme. Y. One fact was readily evident: She suffered from no mental illness whatsoever. She answered the many questions put to her calmly, precisely, and lucidly.

Only the members of the Society had a voice in the ultimate decision. When the vote was taken, out of twenty-one persons casting a ballot nineteen expressed indignation at Mme. Y's plight. Of the two abstentions, one was a Paris magistrate who explained his stand thus:

"I am very troubled. So far as the truth of the matter goes, I can only agree with you. But should a verdict that has been handed down be questioned? That's a very grave precedent to set. Believe me, it opens the door to many abuses."

I countered by declaring that a tribunal composed of fallible men might be expected to make an occasional mistake, and asked, if this were so, whether the seal of justice should be set on its error. Didn't the most elementary law of justice require that such an error be corrected?

As an illustration I asked whether Captain Dreyfus should have been left in prison merely to save the judges from dirtying their robes.

"If you thwart the court's authority," he answered, "you quickly come to more serious abuses."

Of course, to a degree, I can understand his reasoning, which is like that of many judges who believe that error can be found as easily on one side as on the other. In a trial, there is always a man who loses his case and contests the ruling, and whose arguments are not always negligible. To consider that a decision has no finality after the trial is over would amount to exposing justice to a whirlwind.

But even so, should victims of a flagrant error be sacrificed, as men in the old days used to be shot "as examples"?

((234   ))

I said with some asperity to this magistrate, "A court's moral authority is put to the test by how it deals with error."

I have always thought that the stubbornness of the judiciary and of governments had something monstrous about it. Dr. J. Guilhot and I once wrote a study on a new illness to which we gave the name of "bureaucratic psychallergy," a malady that affects subjects who come into conflict with the powers that be and are not able to make themselves heard. They run into insurmountable barriers, if not complete silence and utter contempt for them as citizens. They are inclined to revolt, and many become extremely neurotic.

Having spent my whole life working for the government, I have often been struck by this penchant for infallibility which affects certain bureaucrats who take themselves for God Almighty. In fact they go even further, for the Bible tells us that the Creator often revises His decisions, something the holder of the most minute portion of public authority would never risk, even if revolution fomented by outraged victims were raging at his gate.

A few days after we had taken our vote in the Moreau de Tours Society, I received a letter from the judge who had abstained, confessing that he was both embarrassed and unhappy at his failure to vote. It was too late. For my part I was delighted at the way the poll had gone, even with the two abstentions. A unanimous vote carries less weight than one composed of an overwhelming majority.

I wrote out and submitted for approval by the Society a motion containing the facts of the case and the following arguments in my patient's favor:

1. Mme. Y showed no mental deficiency, and her attitude before the Society was perfectly normal.

2. Mme. Y had never been notified of the reasons for the annulment of her marriage.

3. In a marriage where there have been eight pregnancies, one cannot claim that the union had not been consummated.

4. Neither could one say there had been no valid consent: At the time of her wedding Mme. Y had engaged in intellectual and spiritual

activities of a high level in Christian preparation for marriage.

5. It was impossible to understand what had been meant by "mental cruelty."

6. The expert opinions obtained in Paris, as well as the Society's own personal examination of Mme. Y, had convinced the Society of her complete mental soundness.

7. It was not possible that at the moment of her marriage she had had any physical shortcoming which she might have concealed from her husband. Her hemorrhages were the result of her pregnancies.

8. The Society was astonished that the Church and the court, in ruling against Mme. Y, had not requested a second opinion, and that Mme. Y had not been attended by a physician.

Therefore, the Society expressed its surprise at the turn of events and especially at the annulment of the religious marriage.

I have given the points of this motion at length, because it illustrates what hard work must be put into such a case. In psychiatry one cannot be satisfied with a medical evaluation, but must come to grips with the case in its entirety, must scrutinize the subject from every possible angle, almost rewrite his or her life. No chapter, no detail of his or her existence is irrelevant.

We sent our motion to the archbishop of Montreal, and set about appealing the court decision. At this juncture the poor woman, whom I had been giving all the moral support I possibly could, fell ill. Suffering first and foremost from being deprived of her children, she was under considerable strain and her resistance was lowered. She contracted chicken pox and had to be hospitalized.

She withstood this trial very poorly. In the hospital she had uncontrollable fits of weeping. The doctor who attended her made no effort to understand her problem, but sent her to a psychiatrist. The latter, equally ignorant of the situation, made no attempt to inform himself further. Mme. Y tried to tell this man her story, but it seemed to him too incredible not to be a fantasy. He classed Mme. Y as a "mythomaniac" and "neurotic," and by this labeling he reduced all we had accomplished to naught. A telephone call from me caused him to modify his position. She was given the treatment she needed and afterward was again free to pursue her goal, which by then was fortunately within reach.

Investigation into the family situation often solves our puzzles. For months at Charenton I had a sixty-one-year-old man under observation without being able to discern the reason for his illness. I gave him every care and still his condition remained stationary.

His wife came to see him regularly and showed him much affection. One day she asked to see me.

"Let him come home," she begged.

I answered her evasively. The fact was that I did not see her husband as a man capable of living outside our hospital walls without medical surveillance. He had been brought to me seriously exhausted from overwork, and after he had had a slight stroke followed by depression and hypochondria. This was the first time he had been hospitalized. His case went back many years and had resisted all treatment. Specialists spoke of him as suffering from senile dementia.

I put off my decision, and asked the wife to be patient. Soon afterward her husband showed some improvement, and since she still insisted that I let him go, I did so, but warned her that she should take certain precautions.

She did not have time to take my advice. Her husband had scarcely come home when he assaulted her; she was barely able to escape and call for help. He was quickly returned to Charenton.

On investigating this incident, I learned what I had not been told before, that our inmate had a sister. This sister had telephoned him as soon as he got home, and it had been directly after his conversation with her that he had had his crisis and attacked his wife.

Why had the wife never spoken to me of her sister-in-law? Why hadn't she told me of the relationship between this member of her husband's family and herself? Had it been reticence or had she underestimated the situation? The fact was that the sister, who had never married, hated her and constantly urged her brother to get a divorce and come live with her, where, she assured him, he would be much happier. Dominating sisters are not rare, and in cases where the subject is weak they are just as dangerous as possessive mothers.

It must be added that very strong motives of self-interest also contributed to this emotional conflict. The patient, suffering from overwork and vascular disorders, had been torn between his sister and his wife.

I sent for the sister and laid her responsibilities before her.

"If you continue in your present vein you'll succeed in accomplishing only one thing," I told her, "and that will be your brother's permanent hospitalization."

At first she protested. She was not the only one to blame; her brother's wife was far from perfect. She did not insist long, however; I was able to convince her that her sister-in-law was a loving and devoted wife. She promised to stop her machinations, and she was as good as her word. From that day on her brother's condition improved. He recovered, left us, and went back to a normal life with his wife.

CHAPTER

PATIENTS
WHO ARE ROBBED

FOR SOME TIME I CARED FOR A WOMAN IN HER FIFTIES WHO WAS SUF-fering from epileptic fits. She was on the road to recovery, and one day I announced to her that she would soon be able to leave. She was delighted and I no less so.

She was very wealthy and her return to society seemed to pose no problem. But scarcely had the news of her discharge reached her family than a request for its revocation arrived on my desk. Its source was my patient's nephew, and its aim was to deprive her of her civil rights. In other words, she would no longer have access to her money. Placed under guardianship, she would become legally incompetent.

The motive behind the nephew's request was baldly stated:

"My aunt leads a dissolute and extravagant life," the letter read, "and she must be protected from herself."

This was excessive vigilance. After all, everyone has the right to live as he wishes, if no one else is harmed, and can use his money as he sees fit if his excesses cause no hardship to his dependents. Besides, I had done some investigating of the subject, and the nephew's description of the life his aunt led was clearly exaggerated. Unmarried and a lover of the good life, she went out often, saw friends, and from time to time amused herself by going to have a drink in a nightclub. Nothing excessive, and certainly not indicative of insanity.

The nephew's request, proceeding from obvious motives, came as no surprise to me. As his aunt's doctor, I wrote out a certificate attesting that my patient's condition did not warrant her continued hospitalization, that she had recovered, and that on her release from the hospital she could resume her former activities without further medical surveillance.

The nephew was not discouraged, and the court was brought into the picture. As the law required at the time, the judges assigned to the case came in person to the hospital to examine the patient. At the end of an interview which lasted nearly four hours they concluded, as I had, that she was completely normal.

They dismissed the nephew's claim, found him guilty of attempting to rob his aunt of her money, and assessed him heavy damages.

This example illustrates extremely well the problem posed by the administration of patients' property. It is a delicate matter which has been the subject of an abundant literature. Thanks to the ruthlessness of many of my own patients' relatives, I have lived through enough adventures to fill many hair-raising novels.

The law has been changed and not, in my opinion, for the better. I wish to speak of this because the misappropriation of funds, like arbitrary commitments, is a universal ill. A discussion of the ways in which a poorly conceived law may favor the very abuses it had been intended to prevent will be of interest to the citizens of all countries.

A seriously ill mental patient is, of course, unable to manage his estate or even at times to retain possession of it. Therefore it is prudent to provide such a person with a guardian. Then, when recovery takes place, he will once again be able to take over his property, which will have been protected from the designs of his family and friends.

Because of the influence of Esquirol, the law of 1838 had a number of beneficial provisions. Its framers wisely avoided the legislation which in other countries provides that the patient be relieved of his rights, considered as a minor incapable of looking after his own interests, and assigned a guardian.

This is an excellent principle so far as its intentions go, but in practice, in certain exceptionally serious cases, the guardian is assigned too much authority over both the goods and the person of the individual declared to be incompetent. As far back as the last century French psychiatrists feared the possible excesses inherent in certifying insanity and made efforts to control and limit it.

In a famous letter which Esquirol wrote to the prefect of police, and which still applies today, he said that "mental illness is a malady, but it is also a misfortune, and it is very difficult to see why society should add to it still another hardship. If only we can provide for the safekeeping of the patient's property during his illness, that would suffice!"

His point was well taken. Under the law of 1838, the loss of rights could only be applied to a few exceptional cases. The suspension of rights therefore became quite rare. Carefully controlled, it was only applied to very gravely ill persons suffering, for example, from "imbecility, lunacy, or a permanent state of mania."

The courts took strict precautions lest an individual's loss of his prerogatives favor criminal interests. Judges were required to examine him carefully and to question him personally. The intention of the framers of the law was clear: An individual could not be deprived of his rights except in cases in which insanity was striking enough to be clear even to the eyes of those not advised of it in advance. It was this limitation which saved my patient who was threatened by her nephew.

On the other hand, for the majority of mentally ill persons committed to institutions there was, in the law of 1838, no provision for certifying them as insane or for relieving them of their property. Their estates were simply managed for the duration of their confinement by a provisional administrator who had an office in each psychiatric institution. The persons thus protected were not "incompetent" in the sense of the civil code, since they retained their rights, even that of voting. Of course most of them never went to the polls, but this was only because they were unable to leave the hospital. It was excellent for the morale of these persons not to be disenfranchised.

These provisional administrators were persons of absolute trustworthiness, either lawyers, notaries, or magistrates. There were, of course, some difficulties in appointing them, since they were not reimbursed, and this in some cases prevented gifted persons from serving. Still, those that I knew vigorously defended the patients for whom they were responsible. I remember a man whose wife energetically opposed his release. She received a handsome military pension in his name, had the free use of it, and was as a result very comfortable. If he were discharged, she would have found herself once again in the position of most women, that is, she would be obliged to share her income with her husband.

She opposed us for weeks, assuring us that we were mistaken in thinking our patient should be allowed to leave. The first thing the provisional administrator had to do was limit this woman's demands for money, for which she haggled endlessly. Then he searched for a way to break her opposition. We found the means in an article of the law of 1838, which provided for the appointment of a "personal guardian."

By this was meant a person charged with seeing that the patient's estate was used to his advantage and with working toward his release and his reintegration into society. In short, under this trusteeship, the protection would no longer be abstract and administrative, but performed on an individual basis. Our patient's sister, who was very devoted to her brother, had agreed to accept this responsibility, and he was released. The wife, kept at a distance by her sister-in-law, was obliged to accept the situation.

Several problems arose in applying this provision of the law of 1838. In particular, it became increasingly difficult to recruit administrators, not only because of the lack of remuneration but because the work became increasingly complex and time-consuming. Some study should certainly have been done in order to arrive at a reasonable compensation for the administrators.

Other changes might also have been made in the old law, and I spoke on the subject several times, proposing a specific reform, which I shall describe later, and pointing out parts of the law that

I believed should be kept and those that I thought ought to be changed. I failed to convince those offices of the Ministry which, in the aftermath of a very unpleasant incident, known as "the Toulouse affair," undertook a complete overhaul of the methods of administering patients' property. In the Toulouse scandal, the director of a psychiatric hospital tried—and very nearly succeeded in his attempt —to take over the apartment of a wealthy inmate.

The machinery of supervision had undoubtedly functioned badly. The hospital's overseers should have stopped the director short, but did not do so, through stupidity or negligence. Fortunately, the establishment's chief of service intervened and released the patient, who then took action to prevent the guilty officials from robbing her.

The press got hold of the story and the government panicked in its haste to act swiftly. Instead of reprimanding the overseers, who had failed in their duty, it fired the doctor who had redressed the wrong. In any hasty action it is most often an innocent person who pays.

The government did not appear to have been better advised when it prepared the new statute, which was voted into law on January 3, 1968. It is deplorable from every point of view. Instead of defending patients, it suppresses the guarantees formerly provided for in the text of 1838.

One can now evaluate it, since it has been in effect for several years and its results are public knowledge. I hope that foreign governments do not take it into their heads to copy it, for it has resulted in a highhanded attitude toward all those who throughout the country are in close contact with mental patients.

Putting someone under legal restraint is now done with the greatest of ease. The court has been stripped of its power of control. Any patient may be declared legally incompetent on the simple complaint of a member of the family presenting a medical certificate. In a first draft of the law, the author of such a document could have been any medical practitioner, but the text has been altered on this point. Now only a single magistrate, the judge in charge of guardianships and trusteeships, is competent to perform this office. This is a most troubling provision and as far removed as possible from the law of 1838, in which one used to see an entire court travel from one place to another for the purpose of questioning the patient.

From the outset, vociferous criticism of this change has been made by many jurists and physicians. They have especially pointed out that a patient who recovers continues to be deprived unfairly of his rights. Though it may seem unbelievable, nothing has been done to correct this text, and I have seen many instances of its terrible consequences, some of them quite recent. Some of my patients have found themselves unable to dispose of their property, even though I have testified that they were on the road to recovery and well fitted to manage their affairs. Instead they have remained in the hands of their guardian. It is bad enough when the guardian is honest and humane, but if he takes little interest in the welfare of his ward the latter may be reduced to penury with no possible means of correcting the situation.

It is unnecessary to emphasize that complicated and interminable legal action does nothing to restore the morale of the convalescents. Why has it been necessary to change the old system, where as soon as a patient left the hospital, he automatically got back all his rights? This is an administrative as well as a political mystery to me. It may be due to the fact that jurists often see only problems and not the individuals affected by them, just as some doctors give all their attention to the illness and none to the patient.

I am certain that there has rarely been such unanimity of feeling against the text of a law as there is against this one. I can point to the following organizations which categorically oppose it: the Medicopsychological Society, the Moreau de Tours Society, the Order of Physicians, the Academy of Ethical and Political Sciences. In the Senate, a few informed men succeeded in getting some useful changes voted. But the Chamber reinstated the law in its original pernicious wording. Today it causes incalculable harm.

* * *

I sound severe. But my remarks, I repeat, do not apply to France only. Every country in the world is prone to such mistakes. They are terribly serious, as I became convinced after an investigation I carried out with Commissioner Lesueur, who was general administrator of the properties of mental patients, and who devoted his life to this subject, at the behest of the Academy of Medicine. We queried doctors throughout France and the answers we received were extremely illuminating.

For example, there was the case reported by Dr. Mathey, chief of service of the psychiatric hospital at Angoulême, regarding the peasant whose farm was completely pillaged and whose animals were carried away during his hospitalization. What happens in such a case is that to obtain protection for the inmate's goods, that is, to declare the individual incompetent, requires at least from six to eight months. During that time, the property is under no care whatsoever. The peasant left the hospital at the end of eight months only to find that none of his belongings was left, and, as a crowning blow, that the period of legal guardianship was then over. He was not only ruined but was left with no means to defend himself.

Dr. Mathey also reported the case of a 73-year-old manic-depressive who had been hospitalized for melancholia. He received no visitors. It appeared that his wife was only preoccupied with getting control of a pension to which he was entitled. In order to protect his patient, Dr. Mathey requested that a legal guardian be appointed, and specified that under no circumstances was it to be his wife.

Nevertheless, his wife was appointed as trustee. Then what Dr. Mathey had feared might occur did indeed come to pass: From that day on, the patient was neglected completely and did not even receive pocket money. Before the law of 1968, the provisional administrator could have compelled the family to provide a small allowance, or else he himself could have administered the pension, which would then have been paid into a special account.

In Niort Dr. Burguet told us about a male patient, confined in the psychiatric hospital of the city, for whom guardianship was required. The procedure went on for a year, during which time the patient's brother "bought" real estate belonging to the patient, removed furnishings and linen from the premises, and helped himself to his money. When the guardianship was finally put into effect, nothing could be recovered.

At Agen Dr. Kugener told of a patient who arrived at the psychiatric hospital with a million old francs in his suitcase. The director of the hospital deposited this sum in a savings bank. When the patient was released, the bank refused to give him his money because the hospital and not he had made the deposit. Under the old law everything would have been easy: The director of the institution would have simply taken out the passbook in the name of the inmate.

Commissioner Lesueur summed up this preposterous situation admirably in his report:

> The management of property [he wrote] is now entrusted either to an officer of the psychiatric hospital, who has no special training, and who is remunerated; or to a guardian, chosen most often from among members of the family. Now twelve years of experience have put me in a position to say that most often the family seeks to profit from the patient's confinement in order to get as much out of him as they can.
>
> The law of 1838 stipulated, in article 38, that the guardian may not be chosen from among the presumptive heirs. Many patients are neglected by their families, and are never visited until the day when they come into an inheritance or are compensated for expropriated property, or when some other event of this nature occurs, at which time family interest springs to life.
>
> Moreover, the regulation of patients' leaves of absence, over which there is no legal control and which the new law does not touch on, presents extremely serious problems. The main object of giving an inmate a leave of absence is to determine whether he is ready to take his place again in society. Such leaves may last several months, during which time the individual may deal with a third party, who acts in

good faith, unaware of the patient's legal incompetence, and may injure him or be himself injured; or else the family may involve him in some transaction advantageous only to themselves. In his ignorance of these events, the administrator of the inmate's estate is powerless to correct their effects. When the patient returns to the hospial, it is too late.

Another questionable provision of this law is the lumping together of physical defects with mental shortcomings. A man who has a physical difficulty in making himself understood may be declared incompetent. Thus a patient who may have had a paralyzing stroke or who suffers from Parkinson's disease, or a blind man might be declared incompetent even though his other faculties are unaffected.

Vae Victis: This law is the faithful application of the famous Roman motto. The two Latin words came to my mind when a fellow physician, of great moral and intellectual endowment, who at the age of over seventy survived an incredible adventure, came to my office.

She had suffered a heart attack complicated by pleurisy, and had been utterly prostrated, when a relative had taken advantage of her condition in order to try to get hold of her property. This member of her family acted with great swiftness, asking that the sick woman be declared incompetent on the grounds that she was mentally debilitated.

She presented a vague medical certificate to the judge of guardianships. Fortunately, the patient marshaled the strength to get out of bed and take a taxi to my office. I examined her, found her extremely fatigued but mentally sound, and wrote out a clearly worded certificate. Meanwhile, the president of the council of physicians, who had been alerted, also prepared to defend our threatened colleague. What might have happened if she had not been a doctor and if she had not succeeded in reaching me? There is no doubt whatever that she would have lost her property.

Old people are particularly vulnerable. I rescued an eighty-year-old former engineer who possessed several properties in the south of

France. He sold one, and his son became worried that his father might be preparing to liquidate an inheritance which he—as he cynically expressed himself to me later on—was impatiently waiting to enjoy.

He sent the old man to a doctor, who in the space of a few seconds formed an opinion about the old fellow's mental acuity, and drafted a certificate to be sent to the judge in charge. It was urgently important, he wrote, that he be declared incompetent. Judging only on the basis of this evidence (the opposite of the old law, which required a personal visit from the judges), the magistrate agreed with the doctor, and the retired engineer found himself stripped of all his rights.

He came to see me. After repeated tests, I found that he had all his faculties. I gave him a certificate to this effect, and he went to court. He won his case and recovered the rights he had lost. At his age the worries and unhappiness caused by his son's attitude might well have killed him. Cases of this sort are becoming more numerous and occur in the wealthiest families; the multimillionaire owner of one of Paris's largest hotels was made the object of such an attempt on the part of a young niece whose greed was equaled only by her impatience!

I particularly deplore this legislative barbarism since until recent years France was considered to be a model among nations in this area. Foreign countries envied us, and colleagues, outraged at the abuses in their own countries, often told me they wished their governments would look to our system for their inspiration. Indeed, patients used to take refuge in France in order to enjoy the advantage of our laws and to escape the abuses of their own.

When Palestine was under British mandate, I received a visit from a man who found himself in a ridiculous position. He had been a patient in a psychiatric hospital, had recovered, and had been discharged. He had then decided to marry. As is now the case in our country, the legal restraints against persons who had been certified to be incompetent continued in his native land after their release.

My visitor had advised his guardian, who happened to be a woman, of his intention to marry.

"I don't like your fiancée," the custodian of his rights told him, and categorically refused to give her consent.

"I'm the one who's going to marry her," retorted the man, still under legal restraint.

But there was nothing he could do. His guardian would have none of the union. As a last resort, the former patient then came to France and consulted me. I reassured him that he had every right to marry whom he chose. He took my advice and was happy, against the will of his guardian.

In relation to the history of psychiatry in the last hundred years, it can be seen that what we have been discussing amounts to an unforgivable step backward. When I was at Charenton and could take advantage of that marvelous, now neglected library, I spent long days studying the evolution of the science to which I have devoted my life. What extraordinary teaching there was in the old days, and how those men could have given the lie to today's doctors who only seek to innovate, to ignore the past, and who live and act as if they had invented psychiatry.

Since the time of the Pinels and Esquirols, who left their mark so strongly on our science, our great concern has been to avoid arbitrariness in the administration of the rights of mental patients and to protect individual liberty. The law of 1838, so often attacked, was the product of this conception and reflected the great principles of the Revolution. Was not the taking of the Bastille the symbol of the end of arbitrary arrests, and particularly of the confinement of patients for life? Under the old regime it had been customary to lock up "undesirables," an example being the Marquis de Sade, who was incarcerated at Charenton not as a mental patient but for his sexual perversions, and because his talent for publicizing them had led authorities to fear he might corrupt public morals.

The chief of service at Charenton at that time was M. Royer-Collard, who many times protested against the confinement of his famous inmate, whose case seemed to him not to be psychiatric, especially since the marquis, who was remarkably intelligent, had ended by assuming great powers in the establishment and did as he pleased.

Since the success of the play *Marat-Sade* throughout the world, the public knows that the Marquis de Sade was the inspiration of Moreno's psychodrama, in which mental patients rid themselves of their complexes through their play-acting and the interaction which takes place between the performers and their audience. "The divine marquis," as he has been called, is given credit for founding the famous theater at Charenton, set up near the Marne; there he directed plays which were acted out by the hospital's inmates, who were often derided by the spectators. A series of unfortunate incidents gave rise to unfavorable publicity in an English medical journal, and the theater was suppressed.

To return to the law of 1838, I regret that it has been seen fit to alter the text, which needed only a certain number of corrections. In 1938, M. Benzimbra, of the Ministry of Health, and I studied desirable changes, one of which concerned the investigations conducted by magistrates of the circumstances of new commitments. These used to be carried out so conspicuously that the patient's neighbors and relatives could not fail to be aware of his commitment, with often unfortunate effects on his future. As members of a commission set up through the auspices of the Ministry of Health, M. Benzimbra and I composed an amendment providing for total confidentiality of investigations, which were to be entrusted not to the police but to caseworkers committed to secrecy. Our efforts resulted in a memorandum, and I had hopes that in this way we would gradually be able to modernize a law which we believed to be still efficacious.

A second success of ours provided for voluntary admissions free of charge for those who, because they hadn't the means, were unfairly committed by the courts. I remember that the first free voluntary admissions took place in the Maine-et-Loire at the instigation of my father when he was the head of the hospital of Sainte-Gemmes-sur-Loire. M. Benzimbra and I succeeded in making this procedure general throughout France.

I regret that we were unable to do more in bringing the law of 1838 up to date, especially as concerns the administration of inmates' property. I also deplore the practice of condemning psychiatric hospitals merely for the sake of making room for new methods, open wards, or new pavilions, to say nothing of antipsychiatry. This urge to follow fashion, this will to destroy what exists solely to make way for the new, finally accomplishes no more than is brought about by slow evolution. In psychiatry our first care is man, and upheaval and revolutionary change have the effect of turning him into an impotent guinea pig.

Therapeutic advances are precious in modern psychiatry. What seems to me to be dangerous is the haste with which the promoters of new treatments rush to put their creations into effect without sufficient study of the results. It is the patients who suffer.

CHAPTER

ILL-CONCEIVED
REFORMS

HOW DELIGHTFUL THE TERM "OPEN WARD" SOUNDS. IT EVOKES VISIONS
of an idyllic situation, of mental patients free from all constraint,
coming and going as they please, liberated from the chains in which
repressive psychiatrists have bound them and from the high walls of
hospitals behind which those ogres have detained them for the purpose of subjecting them to inhuman treatment. Sometimes, upon
reading the speeches or essays of young psychiatrists, or of those who
use the title without actually having the right to do so, I get the
impression that the struggle is between the wildest of revolution-
aries and those who believe in a quiet, measured evolution.

The facts of the case are quite different. The open ward, because
of the manner in which it was conceived and put into practice, has
led to contradictory abuses, that is, either to an excess of freedom or
to a return to inadmissible constraints. By a singular paradox, we
have reverted to the errors which were once deplored, in particular
the lack of respect for the patient in psychiatric hospitals, a serious
fault against which I have fought all my professional life.

A good example is an affair in which I became involved in 1971,
concerning a young girl of twenty, the daughter of a high government official. The case was the talk of the town for a long time.

The girl came to see me of her own accord, to ask my opinion
of her case. She told me that her life had been completely "messed
up," that her parents were concerned about her father's career and
that she had been turned over to the care of nurses and governesses.

"I never lacked for a thing—except the climate of affection I
wanted," she declared. "So I curled up in my own shell, or else I
struck up friendships, for instance, with a governess I liked a lot.

But at that moment my family took exception to this attachment, reproached me for it, and now we live in a disagreeable atmosphere of suspicion and distrust."

At the beginning of her adolescence, Mlle. R had suffered a fit of depression and had attempted to take her own life by swallowing sleeping pills. She had a brother and a sister but the sister was married and had left the family. But her brother, she informed me, had reacted differently.

"My brother rebelled and refused to be disciplined. They sent him to several psychiatrists, but nothing seemed to work. Then he was sent to an institution run by a man who used an unorthodox method of teaching that suited my brother perfectly. He passed his exams and started college."

It was this teacher who had led to the conflict between the girl and her parents. In fact, she trusted him and felt very comfortable with him. I met him later on and he impressed me favorably. His educational methods, which took account of the individual emotional needs of disturbed adolescents, bore scarcely any resemblance to those used in ordinary schools. He placed great stress on the art of living and on human relations. His institution was a sort of community in which love of one's neighbor and understanding were the rule, and the teachers he had gathered around him followed his precepts to the letter. Many people believed that he exercised too much influence over his students, so he became the object of an unfair campaign in the press. He was a foreigner, and, although he was doing no harm—on the contrary—he came near to being expelled from the country.

To return to my patient, she, like her brother, recovered her emotional balance under the tutelage of this man. However, instead of being pleased, her parents tried to force her to leave the school, where she wished to remain in order to study for a degree in English. Mme. R, who had been living abroad with her husband, returned to France and asked her daughter to come abroad with her. The argument between the two became extremely acrimonious. Finally the mother proposed to her daughter that she accompany her to consult a neurologist, to which Mlle. R agreed.

She told me that the neurologist had been very nice to her on that first visit and had promised to serve as a buffer between her and her parents. The girl remained in the school, waiting for the end of her mother's stay in France. Then her mother phoned to say good-bye and suggested that they meet at the neurologist's, as she wanted to bid him farewell also. Mlle. R believed that she had won her mother over to her view of things.

They met at the neurologist's office, where Mme. R declared that neither she nor the girl's father would permit her to remain at the school any longer.

The neurologist informed the girl that he had decided to keep her in his clinic since she obviously needed treatment. At that point, two nurses entered, grabbed both her arms, and forced her into another room, where they gave her an intravenous injection that caused her to lose consciousness.

When her schoolmates and teachers discovered what had happened, they asked the court to appoint experts to examine Mlle. R. This was done; the experts discovered that the girl had been given three doses of a mild narcotic drug and eight electroshock treatments, as well as powerful doses of tranquilizers, antidepressants, and barbiturates. They concluded that Mlle. R was not suffering from any psychopathology which could justify such drastic treatment. She was free to leave—the words being especially significant since she had been detained in an "open ward."

A minor, she was turned over to her mother, who forced her to accompany her abroad to join Mlle. R's father. Her friends at the school, including the director, launched a campaign in the press. The pros and cons were argued interminably, and, as I have said, the director was almost expelled from France. Meanwhile, Mlle. R came of age and returned to France and to the school, and the hullabaloo around the affair died down.

I can testify that she had at no time shown any pathological symptoms. It is possible that the bitter conflicts between her parents and her had led to some nervous trouble, but it had been absolutely unnecessary to hospitalize her forcibly, using a stratagem reminiscent of the worst instances of arbitrary commitment. It would have been better if the law of 1838 had been applied because then she would have been committed to a psychiatric institution where she would at least have benefited from certain guarantees.

My remarks may seem paradoxical, yet they are not. Mlle. R had been treated in an utterly arbitrary fashion. My colleague, the neurologist, may have believed that he was doing the right thing, but he had no right to practice forced therapy. This case has a bearing on a whole series of clinical and medicolegal problems, among which is the question of open wards, which, as I have demonstrated, can in practice become closed and secret wards. It is true that such a subversion of justice is an exception, just as arbitrary commitments were exceptions rather than the rule. But the absence of legislation regarding open wards can lead to abuses. Even if those abuses are rare, they prove that the system is not the miraculous answer that some persons would like it to be.

The loopholes in the law which allowed the foregoing unpleasant situation to develop may also work in the opposite manner. Because of them, dangerous persons have been released and have later committed crimes. The danger in an open ward is the fact that the patient is at the mercy of the good or ill will of his family and of his doctor. He cannot complain to the authorities, since no recourse has been provided for by law. The magistrates have no visiting rights; no document exists that can be offered in evidence, such as the certificate of commitment provided for in the law of 1838.

The above reflections do not apply to France alone. Open wards have been introduced in many countries. Legislation varies from country to country, but the idea is the same: Since the patient's freedom is the rule, it is unnecessary to bring it under regulation. This is a gross error. Whether a ward is open or closed, one cannot get around the fact that mental patients, even those suffering from little more than a simple neurosis, are more vulnerable than other people and must be protected against those who might take advantage of their weakness. It is no less important to protect them from themselves.

As an illustration, I remember the case of two unfortunate old women who were being treated in an open ward. They requested permission to go for a walk. No one paid the slightest attention to them. A few days later, they were found dead of hunger and exposure, having lost their way.

Freedom can also degenerate into license. This happens in certain psychiatric services where, under the pretext of ridding inmates of their obsessions, men and women are mixed together in utter promiscuity. Such services are deliberately turned into centers of debauchery, and those who express indignation at such a state of affairs are ridiculed as "reactionaries."

From the strictly medical point of view, one cannot even say that such a relaxed atmosphere actually helps the patient. Most mentally ill persons are afraid of life, and particularly of sexuality. It is therefore important to protect them from shocks they might receive when plunged into a climate of eroticism. I have always found it best to proceed gently with ill persons, guiding them little by little toward the view that sexual reality is one of the more pleasurable factors of our life. If there is one area of psychiatry where prudence is advisable, this is it.

The fundamental idea behind the system of open wards, however, does have its uses. One of the first open wards was, I believe, founded by my father in Angers, at the end of the First World War. As soon as I was able to do so, I created one at Charenton.

In my opinion, Charenton became a model institution for the treatment of the mentally ill. When I left, the premises had been modernized, and I had put into effect a system composed of three interrelated parts.

I personally took charge of an outpatient service in neurology and psychiatry, to which patients came from other Paris hospitals and from all over France. Among them were men and women who had formerly been inpatients. This service functioned like a real clinic. It gave me a fine opportunity to follow the progress of my old patients, though I exercised no policelike supervision over them. They were completely at liberty to come to see me or not. This was far removed from the repression which those who believe that psychiatry in itself is not valid criticize rather vaguely in speaking of the "horrors" of the past.

The second part of the system at Charenton consisted of the closed ward provided for in the law of 1838. The inmates could be of two types: court-ordered inpatients who came to us through public agencies, or voluntary admissions (patients whose commitments had been requested by themselves, their families, or an intermediary acting in their interest). It was my policy to increase the number of voluntary commitments and to curtail court-ordered ones.

In practice, voluntary admission was very elastic. Hospitalization stopped automatically on the day the person who had requested it so desired. Unless there was a special therapy or medication problem, the patient was given leaves of absence, the only requirement being that he ask his physician's permission. Leaves were obviously not conferred on those patients who belonged to the involuntary admissions group, as they could leave the premises only on the express authority of the police.

During my stay at Charenton, I made every effort to give the closed ward the most liberal character possible. The name itself conjures up visions of restraints, and I realize that in some places this impression matches the fact. But I had grown up in the shadow of my father, who opposed arbitrary constraints, and, as I admired him profoundly, I tried to follow in his footsteps.

I took care to endow Charenton with the most complete up-to-date equipment, allowing for medical treatment, psychotherapy, and reeducation and rehabilitation of every kind. One of the best methods of restoring men's minds is to keep them occupied and thus give them a goal in life.

With the help of my friend Dr. Douady, a member of the Academy of Medicine, and with the cooperation of the Ministry of Education, I was able to get teachers to come to Charenton and give lessons in literature, history, art, languages, and geography, so that the inmates were not only kept busy but received an education as well.

We also set up an arts and crafts department. A Swiss friend from Basel provided us with a kiln to make china and pottery. Later on, we added a studio in which decorative objects made by the patients were put on display. I persuaded an artist who was under treatment at Charenton to teach the patients painting and drawing. The works of art which were produced served to give the place a less severe appearance. The patients enjoyed ornamenting their rooms, an activity which was of great help to them in surmounting their troubles. We also had organized sessions in gymnastics, dance, and music, which again did the patients much good.

And so Charenton, as you can see, was far from being a prison. The wards had become lively and attractive. These leisure activities were not forced on the patients, who were free to choose those most suitable to their tastes and talents or, in some cases, to opt for doing nothing at all.

Last of all, we had the open ward, which sprang naturally out of the needs of the times. Besides those patients suffering from major mental illnesses, there were ever-growing numbers of neurotic and depressed persons whom it was not necessary to confine. Admission to our open ward was the same as admission to an ordinary hospital.

This creation, which seemed to mark an evolution toward a more liberal practice of psychiatry, did not come about without a jolt or two. From the beginning, many psychiatrists feared that initiative on the part of mental patients was too dangerous, and they immediately spoke of the risks inherent in the project, which seemed to them to be greater than any possible benefits. They were not entirely wrong, of course. They asked what guarantees patients admitted to an open ward would have against a doctor who might attempt to detain them by force, and also who would protect their property.

There was, therefore, much heated controversy when the first open wards were introduced. At the start, I was in favor of open wards, though I was not unaware of the dangers. As early as 1932, when I had wanted to create one at Charenton, I had sent a letter to the Minister of Public Health, informing him of my feelings. Then, with the help of Inspector General Raynier, I was permitted to go ahead with my project. I regret that our theories are still not generally applied today, for if they were, open wards would be successful everywhere.

As a first principle for success, an open ward must be truly open. The patient must be able to come and go as he wishes, even if the doctor does not agree that he should. He should also be allowed to look after his affairs and manage his property as he sees fit, without benefit of a guardian or an administrator.

But this complete freedom can work only if there is a very strict selection of patients, so that those who are too disturbed are not admitted. It is obviously absurd to permit a suicidal man suffering from depression or a murderous man suffering from a persecution complex to enter an open ward. All patients who need supervision must be confined.

At Charenton, the open ward was made up of patients suffering from minor ailments: neuroses, migraines, neuralgia, simple nervous or neurological disorders. And I can state that our vigilance produced excellent results.

Through the years another conception has unfortunately come into being, advocated chiefly by Professor Heuyer, who had claimed that open wards should accept all comers and treat acute as well as other psychiatric cases. According to him, psychiatric hospitals were meant for the chronically ill who need treatment over a long period of time; in his view, it is not the illness which is the criterion to be used for deciding whether to lock up a patient or to care for him in the open ward, but the length of time required to treat him. Professor Heuyer would like open wards to become the norm for treatment of most illnesses and the closed ward to be a sort of depository for chronic cases. His name for this arrangement is "psychiatric assistance on two levels."

I opposed Professor Heuyer's idea, but my opinion was ignored. What happened was easy to predict. Since gravely ill persons were being admitted to the open wards, it became necessary to keep them there by force, a contradiction of the fundamental principle on which the system itself had been predicated.

Today the law is still silent on the subject of open wards, in which a patient may be shut up as in a psychiatric hospital without, however, any certificate of commitment. The majority of doctors are undoubtedly careful to see that there are no abuses. I am sure that arbitrary action is the exception. Nevertheless, it is not healthy, in my opinion, for the law to ignore a system which can allow members of the patient's family, motivated by questionable goals, to perpetrate new versions of abuses formerly deplored in connection with commitments. This is all the more regrettable in that the term "open ward" gives the illusion of being something else. The public cannot imagine that in such a service patients can be restrained against their will, since the term itself appears to be a guarantee of the contrary.

In 1965, I brought this problem to the attention of the Academy of Medicine, and a commission was set up to study it. As a result, on July 27 of that year a memorandum containing the following passage was sent to the government:

> The Academy deems it necessary that there be legislation passed on open wards in order that said wards be reserved for patients able to control their behavior; that these wards not become secretly closed wards in actual fact; that the patients may not, as in an ordinary hospital, be detained against their wishes; that control via judicial authority be exercised in this regard.
>
> That in cases where an individual is shown to have dangerous

tendencies, he be transferred to a protected service; that in open wards the use of security rooms be rigorously forbidden, except in cases of extreme necessity; that the same be true of the forcible use of therapeutics, restraining apparatus, or any form of physical or mental coercion.

That emergency medical service and house calls become the general rule; that a control of emergency psychiatric services in general hospitals be provided, with a maximum observation period of fifteen days designated.

The above recommendations were based on common sense, but they failed to impress the Ministry of Health. Every reform that saw the light of day was oriented in a very different direction.

It is the fashion today to denigrate psychiatric hospitals. It is true that a certain number of such institutions are unable to render the services expected of them because of lack of sufficient funds. There is cause to fear the future deterioration of this public service because of obsolescence of equipment and installations and difficulty in recruiting qualified personnel. Certain asylums have furnished ample material for an abundant literature describing the dilapidation of premises, the anachronism of some of the routines, the crowding, the insufficiency of medical care. There is truth in all such criticism, but the tide could be turned by modernizing such mental institutions as I did at Charenton.

There was a time when many psychiatric hospitals were renovated. Before the war two men, Inspector General Raynier and the adviser to the Minister of Public Health, Dr. Lauzier, did much laudable work in this direction. Under their influence, modern pavilions were designed, built, and equipped, services were liberalized, improvements in therapy were instituted, and the general ambience was improved. This is the direction we should have taken rather than wantonly jettisoning everything.

There are many who have charged that shortage of help and the difficulty of recruiting qualified personnel compromised the principle on which the hospitals were created. But contrary to what one might think, too many employees can spoil the quality of mental care. On the medical level, I insist that the doctor in charge must see to everything himself. That is why I always campaigned so strongly against the idea of having a crew of assistant doctors, who in my opinion hindered the chief more than they helped him. They became a screen between the patients and the man who finally bore the responsibility for their fate.

It is important to understand that in mental illness, more than in any other malady, the patient's future may depend on the attitude of the doctor who has charge of him. The physician does not act for the ill person, but he does guide him step by step. It is impossible for the doctor, who bears such responsibility, to fulfill his duty without knowing the subject intimately, through studying him closely and personally keeping abreast of his development.

It is the physician's duty to see his patients as often as possible and to make contact with their families so as to understand the milieu in which they have lived and to which they will eventually return. At the same time, he must supervise his staff closely, keep on good terms with them, carefully control the treatments given, and watch over the morale of patients and staff. Such a task is difficult and dangerous to delegate.

"In the hands of an able doctor, an insane asylum is an instrument of recovery," wrote Esquirol. His observation is still true today, which is why I remain an advocate of the renovated psychiatric hospital. If such hospitals are done away with, a fearsome breach will be opened in the wall that protects not only society but mental patients themselves.

I have heard supposedly qualified persons state that a psychiatric hospital is nothing more than a prison for the permanently rejected. If in some cases this is true, it is only because the system has been totally distorted in the institutions referred to in such a remark. And this is so throughout the world.

That is why I resigned from the Association of Psychiatric Hospitals when that organization requested a change in the status of chiefs of service. This reform was put into effect, with devastating results for the hospitals and their inmates. The chief of service, stripped of official status and no longer required to live on the premises, appointed to his post as an ordinary doctor, now comes to the hospital for his consultations and then leaves. No matter how conscientious and professionally competent he is, it is impossible for him to organize his service, to oversee and provide the best care for his patients. He now depends on assistants who share the duties among themselves, while he supervises from afar, without having the intimate knowledge of what is going on in his service that his predecessors had when their lives were consecrated to their work at the hospital.

Everything has been done to give the chief of service a feeling of impermanence. There is an administrative commission in each establishment which may, for diverse reasons, revoke his contract and send him away. The ties between the staff, the patients, and the chief of service have been broken by this new system.

I have an idea that the new method will fail and that we will one day return to renovated psychiatric hospitals. When one reads certain texts dating from the last century, their striking application to today's problems becomes evident.

Several years ago, I had a lively discussion on a radio program with Professor Michel Foucault, who, though not a doctor, was an enthusiastic student of the history of psychiatry. He did not believe in psychiatric hospitals and declared that they were responsible for locking up patients who should have been permitted to go about freely and indulge in their normal occupations. I replied with a few historical facts:

"You say that you want patients to live freely in society. Do you know what it was like before the advent of psychiatric hospitals, which used to be called lunatic asylums? The mentally ill were the object of appalling mistreatment. They used to be arbitrarily confined; they were beaten, robbed, reduced to abject misery and ridicule. People would laugh at them, children would make fun of them, and they became the buffoons of the street or the neighborhood. It was a reaction against this situation that led Pinel to propose the creation of true 'asylums' for them."

Is the world today so different from that world that the mentally ill can really be integrated into society without being forced to suffer for their freedom? I wish that I could be such an optimist. But I believe that as long as human nature remains what it is, it is better to place mentally ill persons in a protected environment.

Pinel himself was quite aware of the risks involved in creating such institutions. In his treatise on insanity, published in 1809, he wrote:

> The administration of a home for lunatics amounts to a small government in which one can see, as in the government of a country, vanity and ambition pulling in different directions; the result is tumultuous conflicts of authority which are continual sources of trouble and discord. . . .
>
> It is obvious that the director of an institution for the insane exercises a powerful influence. If he is a man who is crude and of limited perceptions, he allows beatings and the most barbarous treatment of inmates by the staff. The wise and enlightened man, on the other hand, works on principles of the purest philanthropy, chooses his personnel well, and restrains them by severe discipline. He views his patients' maniacal explosions as nothing more than automatic impulses, or rather the necessary effects of nervous excitement, against which neither he nor his staff should feel any more indignation than they would at the impact of a stone obeying the laws of gravity.

Pinel understood perfectly that great firmness must be added to inexhaustible kindness when dealing with mental patients:

> I have seen the happy effects of gentle ways, of a courageous and strong determination free of all acrimony or anger and full of respect for the rights of mankind, as well as of a steady opposition to the obsessive ideas and inflexible stubbornness of some insane persons.

Scarcely less than a decade later, in 1818, Esquirol published a report which led to an inquiry into the conditions of the mentally ill throughout France. At that time, most such persons were kept at home or placed in ordinary hospitals, a very small number of them being placed in asylums approved by Pinel.

> I saw them naked and in rags [wrote Esquirol] with only straw to protect them from the damp cold of the stone floor on which they lay. I saw them fed as animals are, deprived of air to breathe, water to quench their thirst.
> I saw them at the mercy of the brutish ministrations of veritable jailers. I saw them in narrow, filthy, unsanitary, airless, lightless holes, chained in foul dens, into which one would hesitate to consign the wild animals that governments maintain so luxuriously in the major cities.

It was precisely in order to remedy this scandalous situation that mental hospitals were created, subject to the supervision of public authority, that is, of special commissioners, and strictly controlled. The doctors were government officials and therefore responsible for legal guarantees. Only under these conditions is it possible for the system to work.

Under the influence of the powerful movement against confinement, inspired in large part by the work of Professor Foucault, the unit system of mental health care has come into being. The idea is to assure treatment and prevention of mental illness at home, avoiding commitment as much as possible. Before going any further, I should like to say that this could be a good system, provided it were not given blanket application and were perfectly organized. But this has not been the case; far from it.

During my stay at Charenton, where I was aided by dedicated social workers, I did not stop caring for "free" patients in my outpatient clinic. My goal was to help them so that they could be saved from institutionalization, and often I succeeded.

But that was not the spirit in which the new system was conceived. A rigorous administrative arrangement has been substituted for the old system, and I can only qualify it as bureaucratic and impersonal. Every territory is divided into sectors. Each hospital can receive patients only from its own sector. Thus, the ill person and his family are deprived of a free choice of doctor. Moreover, office consultations are compulsory, which makes the system resemble the judicial supervision of offenders on probation.

Add to this the fact that the district unit is most often run by the psychiatric hospital's chief of service, who must not only watch over the functioning of his institution but also over the clinic where the patients come for their consultations. This is a heavy work load and the result is that the unfortunate man is spread too thin.

I have been consulted by patients who have turned to me after being treated within this system. I do not claim that it has produced only failures, but the examples I have seen have helped me to put a finger on the dangers of the method, which can take on the aspect of police harassment.

One day I received a telephone call from a young man who was quite brilliant, and whom I had formerly treated for simple depression. He was about to take an important civil service examination, but first he wanted to talk with me. He specified that he was coming with a social worker.

When I heard his story, I was astonished, then disgusted. The caseworker intended to warn the examiners who were to grade the young man that he had been a mental patient. He had learned of this and had persuaded his would-be denouncer to agree to come with him to see me. I asked the young woman why she was interfering in this way. Her answer was rather vague. She spoke of her duty, the need to protect society, et cetera.

I brought up the question of professional confidentiality and tried to scare her. I pointed out that she was taking a great responsibility on herself, that she would be harming a boy who was perfectly sound and that through a misconception of her duties she was likely to cause irremediable damage.

She agreed not to inform the board of examiners. The young man passed his examination and did distinguished work in his field. He remained in perfect health, married, and had two children. Every New Year, without fail, he sent me a long letter expressing his good wishes and his gratitude. If I had not persuaded his caseworker that he was perfectly healthy and in effect frightened her a bit, he would never have been passed by his examiners, despite his obvious intelligence.

Of course, most caseworkers are very conscientious and devote themselves wholly to their work. But in addition to their legal and administrative training, they should be given a social and moral education to equip them properly for their task.

Here is another example of a caseworker's overstepping her bounds. An Iranian student whom I was treating for a depression similar to that of the patient I have just discussed lived in a student hostel in the Latin Quarter. I do not know what got into the social worker assigned to his case, but she went to his hostel and told the people in charge that he had mental problems. They asked him to leave, and he was unable to get another room since she had made the rounds of all the hostels with her ill-informed message.

Meanwhile, the young man's father arrived from Iran. He fell madly in love with his son's girl friend and tried to seduce her. The young people were both indignant. Outraged at his failure, the father tried to take his son back to Iran with him. The boy refused and, supported by his girl, started proceedings against his father. Finally, by I know not what trick, the Iranian succeeded in getting his son to Orly airport and aboard an airplane. I have learned, and this will surprise no one, that the unfortunate young man is now in a psychiatric hospital.

As for the caseworker, who was primarily responsible for this affair, she was steeped in her administrative training and believed she was invested with police powers. Instead of taking a humble attitude toward her work, the caseworker had made it an instrument of repression and bureaucratic surveillance.

The social workers I knew in the past were quite different. They did not have the advantage of their younger sisters' training, nor the benefit of a statute which made them untouchable. But their attitude, the quality of their feelings, their tact and understanding made them friends of the patients they worked with. Social workers should bear in mind that they must not resort too quickly to the administrative solution, or believe that by placing the subject in the hands of a public service one has solved the problem. It may at times be a harmful choice.

In short, the complaint I have against the sectorization method of caring for the mentally ill is that the administrative mind has replaced the heart. The method might have succeeded if it had been carried out on the basis of trust. Even more than in hospitals, home care requires a "psychotherapy of open arms." I know that the least relaxation of the giving of oneself, the slightest bending, can lead to catastrophe. One of the most painful failures of my career was linked to this problem.

The victim was an unfortunate woman, Mme. S, whose family had been decimated in the concentration camps. She had been so wounded by life that she had a profound distaste for the mere fact of being alive. She lived in a permanent state of depression, punctuated by periods of insane excitement, during each of which she had been hospitalized. She was called a "schizophrenic," and it was taken for granted that she would never get well.

She had married, but finding marriage difficult had obtained a divorce. She was given custody of her small daughter. Soon afterward, she began to show symptoms of mental problems. Each time she became too excited or too depressed, the authorities in her sector contented themselves with institutionalizing her. Finally the administrative mechanism, with its fearsome efficiency, placed the daughter in a child-care service. The child's father, profiting from his wife's situation, attempted to gain custody of his daughter.

I cannot deny the logic of the system, but it did not take into account the important fact that the little girl was Mme. S's only tie to life. Instead of trying to sever this link, there should have been an attempt to strengthen it and use it as an instrument for Mme. S's recovery.

The action I took was based on this view of the situation. I wrote affidavits for the court, got in touch with the lawyers involved in the case as well as the judges, and succeeded in making an impression on them. They permitted Mme. S to keep her child, and I took responsibility for the consequences.

I kept Mme. S under my wing for months. I convinced her that she was not a schizophrenic. She began to work. Her improvement was uneven but noticeable, and the child began to grow up in rather good, stable conditions. I was certain that with the help of the medication that I was giving her, Mme. S would make a complete recovery.

Then came the blow. Mme. S had serious financial reverses in the business she had started and became profoundly discouraged, disgusted with everything. We were back where we had started. My wife and I went to see her a number of times. She had said she was thinking of killing herself but we succeeded in dissuading her. But to her financial worries were added a concern for her daughter, who had returned from summer camp in poor health. Mme. S's demands on me became incessant. Since she lived relatively far away, she telephoned continually, even at night. In the end, I could not cope with the burden, and I was delighted when she suggested that she might go to the district clinic.

I telephoned to the doctor in charge, who answered me very pleasantly and promised to do everything in his power to help Mme. S. I became concerned when, after several months, she began to telephone me once again. I called the doctor and asked him to check on her more closely. I was especially uneasy about the child as I was responsible for having helped her mother retain custody over her. The doctors from her clinic had gone to see Mme. S and had found her very well. Though they told me not to worry, I spent several sleepless nights.

Several days after they had been to see her, I received a call from the police station in Mme. S's neighborhood. They informed me that she had jumped from a tenth-floor window and had been killed instantly. Her daughter was safe and sound.

To this day I still feel remorse, because I might have saved her. I had behaved more as an administrator than as a doctor. One must be untiringly diligent in caring for mental patients. Every hour of the day and night is important. I wonder if that is possible in a unit system of mental health care, in which an attempt is made to keep watch over a whole district of the city, with its extremely varied sorts of patients, some of whom should actually be committed.

For example, today we have the terrible drug problem. It is doubtful that this scourge can be controlled through the district-care system. Some persons have proposed that it can be, but I am not convinced, and nothing I have observed has led me to change my mind.

I became involved in the case of a former high official, now retired, who was gravely afflicted with diabetes and suffered agonizing pains in his legs. A doctor finally prescribed a pain-killer that worked, a synthetic analgesic, more powerful than morphine, which he used and abused, perhaps procuring some of it without his doctor's prescription.

He was summoned to appear at the clinic in his sector. Since he was too tired to move, his wife went in his stead. She was told that her husband was addicted to drugs and would have to be hospitalized. She indignantly replied that her husband was seriously ill. They did not listen to her at the clinic. She had a clash with one doctor partial to the new methods who questioned her like a psychoanalyst. He asked her why she stayed with her husband and did not seem to understand that she was old-fashioned enough to believe that loyalty was one form of conjugal love. To him, this notion was passé. It ran counter to personal interest, to the liberation of the self.

Disgusted by her experience at the clinic, she came to me. I wrote out a clearly worded certificate, with the result that the administration desisted from pursuing her husband, whose case did not merit such extraordinary surveillance or enforced hospitalization.

I have another example which is, in a sense, the exact opposite of the foregoing one. I treated a young woman who had had a fairly checkered career. For many years, she had been the mistress of a rich married man by whom she had borne two children. Their father gave his two sons hardly any attention, and she herself was frequently absent. Absorbed in her liaison, worried about losing her lover, traumatized by the bad situation in which she found herself, she eventually became depressed enough to require hospitalization.

When the woman became my patient, I urged her to assume her responsibilities as a mother, showing her that this would help her to recover her mental stability. As soon as she was well enough to do so, she took her two sons in hand. Unfortunately it was too late. The boys had become bitter and violent, their aggressiveness manifesting itself especially toward their mother, who they felt had neglected them. One of the boys left home and never returned; the other took to drugs, especially LSD and hashish. He attached himself to a group of young drug users and supported himself by peddling the products he used.

Sometimes he would reappear at home, looking extremely emaciated, completely worn out, but still rebellious. One day he announced that he planned to go to the East Indies where he might die, and that that would be the best thing that could happen. The frightened mother made the rounds of the organizations that handled the problems of young drug users. They all told her that her son must come himself and of his own accord. She came to me for help, and I turned to the district clinic. Here too we received the same answer: Drug users who did not ask for help themselves must be left to their vice. It is fortunate that this policy is not pursued with the mentally ill. In any case, here was a second instance of my attempt to work with the district system that came to naught. The boy left home and continued to take drugs in ever-increasing doses.

It is certain that the means put at the disposal of the district were miserly. Also, the theory was that by emptying the psychiatric hospitals of patients who came under the jurisdiction of the sector, progress was being made and the system was being shown to its best advantage.

I must reiterate that hounding ill persons in their homes or summoning them to appear for consultations can give the appearance of being a police action and consequently arouse fear in the patient. There must be trust, and in order for that trust to exist those working with the mentally ill must demonstrate respect and dedication. Trust cannot be extorted through the use of clever tricks, but is won by proving that those who wish to treat the ill are humanitarian and sincere.

Psychiatry is an "affair of the heart," or, to use the words of Saadia, the great Jewish theologian of the ninth century, "a leap of the heart tempered by intelligence." A great psychiatrist, Dr. Parchappe, said in 1862 at the dedication of a statue of Esquirol, that asylums for the insane must be protective shelters for human suffering, and that the warmth of the heart must be added to scientific knowledge in order to comfort the deranged.

I can assure you that the great majority of chiefs of service in psychiatric hospitals have loved the insane in the past and were dedicated to helping them. Fortunately people of that caliber still exist; some of my students are among them. We must listen to them when they decry the errors committed in a science which neither man nor society can do without.

CHAPTER

THE ROLE
OF THE FAMILY

I HAVE CRITICIZED SOME OF THE MISTAKES MADE IN THE ORGANIZATION of the open wards and the unit system of mental health care, which in France and abroad has complemented or extended the sphere of the psychiatric hospitals. I am not attached to the old ideas per se but I do find it regrettable that the useful parts of the old system should be ignored or destroyed.

Psychiatry is a whole which cannot be pulled to pieces with impunity. Mental illness takes many forms and cannot be reduced to one type of affliction, amenable to a single mode of treatment. This is why the ideal mental health service consists in a harmonious combination of the different useful procedures perfected by our science. I have often been among the first to use new disciplines; I know of no single one that could replace all the others.

I have already spoken a great deal about the family and the role it must play in the treatment of the patient. I have never treated a man or a woman without knowing well the milieu he or she has lived in. I have often arranged confrontations between my patients and their families in order to observe the reactions on both sides. Some of these sessions have been upsetting, and some stormy, and have left me with extraordinary memories. I regret that today's doctors do not make a systematic study of their patients' backgrounds, but leave this task to caseworkers who merely fill in questionnaires.

This is in no way comparable to the direct contact of the doctor himself with his patient's parents, spouse, acquaintances. It has always seemed to me important to obtain the greatest possible amount of information on how my patient's illness began and what incidents preceded it. I have always established with each family a complete curriculum vitae, including not only physical details but emotional, psychological, and social ones, from the subject's day of birth until the moment he arrived in my office.

I look for the hereditary sources of his illness, and I examine the character of each family member, the individual's own education, the habits, peculiarities, beliefs, or convictions current in his milieu, his way of life, his special joys and disappointments.

I have usually tried to involve the family in the therapy; often it can play a decisive role in the patient's eventual readjustment. Now, families will not always agree to help. Some are models of devotion, while others have only one idea, which is to rob the unfortunate person of his property or to keep him confined.

Should we go as far as Canada has and create a corps of doctors who specialize in the treatment of the family? I don't think so. Such a division of work, in my opinion, leads only to inefficiency. I can never insist enough on the indivisible nature of psychiatry. It cannot be carved up among specialists in this or that field, who pull in opposite directions, leading the patient first right and then left. Only one man must deal with the patient. The psychiatrist must be a trained medical doctor who, when face to face with his subject, has at his fingertips all the data of general medicine. If he is not, psychiatry falls into confusion.

The physician must be absolutely impartial in the research he undertakes with his patient and his patient's intimates. There are psychiatrists who automatically take the part of the family or that of the patient. This is a serious mistake, for each case is different. If it is true that some families wish to be rid of their relative, there are also patients who tyrannize and martyrize their family and friends. It is not only paranoiacs for whom slanderous accusations form an integral part of their illness. As Adler discovered, persons suffering from an inferiority complex can fall into this category too.

One of my patients, a man of forty-nine, of a frail, sickly constitution and markedly tubercular, suffered from a progressive, deforming ankylosis, or stiffening of the joints, which made him almost an invalid, unable to pursue any activity. He savagely accused his family of being the cause of his misfortune. The following passage from a composition he wrote on the subject will give the reader an idea:

> Whereas I formally accuse my family of murder, and am prepared to stand by said accusation before whomsoever . . .
>
> Whereas I have experienced nothing except unpleasantness through having a father, a mother, sisters, a brother, who have never made it possible for me to derive any good or pleasure from the relationship . . .
>
> Whereas these almost monstrous, ridiculous creatures, molded of folly, vanity, conceit, spinelessness, and selfishness, certain of whom believe themselves adorned with beautiful halos which no one perceives save themselves, have in a cowardly fashion exploited my greatness of soul, my courage, my magnanimity, my tact, my pride . . .
>
> Whereas I myself was one of those creatures marked by destiny, hardworking, honest, proud, brave, little given to vanity, simple, possessed of ideals of beauty, justice, perfection, and greatness, born with the awareness of a mission to accomplish, I declare without boasting or false modesty that few men would have been capable of making the superhuman effort I have, given the conditions in which I have struggled . . .
>
> Whereas this superhuman effort will bear no fruit, since a great force has been destroyed, and a great voice silenced . . .

This is all I shall cite of my patient's libelous opus, which ends with a demand for money and a threat of scandal; in this mixture of pride and blackmail one sees the compensation reaction.

Such responses, due to humiliation and a sense of inferiority, are frequent, as I have stressed, in persons of low intelligence. Contrary to what is too often believed, the problem of working with such people is not simply to measure their deficiencies through testing but to remember that an awkward revelation of their shortcomings humiliates them and inspires in them a desire for revenge.

An example is the feebleminded young man who, in retaliation for an unfortunate remark made by his employer, stole the latter's cash box. The following morning, after his boss had spent a sleepless night, the boy brought the cash box back. Another illustration is seen in cases of arson where the fire was set by children.

Often, however, these weak-minded individuals exhibit exceptional gifts in very limited fields, and these can be put to use in their treatment.

Another family problem consists at times in correcting misunderstandings or wrong attitudes on the part of the family members, as happened with Mme. B.

The wife of a doctor, Mme. B was afflicted by manic-depressive psychosis. Whenever she had an attack her husband sent her to a mental hospital, where she was given either electroshock treatments or medication—those famous "medicinal cocktails" whose evil I have mentioned.

In time Mme. B came to dread her hospitalization. She began to look on her husband, who sent her to such painful and perfectly ineffective therapy, as her "public executioner." She began to hate him and he became part of her nightmare.

Meanwhile, she met a childhood friend who was in the midst of a divorce. After several meetings this man began to exploit the situation. He listened to Mme. B sympathetically, encouraged her to blame her husband for her condition, persuaded her that with him she would find support, help, and affection, and ended by asking her to leave her home and children and come live with him.

Mme. B agreed, and divorce proceedings were begun. Her children were upset and angry at her desertion. A tempest raged in the entire family. Mme. B herself, caught between her new love and the real attachment she felt for her husband and children, and fearful of the therapy she had been subjected to, was not exactly supremely happy.

My first observations after being called in on this case were pessimistic. A once united home appeared to be in ruins, and I saw that psychotherapy would not be enough to effect a lasting cure of Mme. B. It would be necessary to rebuild a suitable frame for her life.

I interviewed separately all the persons involved: the patient, her husband, their children (one of whom, a daughter, was studying medicine), and the lover. In interviews, some of which were not easy, I brought them face to face with each other.

"I believe that you have subjected your wife to treatments which only did her harm," I told the husband.

Such a judgment on my part represented an affront to him not only as a husband but as a doctor. I tried to make my point cautiously. There were other methods besides electroshock or the forcible administration of drugs, I remarked. Perhaps he had not sufficiently taken into consideration the factor of trust, which could work miracles. He had instead succeeded in frightening his wife and making her more refractory about the treatments.

"You might try letting her be treated at home," I proposed and indicated to him what could be done under the circumstances, proceeding, for example, with graduated medication, which would shorten the manic periods and prevent the return of the depressive states linked to them. In the end, he agreed that I was right.

I reasoned along the same lines with Mme. B.

"You'll never have to go back to a mental hospital," I reassured her. "I'll take care of you. We'll keep in touch by telephone."

The children continued to be very upset. They resented their mother, the medical student especially. I explained to them that what happened had only been an accident, and that soon their lives would return to normal.

I tried very gently to persuade Mme. B's lover that he was engaged in an impossible adventure. After initial hostility, he agreed to hear me out.

"Are you aware of the harm you're doing? And for what?" I asked him.

I assured him that he could never make Mme. B happy because

she would always suffer from guilt at having broken up her home and set her own children against her. I saw that the man sincerely loved Mme. B. He acknowledged that there would always be a shadow between them, and at last he agreed to give her up.

I telephoned the lawyer who was handling the divorce and got him to set the proceedings aside. The husband promised me that he would take no further professional interest in his wife's health, but would leave this to me. A few weeks later Mme. B returned home to be welcomed with joy, with no second thoughts, at least none that anyone could detect on the surface, by her husband and children. Little by little, with treatment, and above all because she had regained her trust in life, her condition improved. Soon she found her equilibrium.

The road to peace seemed clear, but it was necessary to remain on it. Once again, however, quarrels erupted, accompanied by threats to return Mme. B to a mental hospital; the husband had decided after all not to follow my advice. He turned his wife over to her old doctors and that was the last I heard of her.

In the above story, one can see the patience and energy that are required in the comprehensive therapy I advocate, and the ease with which setbacks can occur. The method will not work if the mental patient is not treated first and foremost as a highly sensitive human being.

In psychiatry abuses can take many forms. The development of private ambulance services has led to real kidnappings. A young girl was spirited off in this way to Charenton by her mother, although her condition in no way warranted hospitalization. I of course sent her away again, and at the same time warned the police to be on the lookout for similar attempts in other hospitals.

It should not be possible to commit a person to a psychiatric institution without a house call and an extensive, competent medical examination. Most abductions are engineered by pretending to the patient that he is being conveyed to the hospital for an examination. Now, the very fact that he has been transported by force like a suspect can influence young and inexperienced doctors. Uncertain of their responsibilities, they may decide they risk less by admitting the patient, or so-called patient, than by refusing to accept him. In this way they set in motion a mechanism which, once started, is often difficult to stop.

Family authoritarianism may also lead to tragic mistakes, especially if exercised over persons torn between contradictory influences. I remember a ten-year-old boy I cared for years ago, who, even at that age, had a rich and promising nature. What became of him? Alas, I regret bitterly that I do not know.

He was brought to me with the diagnosis of aftereffects of encephalitis, following diphtheria. He had an absent air about him, was utterly withdrawn, and was interested in nothing. He answered questions with great reluctance.

His parents were in the midst of getting a divorce and I looked for the reasons for their break, which I was sure had played a part in the child's condition, even independently of any pathological origin. It turned out that their troubles had their roots in a serious ideological conflict.

The mother was a fervent believer in the exact sciences and was at heart a communist. She was fiercely opposed to anything that had to do with human affections. She was a devotee of absolute rationalism, and it was in this spirit that she had attempted to raise her son.

The father, sensitive and affectionate, belonged to an old rabbinical family which also included famous actors and musicians. The boy resembled him and, young as he was, appeared to have inherited from his Hebraic antecedents strong notions of right and wrong, and of good and evil.

His vivid awareness of moral values had the most irritating effect upon his mother, who disciplined him severely and constantly pressured him to "be hard," with results that were the opposite of what she hoped. This was when the doctors decided that he had infantile encephalopathy, or chronic inflammation of the encephalon (the brain), a diagnosis to which I did not subscribe.

In the course of my investigation, I made the acquaintance of a relative of the child on his father's side, a very famous actress of whom the little boy was very fond, and I suggested that custody be awarded to this young woman. Experts appointed by the court agreed with me.

After three months of living with his guardian, the change in the child was miraculous. He became active again and recovered all his faculties for contact with his fellows. He blossomed and was beginning to make amazing progress in music. I believed that I had saved him.

But the mother, who had fought to get the court's findings reversed and had failed to do so, kidnapped the child and took him out of France. I have heard that he relapsed into a state of stupor. He had not been really ill, however. All he needed to make him a boy "like the others" was a little understanding and love.

Have these two words any meaning at all today? Throughout the world books appear which analyze in scholarly fashion the malaise from which civilized man suffers. Most of them offer purely technical judgments and forget the human being. Their solutions are despairing and deprive mankind of what he needs most: hope and joy.

Since it is clear that men no longer feel responsible for one another, the government has stepped in and taken in hand the unfortunate, the disinherited, the weak, the uneducated, all those who are unable to defend themselves—and it has done so according to its own bureaucratic logic. It has set rules and applies them evenly to everyone it helps; its rules regulate their lives and often class them forever as "handicapped." I do not deny the good intentions that lie behind all this, but what is lacking is the vital human element and the irreplaceable moral atmosphere which it creates.

I remember a poor woman who lived alone with her two children. She had a heart attack and was rushed to the hospital, leaving the children behind. Faced with the problem of the children, her neighbors reacted in a fashion which can only be called selfish; instead of taking turns caring for them, they alerted the public services, which carried them off to an orphanage.

On her release from the hospital, the mother could not find her children. None of her neighbors could tell her what had become of them. At the town hall she was sent from office to office. In her distress and in her convalescent condition, she lost her temper with an employee and insulted him. He accused her of being a mental case. She was promptly committed to a psychiatric institution and had a very difficult time getting free again.

In addition to a study of the patient's family, social psychiatry involves a consideration of what is very nearly of equal importance: his occupational background. How many of today's neuroses have their origins in the difficulties and anxieties encountered in one's work! Fear of unemployment proceeds from more than financial reasons. The unemployed man waiting to find a problematical job feels useless, purposeless, diminished, looked down on and scorned by society. He lives in a state of constant humiliation.

The unemployed, above all those of a certain level of mental development, are comparable—I simplify, of course—to the boy who at Charenton set a fire in a cellar. One day employees saw thick smoke coming out of a basement, hurried down, and found a young feebleminded boy, whom they snatched from the flames.

"Why did you do that?" they asked.

"Because they made fun of me!" he answered.

I decided to give this boy an important job in the hospital, receiving and introducing the people who came to see me.

"Greet them politely," I told him, "then come and announce them to me."

He acquitted himself marvelously in his duties. He was transformed—calm, smiling, eager to please.

"What miracle cure did you use?" his parents asked me.

"Confidence," I answered.

The boy believed in himself because I had believed in him. I had made up for the injustice done him by those who had not taken him seriously. In their work, men wish to be treated in the same way: with dignity.

An old man had worked all his life in the field of electricity and central heating. He was a real old-time workingman who loved his trade and put in his time without counting the hours. When his boss retired, a successor moved in with his own crew and the old man was laid off.

Not knowing how to fend for himself, he found himself out of work, and he began to despair. He went to his former employer to ask for help, if only in the form of a testimonial as to his value as a worker. This man, though friendly, made not the slightest effort in his favor.

The reluctant retiree then fell into a depression which brought him to me. Rather than give him stereotyped treatments, I undertook to restore his confidence. I turned myself into an employment bureau, for this was the crux of his problem. He needed someone to stand up for him, to take his part, to help him solve the real difficulty, which was his enforced idleness and his feeling of being worth nothing, for he had been a man who had lived only for his work.

It is because of cases like this that I have always been against the idea of making retirement the goal of life. To give a man the assurance that he will have something to live on when the time comes is of course necessary. To assure him of rest when his strength wanes is an elementary duty of society. But I have seen too many examples of the dangers of forced retirement. There are men who cannot bear inaction, and die of it. Others, without apparent reason, see their faculties declining, while if they had kept on working at the job they were used to they might have remained in full possession of their abilities.

I have given much thought to the fate of old people, psychiatric problems being among the hardest posed by geriatrics, that is, the practice of medicine for the aged. With today's longer life spans the situations of old people afflicted with disorders of the nervous system and especially with mental troubles are often dramatic, and many mistakes are made concerning them.

At Charenton, I set up a section for psychiatric gerontology with admirably dedicated staff who saw to the smallest hygienic and mental needs of these patients, who are often infirm and desperate, and who are prone to painful urinary and rectal problems, and innumerable other miseries!

Ill old people are too often the subjects of an unacknowledged ostracism. Mentally debilitated or merely physically enfeebled, they find it increasingly difficult to secure places in institutions which suit their needs. Hospitals refuse to take them in, nursing homes discharge them as quickly as possible, homes for the aged prefer to accept only those who have retained all their mental faculties. Undoubtedly they make difficult residents, but the real motive comes from what has been stated as a truism, that the aged ill are definitely lost, that they can neither recover nor improve.

Now, it so happens that this idea is perfectly erroneous. More often than is believed old people suffer from acute or temporary psychoses, which exhibit the same characteristics as disorders observed in the young. With suitable treatment, these stages can be made to disappear quite well. One forgets the frequency of confused states in the aged and too often tends to take them for states of dementia. There then occurs the same deplorable phenomenon as in cases of schizophrenia. Some doctors see the latter affliction in every disturbed young person, while others have only to find themselves in the company of an old person who is a bit irrational to diagnose him as a victim of senile dementia. And the damning is just as categorical.

There was the sixty-eight-year-old man whose case I followed for months, who suffered from mental problems subsequent to prostatic hypertrophy (enlarged prostate), for which he had been treated with testosterone. His symptoms were abnormal sexual excitement, excessive euphoria, and flights of fancy, followed by periods of collapse, in which he fell silent, rarely answered questions put to him, had difficulty in remembering, and was disoriented in time and space.

"Incurable senile dementia," several doctors declared.

I began his treatment with tonic restoratives, after which I installed him in a house in the country and limited his case to correcting slight circulatory and hepatorenal (liver and kidney) insufficiencies. After six months he showed improvement. He gradually recovered his health and his mental functions. Soon his return to normal was complete, though he had been categorically declared to be incurable.

All that happened before the war. The terrible events which we lived through did not spare my patient, who knew many hard times, yet he had no relapse whatsoever. Until his death, many years later, he remained mentally sound.

The tragedy of old age is that even when dementia is real and very serious, patients retain an emotional awareness, "a consciousness of the heart," as Scipion Pinel called it, which is unsuspected and extremely strong.

An example can be seen in a patient who was brought to the hospital apparently totally unaware of and indifferent to his family and his surroundings. He seemed not to suffer from this transfer, yet scarcely had his family departed than he began, while declaring that he was still at home, to weep. From the intellectual point of view he had not known that he had been moved. On the emotional level, he realized that he was in the hospital and suffered because of this.

Aged patients are very sensitive to the reactions of those around them. In fact, one of the clearest marks of nervous and mental disorders in old age consists in keeping up a "front" and of maintaining outward appearances. Psychoses in young people and schizophrenic changes, even if they do not affect intellectual functions, are accompanied by behavioral lapses, whereas the greatest deteriorations of old age, loss of memory and intellectual functions, are accompanied by heroic efforts to preserve a facade, to hide as much as possible from one's family and acquaintances the organism's decline. This effort is intended not only to conceal the troubles from the eyes of others but to keep them hidden from the subject himself, so that he not feel them more cruelly. It becomes the doctor's responsibility not to violate nature, but to use tact and sympathy to prevent the patient from feeling that he has become merely an object for study.

If it is indispensable in psychiatric hospitals to set aside special wards for old people, it is harmful to separate the infirm from the able-bodied. The best way of combating senility is to attempt to wake the mind and to maintain emotional awareness. A gerontological ward demands, more than any other, an atmosphere of optimism and activity. It is, moreover, very important to be careful that the staff, in the interest of ensuring their own peace, do not misuse tranquilizers, that is, that they do not substitute massive medication for the small attentions the condition of the aged requires. Such a practice leads quickly in these subjects to befuddlement, sleep, then coma, with the appearance of bedsores, and death.

No group of patients requires more therapeutic attention than the aged. One of the most serious problems is bedsores, an ulceration of tissue at pressure points, at the sacrum, heels, and buttocks, which may spread to the bones and become infected. A sensational discovery was made by Professor Lefèvre, a research scientist for the National Center for Scientific Research, who established the efficacy of certain algae of the genus *Cyanophyceae* (i.e., *Myxophyceae*) in curing bedsores. In a comprehensive study I made of the effect of extracts of these algae, I saw seriously affected patients, running a fever, completely cured.

Not all the patients in a service for psychiatric geriatrics are sad. Some are full of life, love to sing, and look forward to and enjoy diversions. At Charenton, many of our active old patients took classes in painting, watched television, attended musical gatherings and dances, and even went to the theater; in good weather they also enjoyed automobile excursions.

Nothing favors senility more than the creation of rooms reserved for those suffering from it. Those who are least affected let themselves go; decline, aided and abetted by contagion, sets in immediately. At the end of the last century Archambault abolished such wards at Charenton and observed a consequent decrease in this progressive weakening. I have followed his example.

Restoration, through the agency of the family, of work or of any other activity, and of a framework of life for patients, is not only social psychiatry's aim but is the best means of effecting cures. It is a part of our arsenal for combating dementia, neuroses, and psychoses. In my field, medical treatment is not always enough, and I regret that too many of my colleagues limit themselves to its use, seeming to consider mental illness to consist of no other factors than physical ailments. Troubles of the mind require not only the use of drugs, but also psychological and social support. The psychiatrist heals not only by the administration of medication, but by his very presence, his words, his sympathy, the confidence he inspires and instills. He encourages his patient to regain the friendship or the love of those around him, and to feel useful through his work.

In short, he takes charge not only of the patient but of the man or woman before him. He seeks to restore not only the patient's lost stability, but his reasons for existing. Psychiatry, more than any other branch of medicine, is the study of the person as an indivisible whole. It is also an expression of one form of the fundamental sympathy which unites mankind.

CHAPTER

XVII

TOWARD SERVING
THE WHOLE MAN

FROM THE WINDOW OF MY APARTMENT STUDY I CAN SEE THE PLACE
where I spent thirty-seven years of my life, the celebrated Maison
de Charenton. I retired in 1968. Charenton was originally called
l'Établissement national de bienfaisance de Saint-Maurice. Actually,
today its name is the Hôpital Esquirol.

At the farewell ceremony I was, as you can imagine, deeply moved.
The head of the staff of the Minister of Health, a famous professor
at the Faculty of Medicine, reviewed the high points of my career,
gave me a handsome medal, and asked me this question:

"How did you accomplish the miracle of restoring an institution
which no one believed to be viable any longer?"

I smiled and replied, "I didn't work the miracle. All I did was
apply the rules for examining evidence that are in the Hebrew
writings. All I did was learn Hebrew!"

I have not slowed down my activities. In fact, I have the impression that I am busier than ever. I have profited from my freedom
to travel, accepting, a little belatedly, invitations I had put off.
I have given courses throughout the world and have participated
in psychiatric conferences. I have been able to visit the United States
and Canada, and I have lectured in New York, Chicago, Washing-
ton, Montreal, and other cities. I have visited my students, now
scattered throughout the various European countries, especially England. These have been fruitful encounters for me and have helped
me to gauge the present state of psychiatry.

I still hold consultations at Saint-Antoine and at Sainte-Anne
hospitals. I continue to keep up my private practice, and without
respite I pursue my scientific work, publishing new books and

papers on my own research and on the evolution of psychiatry, which until now I did not have the time to do. I also continue my Hebrew studies.

What I miss most of all is the laboratory I founded at Charenton which, for administrative reasons that are difficult to understand, is no longer in use. But an identical installation, which has been given the name of the Baruk Institute, was inaugurated in Tel Aviv in the fall of 1972. I confess that this event flattered my ego, but the physical distance of the new laboratory from France is regrettable, even though I frequently return to Israel.

The Institute, which I have tried to endow and to which, after my retirement from Charenton, I sent some of the apparatus which had belonged to me personally, is directed by Professor Czerniak, a great doctor who was trained in France at the medical school at Montpellier. He has created in Israel a center for the technical study of nuclear medicine, including radiation, and especially the use of isotopes in diagnosing disorders of the nervous system.

I was of course present at the inauguration ceremony, which was held in the open air at the Tel Hashomer Hospital on a terribly hot day. Such distinguished persons as the rector of the university, Professor Simonsohn, and the director general of the Ministry of Health, Professor Padé, were present and gave speeches. In my reply I described all that the Institute might look forward to accomplishing and expressed the wish that the work in experimental psychiatry on animals which was begun in my laboratory at Charenton, the first in France and perhaps in Europe to study the physiology and psychology of primates, be continued.

I have also done a good deal of historical research, including writing a book on the history of French psychiatry, and I have given many lectures on this subject in different countries, especially in England. My colleagues in that country have the greatest respect for Esquirol and Pinel, but during my professional visits to Great Britain I never once heard mention of the works of modern Frenchmen.* I have attempted to make up for this lack by inviting Englishmen to visit us at the Moreau de Tours Society and by giving lectures in London and in other British cities. This is, however, a long-range project which one man cannot accomplish alone.

It cannot be denied that French psychiatry has lost the dominant position it once occupied. It is not that the science itself has fallen off in our country, for we still have great men, but we no longer have the collective power of a united group that we formerly possessed. Individual jealousies have led to attempts to destroy what existed, and the resulting negative effect has ended in our present loss of prestige.

Psychiatry in France also suffers from the decline of French as an international language, a role which has been taken over by English. A British doctor, Dr. Patterson, came to the Moreau de Tours Society at my request, and afterward invited me in turn to London where he and I dined with Dr. Slater, director of the *British Journal of Psychiatry*. After listening to me talk about schizophrenia, Patterson said, "Write an article on that. It will be published in English and read everywhere."

This promise was not kept, as the English at the time were dominated by an absolute attachment to the doctrine of schizophrenia and were opposed to all criticism and all reform.

I have experienced my greatest joys in Israel. Since 1946 I have made a dozen trips there, each as fruitful as the last, each one a real pilgrimage to that land so imbued with Jewish prophecy, which has contributed so much to mankind. In 1946 M. Mani, a Jerusalem pharmacist, and I made a trip to Hebron to see the tombs of the Patriarchs, where Abraham's moral revolution began. We arrived in a dark, wild town, to be welcomed, the moment we set foot near the famous cave of Machpelah, by a hail of rocks. If our guide had not had the idea of throwing piasters at our assailants we would

---

* Fortunately, a work on psychiatry as practiced on the Continent has very recently appeared in London.

have been stoned to death. While they scrambled to gather up the money we had time to race back to our automobile and flee for our lives.

Twenty years later, after the Six-Day War in 1967, I again went to Hebron with my wife and some cousins, the Benyakov family, who lived in Jerusalem. At the tomb of Abraham on the morning we went there the Israeli soldier on guard duty told us it would be impossible for us to see the famous site early in the day, since mornings were reserved for the Muslims, and the afternoons were reserved for members of other religions. An Arab who was present and understood Hebrew, seeing our disappointment, suggested that the guard ask the Arab authorities to make an exception for us, since we were going back to Paris that same evening. Soon the Israeli returned with the Arab chief, who allowed us to visit the tombs of Abraham, Isaac, and Jacob, of Sarah, Rebecca, and Leah.

In the course of these trips I was present at one of the most extraordinary sessions I have had the privilege of attending, in the chief rabbinate of Tel Aviv.

At that time one of my former patients, Mme. H, whom I had successfully treated at Charenton for manic depression, was in Israel. She had settled there and married. One Sabbath eve shortly after her marriage, when her family had come together for the holy occasion, her husband suddenly declared, "I forgot something, I'll be right back," got up, left the room and never returned. From his new residence he asked Mme. H for a divorce. He then took advantage of her resulting depression to inform the court and the public agencies that his wife was mentally ill and that since she lived alone the best thing would be to put her in a hospital.

Mme. H was hospitalized in a psychiatric ward and the divorce proceedings began. The judges questioned the doctors, one of whom, a woman, gave it as her opinion that Mme. H was "schizophrenic." This was a stroke of good luck for the husband, who pleaded that he could not stay married to an incurable mental patient.

I was then in Paris and was asked to send a certificate, which of course I agreed to do, to Mme. H's lawyers. But the husband's lawyer objected.

"How do we really know it was Professor Baruk who wrote this certificate? His signature must be confirmed by the chief rabbinate in Paris."

The chief rabbi sent an affidavit. The lawyer then raised a new objection.

"The court can't render a verdict if it doesn't hear Professor Baruk's arguments in person."

It so happened that I was going to Israel to lecture, and so one morning soon afterward I set off for the chief rabbinate of Tel Aviv, where judges, rabbis, and lawyers were assembled in a large room. I was given a warm welcome and the chief rabbi, a man with a majestic, flowing beard, who was acting as judge, said:

"Explain to us, Doctor, what is meant by schizophrenia. The truth is that we do not know much about it. The doctors tell us that Madame H is schizophrenic, but you say she is not. Where does the truth lie?"

I found myself facing the rather difficult problem of making Mme. H's case understandable to that gathering. The fact was that she had at one time been mistakenly treated for insulin shock; the treatment leaves small cerebral lesions and produces aftereffects. In Mme. H the latter were manifested by a phenomenon which had all the earmarks of delirium; she heard a small voice whispering in her ear. An uninformed person might easily have decided she was mad, although Mme. H knew very well that what she heard was an illusion and not reality.

I had against me the opinions of the doctors who, because of this voice, had concluded that she was schizophrenic. In order to make clear the difference between this illness and Mme. H's minor disorder I drew a comparison familiar to my audience.

"Sir, I remind you that in the Talmud the *batkol* is also a *small voice*," I said, "but it too has nothing to do with psychosis."

I explained that this phenomenon, which is well known to mystics, represented the materialization, in the form of a voice, of their contact with God. Unless one decided that mysticism amounted to schizophrenia, it is hard to confuse the two. The judges seemed surprised that I should know the *batkol* so well. My allusion, which transcended the realm of the purely medical, won their confidence.

By a happy chance I had been present a short while before my departure from Paris at a lecture given by one of the most brilliant men in German psychiatry, Dr. Poliakov, holder of the chair at the University of Münster. He had declared, to my great satisfaction, that our German colleagues were then giving up the exaggerated notions held by Dr. Kraepelin (of whom I have spoken) on the subject of dementia praecox and schizophrenia, and were rallying entirely to my point of view.

The judges of the chief rabbinate listened to me with great attention. They asked me for the dates of Mme. H's hospitalization, which I promised to send when I returned to Paris. Upon my return home, I took advantage of the opportunity provided by having to execute this small chore to write a long report in Hebrew on the basic difference between schizophrenia and periodic disorders.

Unfortunately Mme. H's family, under pressure from the lawyer for the other side, would not allow the information to be used, and as a result she lost the case.

Since my retirement I have had more time to participate in the learned societies to which I belong. But a tendency is appearing which troubles me: the opposition of certain persons to free discussion.

This is intellectual terrorism in its methods and its goal, which is to impose one's own ideas on others by force.

Only a little while ago, no one in the scientific world would have dreamed of acting otherwise than Pasteur did when he announced his discoveries. He appeared with his theories before the Academy of Medicine, listened to and answered his critics—some of whom were very hard on him—and was obliged to make new experiments. In the end he emerged victorious from the pitiless joust. Real progress is made in this way, for with thorough discussion no aspect of the problem is left in the shade.

But today's new theorists dislike appearing before learned societies, as if to do so were an attack on their talents and their knowledge. Their presumption adds nothing to their stature; on the contrary. When I was president of the Medicopsychological Society, I urged the advocates of revolutionary ideas to come and discuss their theories freely.

"We may not agree with you," I told them, "but you will be heard. And perhaps you will convince us that your theories will make a contribution to science."

I succeeded in getting the antipsychiatrists to air their views before the Moreau de Tours Society. The discussion was sharp, but at least it took place. Others failed to answer our invitation. They prefer to affirm, to proclaim, to be dogmatic, without having to come face to face with their opposition. This is an attitude completely devoid of any scientific spirit.

One of their favorite moves is to address themselves to the press, which too often falls into the trap they have set for it. Newspapers and television are chiefly interested in novelty, and so they accept new ideas right away, without discussion. Then pressure groups are formed, and public opinion exerts influence on public agencies. This is far from the prudence that should govern such delicate subjects.

Next, in a hasty response to the public's impatience, laws are passed without study or deliberation. This is a dangerous phenomenon. It happens daily and it can destroy all that is worthwhile in our society. It suffices for a pressure group to clamor loudly enough that such-and-such an aspect of our legislation, or of our customs, is "repressive" for it to be abandoned and replaced by a system which more often than not is merely improvised.

One typical result is that in psychiatry today the patient has no means whatever of protecting himself against the excesses to which his troubles may expose him. We have passed from a freedom which allows the doctor to intervene, and which I believe in, to an absolute freedom in which the patient is left utterly to his own devices. We will see the day when it will be claimed that one may not interfere with a man who wishes to commit suicide or murder.

During a meeting of the administrative board of a hospital I am connected with, I learned that the custom of keeping the patients in at night so they can rest has been given up. They may come and go as they please, around the clock. Some of them return drunk. Others return armed with knives and even with revolvers.

In regard to euthanasia, how can one not be alarmed at the news that forty scholars, of whom several are Nobel laureates, have issued a statement to the world in which they advocate mercy killing? I could not contain my indignation. I immediately contacted the Academy of Medicine and got in touch with numerous friends who I knew were, like myself, absolutely attached to the life principle. The result was an official resolution against the statement. For me a fundamental tenet of our profession was in question: A doctor should never in any way contribute to the death of a patient.

Persons who advocate euthanasia speak of "pity" and "charity" and of "delivering the sufferer from his agony." What is such a sentiment worth? I refer the reader to the Bible, where the word *hesed* or *charity*, is always used in conjunction with the term *emet*, which means *truth*. The two cannot be employed separately. Charity cannot bring peace unless it is accompanied by rigorous investigation; the *tsedek* as I have practiced it is not a vague religion but a real science.

Can a patient be judged on the basis of his outward appearance or on a superficial interpretation of his condition? Are we capable of gauging the hidden force that lives within him? Who shall dare to decree that he shall have no more chance to live?

At the Academy of Medicine, my friend Professor Gutmann has reported the case of a patient who was practically in a coma. An X ray of his lungs showed that he had cancer, and, since he was no longer taking nourishment, his doctors believed that the cancer had spread to his stomach. Professor Gutmann, a specialist in diseases of the stomach, was consulted.

The patient had made an agreement with his wife and son-in-law, a colonel, that in case the doctors decided to give him up, they were to end his life. The poison and the syringe had been made ready.

"Let me take him home," the wife pleaded with Professor Gutmann. "I gave him my word."

Gutmann asked for a few days in which to observe the patient. Before the observation period was over, the doomed man vomited up two liters of liquid. This appeared to relieve him considerably. He then began to eat again, and to speak. He improved steadily. A new X ray of his lungs showed no trace of cancer. What he had suffered from was a virus pneumonia that had caused pressure on his stomach. He left the hospital a well man, an escapee from the imprudent contract he had entered into with his wife.

Nothing is more fragile than a diagnosis of a fatal condition, above all a diagnosis of cancer. At Charenton I had as a patient an inmate who, according to the most eminent specialists, had cancer of the tonsils.

"We'll have to operate," they said.

"Out of the question," answered the inmate.

I respected his wishes, although I had high regard for my colleagues and believed they were right. Now, as if by a miracle, the tumor melted away. I sent the patient back to the specialists who had diagnosed it; they were incredulous. My so-called madman had seen more clearly than his doctors!

A physician without faith is like a general who believes he will lose. He courts defeat. It is not he who pays, however; a doctor who thinks he will fail shatters the confidence of others. I saw an example of this in the wonderful mother of a fourteen-year-old son suffering from infantile encephalopathy. She never once gave up hope. Every hour of her day was devoted to the child. I encouraged her all I could, and the reeducation she and I worked on bore fruit.

Then the family moved to Alsace. A few years later on a trip I made there I saw her and the boy again. The change in both of them was terrible. They were literally crushed. I asked why.

"There's no hope for him. I know that now," the woman answered.

"Who says so?" I demanded.

"The doctor. He told me that the damage is permanent."

She had lost her only goal in life, and was verging on deep depression. As for the child, once he felt he had been abandoned, he had regressed toward the animal state. He had lost all he had gained, had become aggressive and disobedient. This is comparable to euthanasia, this condemning without appeal of a creature who could be saved by an intelligent psychotherapy ruled by the heart.

It was such thinking that led to the powerful schools of thought on first, dementia praecox and then, schizophrenia. I have told the story of the controversy over these two disorders, which very nearly led to the bankruptcy of psychiatry. The advocates of euthanasia are believers in the "doctor-as-God." He holds the right to life or death. The physician who believes this can become an instrument of dictators, can be used by the holders of power to effect their revenge, to exterminate those who oppose them, even to carry out criminal racist policies. He can be brought to demean himself and to be a party to murder. That is what happened with the Nazi doctors.

The lure of death is one of the great threats to humanity today. History has shown that it is strongest during civilization's great crises. At the end of the Roman Empire, an epidemic of suicides broke out, affecting even the stoic. The legions massacred each other. Our disillusioned and faithless epoch resembles that ignoble period. In its attraction to death, its advocacy of euthanasia, in the nirvana of drugs, not to mention the attitude of living death which is popular in certain cults, our era is fleeing from life.

Euthanasia, which is the sign of a grave crisis in our civilization, represents a threat on a worldwide scale, as Professor Dvorjetzki has emphasized. We must combat it by reminding ourselves constantly that life is sacred. We must condemn this glorification of death. Excuses for destroying life in the name of some ideology or another will multiply, and we will end up as barbaric as our ancestors were in the first centuries.

Justice and truth are debased words today. Everyone uses them, assuring us that they represent an untiringly sought-after ideal. This is only talk. One cannot arrive at peace except by actually putting justice and truth into effect, by way of the lengthy and painstaking investigations such as I describe in this book. Who has the patience to do such work today?

In this vein I have given considerable study to the problem of divorce, which is a burning issue in many countries, and the conclusions I have arrived at will not be popular. Yet no reform of the divorce laws can change this fact: The children of divorced parents pay a heavy toll in mental illness, delinquency, and all the scourges which threaten our youth today.

In order to reply to an inquiry made by a widely read newspaper on the subject of divorce, my student Goldmann and I made an abstract of the files he had compiled for the Center of Social Psychiatry, an organization directed by Professors Bastide, Morazé, and myself, and we found that there is a crying need for attempts at reconciliation. Only the judge acts at this level, while the doctors and even the psychiatrist should be intimately involved.

I have acted in proceedings in which a spouse, or even an entire family, has conspired to get rid of a mate or a relative who, because he had been committed as a mental patient, had become an embarrassment to them. I have had to fight to make the facts known, and to defend the victims of these plots. The most striking illustration was that of a perfectly irreproachable mother of three children whom a welfare agency had falsely reported to be mentally ill. I was called into consultation along with several colleagues. She was faced with a divorce she did not want. We would have done her no good if, after rescuing her from her incorrect diagnosis, we had not gone further and helped her fight the divorce; not to have done so would have amounted to our delivering her into the hands of her executioner.

This is why I cannot approve of court decisions that authorize divorce in cases where one of the parties has been committed to a mental institution. The door is thus opened to every abuse and to the most unjustified persecutions, such as the suffering of the Canadian woman who for religious reasons refused to be divorced, only to find herself hospitalized and diagnosed as schizophrenic. This is not the only case I know of in which a similar maneuver was used.

A workman of about fifty, the father of five children, was married to a woman who was unable to stay at home and used every pretext to go out. M. R bore the conflicts with his wife very poorly; he became depressed and was directed to an open ward for help in solving his problem.

What happened after that is common enough. In the eyes of his neighbors and acquaintances, M. R was considered unbalanced, or in any case not too stable mentally. His wife made no effort to correct this impression—on the contrary. She even drew into the plot a doctor who had been treating M. R for lumbago. I am always astonished at the casualness with which some of my colleagues make diagnoses in matters of mental health.

"M. R is insane," this physician wrote cold-bloodedly.

One evening the wife and two of her neighbors seized M. R, bound him hand and foot, and took him to a mental hospital. The director of the institution, an honest and clear-thinking psychiatrist, saw that M. R was perfectly sane and discharged him.

Not daring to go home, M. R took refuge with his sister. Since the arbitrary commitment, though it had lasted no more than twenty-four hours, still damned him, his usual doctor sent him to me at Saint-Antoine to obtain a clean bill of health. As Mme. R refused to come to my office to be questioned, M. R reluctantly began divorce proceedings.

At this threat of exposure to the law, Mme. R became frightened, as did her accomplices, and she decided to come to see me after all. I attempted to reason with her, to show her the consequences of her attitude, especially the effect on her children, whom, in spite of what might be assumed, she loved.

"I made a mistake," she said finally.

M. R, however, no longer trusted his wife, which can be readily understood, and refused to stop the divorce proceedings. I spent long sessions attempting to bring the pair together again, efforts which, alas, ended in failure. One does not reunite in a few moments a couple so profoundly divided as this pair; and, above all, one wishes to make sure that the reconciliation will last. I am aware that the judiciary lacks the human and material resources to make inquiries as careful as this one into forty thousand divorces annually. The need is paramount, however; only when legal conciliation ceases to be a formality in which no one really believes will divorce cease to be the plague it is today.

I now come to the end of this survey of a life and a career which have but a single aim: to know man through the disorders that affect his mind. Have I succeeded in showing what mental illness is: two words which, though singular in form, cover an infinitely varied world? Have I made it clear that there is not just one disease that may affect the human mind, but ten, twenty, fifty, and that their causes are many?

The following represents the merest skimming of the possibilities: meningoencephalitis, brain tumors, infectious or toxic encephalitis, alcohol, drugs, mental confusion caused by exhaustion, periodic depression, periodic psychoses or neuroses, infantile encephalopathies (diseases of the brain), problems with mental development, feeble-mindedness, and so on.

The causes of all these troubles constitute a multicolored array, all of whose nuances I have tried to render in this book. By describing my first research into catatonia and its toxic origin, or into the biological origin of certain psychoses, I have aimed at giving the reader a complete inventory. A poison circulating in the blood can cause damage resembling a purely mental breakdown, with results such as hallucination or delirium that submerges the will, guilt-ridden melancholia, or permanent and unassuageable moral suffering.

The whole organism affects the mind. We know now that mental disorders can be caused by disturbances which may be digestive, biliary, hepatointestinal, vascular or circulatory, endocrinal or ovarian. Aristotle said, "The character of the soul depends upon the condition of the body." The Talmud tells us that "the blood is the organ from which the soul is suspended." It follows that psychiatry, as I hope I have shown in the specific examples in this book, requires not only a complete and comprehensive knowledge of medical science but also a profound moral cultivation, and a ceaseless, alert openness of mind.

In the same way, moral conscience exerts a considerable influence on the body. Psychological torments translate into disturbances of every physical function and destroy the organism's defense reactions. Psychosomatic effects can lead to extremely impressive physical maladies before which a doctor will puzzle in vain if he thinks only in terms of the body.

Our era has seen a formidable and unprecedented increase in mental illness. It has become a tidal wave which we have been powerless to stem. A major role has been played by alcoholism, with its ability to cause acute and chronic psychoses, and its deleterious effect on future generations, which can be observed in certain areas such as the west of France. Drugs are an especially serious problem since, unlike alcohol, their use is accompanied by a whole ideology aimed at their justification. Despair and society's disapproval lead to an attitude of withdrawal, negation, then partial death. Once merely an individual problem, drug addiction has become a social one.

I shall add to these words a point I stressed at a conference held in Vienna in 1960. In a study entitled "The Influence of Postwar Living Conditions on the Mental Health of Nations," I spoke of the way in which such collective emotions as fear, generated by arbitrary arrests and the political and social conflicts which are now daily events, and which are abundantly diffused by the communications media, create an atmosphere of anxiety. This is made worse by the wars which are constantly breaking out around the world, and the threat that one day one of them may become a global holocaust.

The too rapid pace of our lives literally exhausts the nervous system. Poor working conditions give rise to contradictions which are scarcely propitious to tranquillity. In our time, everything serves as a pretext for conflict. The most resolute souls become worn down.

This book has been written in order to demonstrate that one cannot be a good psychiatrist by applying only what one has learned in medical school. Though it is important to know everything medical science has to offer, that is not enough. The spiritual factor must have the last word.

The man who flatters his patients and encourages their instincts instead of channeling them, is turning his back on the rules of our profession. Antipsychiatry, group therapy, total freedom for the most seriously afflicted patients—all that jumble which is kept going at great cost and in a hullabaloo of publicity—can only lead to excesses that will end in various bloody results. In making such a statement I realize that I expose myself to attack. I wish I could be wrong, but there are many signs which show that the danger is real.

The great harm which antipsychiatry does—in England especially —is to make of the mentally ill a group apart and free of social constraint, an assertive, demanding element that rises up to accuse society and is bent on having its revenge against its fellowmen. It is supported by persons whose aim is to destroy the social order, using mental illness and mentally disturbed people as their instruments. By encouraging ill persons to believe themselves oppressed, these agitators, who intend to use psychiatry for purposes of subversion, conveniently fail to mention the fact that throughout the world and throughout history, regardless of regimes, mental troubles have been universal.

How far away I feel myself to be from such a conception! The art I have practiced has confirmed me in my respect for the fundamental moral values, whose reality and psychological efficacy I have attempted to show in the cases described in this book. These values must be intelligently applied, with respect for the truth and by setting an example! Isn't that—respect for the truth and setting an example—the best motto for a psychiatrist? I have adopted it as mine, taking my example from my father, who left me the marvelous heritage of belief in the specific worth of man. This inspiration is also found in Hannah's prayer, in the first book of Samuel, which became the Magnificat of Christianity.

We must not forget that what the Bible teaches us penetrates to the depths of man's nature. My experience as a psychiatrist has led me to discover in experimental fashion the living God who exists, as Ibn Gabirol said, in our viscera. I have seen patients harden their hearts against accepting responsibility, and then turn their repressed guilt feelings against others. Their overburdened conscience then causes them to become mad with uncontained rage and hatred. The repercussions of this are felt in the lives of nations and of peoples.

The foundations of the moral psychiatry which I practice can be summed up as follows: identification with my patients, faithfulness to my promises, vigilant understanding, humaneness, the whole combined with as good medical and social orientation as I am capable of. *Midah kneged Midah,* measure for measure, the notion of reciprocity, plays an essential role in the history of psychiatry. Because through the centuries people rejected this reciprocity, the mentally ill remained society's pariahs, endured atrocious mistreatment, were robbed, and were terrorized by inhumane methods which have their equivalent today. It is inspiration, aroused by the Prophets of Israel, which has caused their liberation, thanks to the intervention of Father Joffre in Spain, then the work of Saint John of God, followed in France by the work of Pinel and Esquirol, imbued with Biblical culture, and in England by Puritans like Tuke, and finally, in Italy by Chiaruggi.

In attempting to aid the ill, some of my efforts have been inadequate; I have had my share of failures, which I have made a point of departure for new efforts. I have traced the idea of right and wrong in groups and in individuals. By restoring or strengthening moral conscience in my patients, I have brought peace to families and I have healed individuals physically as well as mentally.

I have always clung to a belief in truth and in justice, in which science and faith are reconciled. Through my work I have come to know the meaning of that beautiful Hebrew prayer, in which the role of the God of Abraham, Isaac, and Jacob is defined: "He raises up the fallen, He heals the sick, He frees the oppressed!"

BY THE
SAME
AUTHOR

PRINCIPAL PUBLICATIONS

Mental Disorders and Cerebral Tumors. 1 vol., 396 pp. Doin Editions, 1926.

Experimental Catatonia and Bulbocapnine. With de Jong. 1 vol. Masson, 1930.

Experimental Moral Psychiatry (Individual and Social Hatred and Guilt Feelings). P.U.F., 1945. 2nd Edition, 1950. Translated into Spanish and Japanese.

Physiological and Experimental Medical Psychiatry. 1 vol., 827 pp., Masson, 1938.

The Tsedek Test, Moral Judgment and Delinquency. With Bachet. P.U.F., 1950.

A Short History of Psychiatry. Treatise on Pediatrics. With Lesné. Doin, 1954.

Child Neuropsychiatry. Treatise on Pediatrics. With Lesné. Doin, 1954.

The Disintegration of the Personality. P.U.F., 1952.

Monotheism and Science. 1 vol. Editions Synthesis, Geneva, 1952.

Psychoses and Neuroses. Series "What Do I Know?", No. 221, P.U.F. Translated into Italian, Spanish, Serbo-Croatian, and Japanese.

Psychiatric Therapeutics. Series "What Do I Know?", No. 691, P.U.F. 1955.

Treatise on Psychiatry. 2 vols. 1,670 pp., Masson, 1959.

Moreau de Tours Annals. 5 vols., P.U.F., 1962, 1968, 1970, 1973.

Experimental Psychopathology. Series "What Do I Know?", No. 1128, P.U.F., 1964.

Psychiatry and the Science of Man. Editions du Levain, Paris, 1963.

Hebrew Civilization and the Science of Man. Editions Zikarone, Paris, 1970.

French Psychiatry from Pinel to Modern Times. P.U.F., 1967.

Tsedek, Hebraic Law and the Science of Peace. Editions Zikarone, Paris, 1970.

Tsedek, Modern Science Reviewed in the Light of Hebrew Civilization. 1 vol. Binghamton, New York, 1972.

Hypnosis and Related Methods. Series "What Do I Know?", No. 1458. 2nd edition. P.U.F., 1972.

Freud and Hebrew Monotheism. The Man Moses by Dorion. Editions Zikarone, Paris, 1972.

Interpreting Supplementary Neuropsychiatric Tests. 1 vol. A. de Visher, Brussels, 1962.

Psychiatry, 1 vol. Series "Medical and Social Professions," No. 17. Editions Foucher, 1970.

Social Psychiatry, 1 vol. Series "What Do I Know?", No. 669. 5th edition. P.U.F., 1974 (including *History of the Moral Conscience*).

Essays on Hebrew Medicine within the Framework of Jewish History. 1 vol. Editions Zikarone, Paris, 1973.

Encyclopedia of Psychology, The World of Psychology, etc. Collaboration with Professor Huisman and others.

INDEX

INDEX

INDEX

INDEX

INDEX

Moreau de Tours Society, 66, 68, 190, 233-236, 244, 289, 293
Morel, Bénédict, 71-72, 156, 168, 203
Moreno, 250
Morlaas, 26
Moses, 151, 152
Motor aphasia, 21
Mouchpat, 182
Mouel de Kérangué, Mlle., 36
Multiple sclerosis, 136
Münster, University of, 89, 292
Musical agraphia, 25
Myxophyceae, 285

Napoleon I, 50
National Center for Scientific Research, 285
Nazism, 140-145, 193, 194, 196, 296
Negativism, 35, 38
Neurasthenia, 154
Neurological Society, 33, 37, 38, 203
Neuropsychiatry
  catatonia, experimental, and, 35-49
  development of, 40
  hysteria and, 136-137
Neuroses
  case histories of, 156-182
  definition of, 154
  Freud and, 211
  obsessions as, 154-155
  present-day reasons for, 154
  psychosis and, 156, 159
  scopochloralose for, 168-169, 170
  symptoms of, 154
Neurotropic toxin, 42, 46
Neuville, M. de, 153
Night Porter, The (film), 209

O'Brien, 39
Obsessions, as neuroses, 154-155
Obsessive-compulsive fear of inadequacy, 160
Oedipus complex, 220
Open wards, 252-261
  abuses of, 259-261
    case histories, 252-255
  Baruk on, 260-261
  at Charenton Hospital, 256-259
  early history of, 256
Order of Physicians, 244
Organic hemiplegia, 130
Organodynamic theory of Charcot, 17, 26

Padé, Professor, 288
Paranoia, 92-102
  case histories of mistaken diagnosis, 92-113
    criticism of public and colleagues, 101-102
  case histories of true paranoia, 113-122
  definition of true paranoiac, 113, 122-123
  hypersensitive, 111
  public reaction to, 92
  schizophrenia vs., 92
Paraphasia, 22
Parchappe, Jean-Baptiste, 51, 272
Pâris, Deacon, 128
Parkinson's disease, 134, 136, 138
Pasteur, Louis, 194, 292
Paterson, Dr., 138, 139
Pathological sleep, 137-138
Patient's property, administration of
  case histories, 239-249
  the law of 1838 and, 240-242, 249-251, 255, 257
  new statute (1968) to, problems of, 243-248
  problems of, 242-243
Patriarchs, tombs of, 289-290
Patterson, Dr., 289
Periodic catatonia, 70
Periodic depression, 299-300
  crime and, 189-190
Periodic psychosis, 72-74, 77, 219
  schizophrenia and, 73, 76-77, 89-90
Persecution complex, 108
Peters, 37
Pharmacodynamic drugs, 60
Picksworth's method, 62
Pinel, Philippe, 16, 51, 52, 56, 197, 249, 264-265, 288, 303
Pinel, Scipion, 284
Pituitary gland, disorders research, 64-66
Pius XII, 194
Poliakov, Dr., 89, 292
Praxes (everyday gestures), 26
Presses universitaires de France, 68
Pritchard, 183
Provence (ship), 125
Psychasthenia, 155, 214
Psychic torpor, 36
Psychoanalysis, abuses of, 205-214
  Baruk on, 209-211
  case histories, 206-208, 212
  sex and, 212-214
Psychological hypnosis, 137

INDEX

INDEX

ABOUT THE AUTHOR

BORN IN 1897, HENRI BARUK spent his childhood at Sainte-Gemmes-sur-Loire in the psychiatric hospital which his father directed. After serving as Chief of Medicine at the psychiatric hospital of Clermont-de-l'Oise, he became director in 1931 of Charenton, the great French national mental hospital. He remained there almost forty years. He is a member of the Academy of Medicine and of numerous learned international societies. In the course of his long career he has presided over many congresses on psychiatry and neurology. He is equally a specialist in Hebraic culture and civilization.

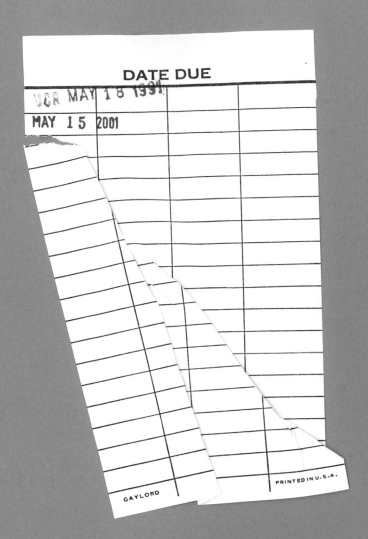

DATE DUE

UCR MAY 18 1991		
MAY 15 2001		

GAYLORD   PRINTED IN U.S.A.